AN EDUCATION IN JUDGMENT

AN EDUCATION IN JUDGMENT

Hannah Arendt and the Humanities

D. N. Rodowick

The University of Chicago Press   *Chicago and London*

The University of Chicago Press, Chicago 60637
The University of Chicago Press, Ltd., London
© 2021 by The University of Chicago
All rights reserved. No part of this book may be used or
reproduced in any manner whatsoever without written
permission, except in the case of brief quotations in critical
articles and reviews. For more information, contact the
University of Chicago Press, 1427 E. 60th St., Chicago, IL 60637.
Published 2021
Paperback edition 2023
Printed in the United States of America

32 31 30 29 28 27 26 25 24 23   1 2 3 4 5

ISBN-13: 978-0-226-78021-4 (cloth)
ISBN-13: 978-0-226-82950-0 (paper)
ISBN-13: 978-0-226-78035-1 (e-book)
DOI: https://doi.org/10.7208/chicago/9780226780351.001.0001

Library of Congress Cataloging-in-Publication Data
Names: Rodowick, David Norman, author.
Title: An education in judgment : Hannah Arendt and the humanities /
D. N. Rodowick.
Description: Chicago : University of Chicago Press, 2021. |
Includes bibliographical references and index.
Identifiers: LCCN 2020047075 | ISBN 9780226780214 (cloth) |
ISBN 9780226780351 (ebook)
Subjects: LCSH: Arendt, Hannah, 1906–1975. | Judgment. | Humanities.
Classification: LCC B945.A694 R646 2021 | DDC 144—dc23
LC record available at https://lccn.loc.gov/2020047075

♾ This paper meets the requirements of ANSI/NISO Z39.48–1992
(Permanence of Paper).

For Dominique,
who never judges me *too* harshly.

The true philosopher does not accept the conditions under which life has been given to man.

HANNAH ARENDT,
Lectures on Kant's Political Philosophy

Contents

Preface

Beginnings are always difficult until one becomes aware that the point where an act begins is really only a step or stage in the disordered flow of time and history, that is, a continuation whether the actor knows it or not. This uncertainty about the when and the how of first steps also happily suggests that the best beginnings arrive unexpectedly as if a gift from time and circumstance.

Five or six years ago, I would have been surprised and bemused if someone told me that I would write a book about Hannah Arendt and her thoughts on judgment, art, culture, and politics. After publishing *Philosophy's Artful Conversation* in 2015, I found myself at something of an impasse. Having intimated in that book that I would continue defining my ideas about a possible philosophy of the humanities, I was at a loss to say more than I had already said. By happy circumstance, in spring 2015 I fell upon Corey Robin's essay "The Trials of Hannah Arendt," commissioned for the *Nation* by my friend John Palatella, who was then literary editor. Robin's thought-provoking account of Arendt's philosophical and political approach to difficult questions of judgment inspired me to return systematically to her writing, especially in the context of work I was already pursuing on Kant's third Critique and his writings on anthropology. This book began to take form through my single-minded reading and note-taking on Arendt's various and multifaceted texts on thinking and judging, which took place out of curiosity and largely independently of secondary sources. The commitment to turn this material into a book arose in the context of teaching Philosophical Perspectives on the Humanities to first-quarter freshmen at the University of Chicago, where in my seminar I added reading from Hannah Arendt to our canonic attention to Plato, Aristotle, and Sophocles. My students' infectious enthusiasm for thinking and judging in company is a major inspiration for this book.

When I finally began exploring selectively the secondary literature on Arendt, I was surprised by two impressions. The first had to do with the persistence of a number of critiques of Arendt's account of judgment in well-known texts by Jürgen Habermas, Ronald Beiner, Richard Bernstein, and especially Seyla Benhabib's sympathetic reading in her important book *The Reluctant Modernism of Hannah Arendt*. I understand these criticisms as unfolding along three lines. First is the expression of skepticism that there is real continuity between the modalities of solitary thinking and public acts of judgment. In essence, this criticism questions Arendt's fundamental argument that there is an important link between thinking and moral considerations. The second line of criticism doubts that one can justify philosophically Arendt's claim that Kant's critique of the power of judgment can or should be read as his unwritten political philosophy, or, in other words, this criticism questions that a bridge can be thrown between judgments of taste and political deliberation. Finally, related to this argument is the accusation that Arendt deliberately misreads or deforms Kant in extending her account of judgment to include moral considerations, or that she inappropriately conflates modes of practical reason and acts of judgment, which Kant felt must be kept separate as distinct mental faculties.

To this last point, I will say that in a close reading of the *Critique of the Power of Judgment* one can uncover a lot of hedging by Kant on the role of judgment in moral reasoning. (Additional evidence can be found in his remarks on judgment in his anthropological writings, especially in "Anthropology from a Pragmatic Point of View.") But my main point in this book is to say that it is worth taking Arendt at her word. I have chosen to look closely at her writings on these matters with the working assumption that her account of judgment is highly original and develops with a deep conceptual consistency, even if her argument is incomplete and unfinished. In contrast to most secondary literature on Arendt, I want to make a clear case, first, for the idea that thinking and judging are closely interrelated and indeed inseparable activities. Second, I want to support and underline the claim that the mental and discursive operations one uncovers in Kant's account of pure judgments of taste can and should be extended to all disputes where qualitative distinctions are in play in assessments of the meaning and value of particular experiences and acts. Aesthetics and politics and questions of culture, history, and memory are deeply interconnected here. Judgment plays no less a role in deciding between what is just or unjust than it does in distinguishing between what is pleasurable or unpleasurable. This amounts to accepting that Arendt's revisionist reading of Kant is original and defensible. (I would say the same about her often-criticized extensions of Aristotle's account of *phronēsis*.)

My proposal to provide a fresh critical account of Hannah Arendt's writings on thinking, judgment, and ethics is meant to extend and clarify these aims in a new context through an original approach to Arendt's account of the postwar crisis in culture, so similar in many ways to how the crisis in the humanities is articulated today. This crisis is certainly real and deeply felt by those like myself who consider themselves committed to writing and teaching in areas not dominated by the modes of reasoning prevalent in the natural and social sciences. To be sure, the humanities contain a great variety of disciplines, methods, and vocabularies that compose an almost indescribable whole that is constantly changing. Nevertheless, in this book I hope to show that the problem and practice of judgment is the Ariadne's thread that guides and links all of the otherwise divergent disciplinary endeavors of the humanities.

However, one may ask why I want to make a case for a *philosophical* education in the humanities as key to the shared task of a humanistic education regardless of discipline. I take this approach because in my view philosophy's primary concern is to describe and evaluate the activity and shape of our thoughts and judgments, the how and the why of their taking place, regardless of the objects or experiences to which our thought and judgment are drawn. In other words, philosophy is concerned with the nature and value of thinking and judgment in themselves regardless of application. In this respect, Arendt has taught me to look more deeply into what I call the operations and aims of judgment—discernment, imagination and reflection, insight, impartiality, revisability, enlarged thought, and sociability—that come into play whenever and wherever we are called to conversations of import and value. In this crucial task, I would hope philosophical criticism to be constructively engaged with the broad range of humanistic activities and thought though in a competition with none of them.

My emphases on humanism and the humanities no doubt raise

questions in the minds of modern readers, especially considering the widespread and important critical work that has been accomplished under the umbrella of the "posthuman." I have deep sympathy and respect for this work, above all in the context of environmental criticism and animal ethics, as well as other domains. However, what has always troubled me about the concept of the "posthuman" is the assumption that at some point we knew, whether mistakenly or not, what being human means. A recurring argument in Kant's political writings and his anthropology is that the human, or Kant might say humanity or human culture, is something yet to be achieved and which in fact may never be achieved. Kant's account of the history of human culture is certainly teleological, but it is also asymptotic. Especially in her readings of Kant, Arendt is drawn to what Stanley Cavell would call certain "facts of the human," perhaps best characterized by Kant's fascinating account of "community sense" (*gemeinschaftlichen Sinnes*), or sensus communis, as the ground of judgments of taste. These facts have nothing to do with an appeal to or discovery of universal human qualities or essences, nor are they grounded in empirical facts. Arendt prefers to follow Kant in writing of certain perfectible "ideas" or "ideals" of the human. Here the question of judgment again becomes important because there are no transcendental or transhistorical standards by which to measure progress toward these ideals, or even to define with certainty what they are and who they count for. Also important here is Arendt's commitment to her concept of plurality, which from one perspective means that whatever our commitments are with respect to human values, rights, or identity, and no matter how they are measured, they have to be worked out collectively. As I will argue further on, in the absence of providence, humans must continually negotiate, in plurality and community, the truth that defines their history and their actions, indeed, their politics, and it is up to humankind, from moment to unpredictable moment, to define collectively the ethical shape of its common existence. There is no prior essence from which humans have departed or must return to and no final end that guides the evolution of culture (*pace* Kant), but rather we are always working out on the terrain of judgment the terms that guide human understanding of what we value or abhor in our current collective and increasingly interconnected existence.

Inspired by the French genre of the *essai*, my book is divided into six sections. Each part takes the form of close philosophical readings of

Arendt and her main interlocutors in the history of philosophy, especially Immanuel Kant. The coherence and consistency of Arendt's perspective on the humanities is often more implicit than explicit. One aim of this book is to bring forward the connecting threads of her arguments about judgment, culture, and politics as they unfold in a variety of texts published in her last decades of writing. I envision my book as less a commentary on Arendt's thought than what I hope will be an original and respectful though critical dialogue with Arendt's ideas about the arts and humanities and her implicit yet persistent suggestion that an education in the humanities is the only appropriate response to the crisis in culture that concerns her.

Readers will surely notice that no archival research informs these arguments, nor am I directly interested in imagining what a reconstruction of Arendt's final contribution to *The Life of the Mind* might look like. I have turned to Arendt as a powerful interlocutor in my ongoing thought about how to picture a philosophy of the humanities, and what she has helped me to understand better and more completely is that the activity of reflective judgments may be the central thread that holds the beautiful but sometimes frayed and discordant tapestry of the humanities together. My aim from the beginning has been to read Arendt closely and to take her at her public word rather than to speculate on what she might have thought or written had she lived longer or witnessed our contemporary historical moment. And in engaging Arendt in a somewhat personal critical conversation, I have been seeking to understand better why I have now been drawn to her thought, and in so doing, I hope I have made more perspicuous my own arguments concerning philosophy, judgment, and the humanities in ways that make apparent whatever originality may be their due.

Within this context, my greatest sympathies are with Linda M. G. Zerilli's provocative and original reading of Arendt in her 2005 essay, "'We Feel Our Freedom': Imagination and Judgment in the Thought of Hannah Arendt," and in her recent book, *A Democratic Theory of Judgment.* Unlike Benhabib, who focuses mainly on Arendt's arguments in *The Human Condition,* in my view Zerilli is one of the very few contemporary authors who understand the importance and conceptual continuity in Arendt's account of judgment. Zerilli's originality lies in reframing Arendt's account of judgment with respect to the philosophy of the later Wittgenstein and his most influential interpreters, most of whom follow in the wake of Stanley Cavell's important readings of Wittgenstein in *Must We Mean What We Say?*, *The Claim of Reason*, and other pathbreaking works. Wittgenstein and Cavell are both key figures in my earlier account of a possible philosophy of the humanities as set out in *Philosophy's Artful Conversation*. While I only discovered Zerilli's book at a late moment in my own research on Arendt on judgment, art, and politics, I have found her helpful in confirming some key arguments. In particular, rather than seeking in judgment confirmation of rational processes of intersubjective agreement and validation of political deliberation, I share with Zerilli the position that judgment is a quotidian practice that is reflexively exercised whenever we fail to find an overarching concept or rule to guide experience of whatever kind or quality; in other words, judgment is the faculty whose recurrent exercise is meant to give coherence and meaning to human experience. Reflective judgments, as modeled by aesthetic experience, occur in singular circumstances where determinate judgments fail, and in this respect, they can only seek to persuade rather than convince or compel. What we seek in judgment, then, is less a claim to reason than an affirmation of our freedom to remake in community our experience and understanding of the world in both local and global contexts as guided by the productive power of imagination.

Zerilli's perspective on Arendt and judgment is thus the closest to my own yet also confirms the surprise of another impression of the secondary literature. While all of these publications contribute to important debates in political theory, I have yet to find any substantial writing on Arendt's account of judgment from the perspective of aesthetics or culture or, indeed, any significant Arendt scholarship that raises important questions for the humanities around art and politics or culture and education.[1] In this respect, I feel my book is unique in my aim to rebalance philosophically the relation between aesthetics

---

1. An important exception is Cecilia Sjöholm's recent book, *Doing Aesthetics with Arendt: How to See Things* (New York: Columbia University Press, 2015), although unlike her I am unconcerned about questions of what an Arendtian aesthetic theory would look like. My focus, rather, is to examine how judgment sets a context for all the activities of criticism, interpretation, and evaluation in the otherwise diverse practices and methods of the humanities. Another important recent event has been the publication of Arendt's numerous occasional works of criticism in *Reflections on Literature and Culture*, ed. Susannah Young-Ah Gottlieb (Stanford, CA: Stanford University Press, 2007). This is an indispensable resource, though yet again I have preferred to concentrate on a limited corpus of Arendt's philosophical works.

and politics in Arendt's account of judgment, especially as a practice of curation, world building, and ethical revision. And while an idea of politics as aiming at the analysis and transformation of large institutional or social structures certainly remains important, I aim to show that an education in judgment, whether in aesthetic, cultural, or other domains, is also a political force that is as local as the classroom where the skills practiced through conversations and disagreements about art, philosophy, and other areas of humanistic concern can be applied to many other domains of decision and action.

What does politics mean here? Arendt's unique, perhaps even eccentric, definition of politics has been a frequent target of criticism within the broad domain of political philosophy, especially with respect to her continual appeal to the ancient Athenian polis as ideally modeling politics as a self-organizing and self-legislating activity arising in debates and conversations guided by reason and the practice of insight or good judgment. Arendt's interest in politics looks at human decision making and action from the ground, as it were, in situations of free and mutual exchange where quotidian discussions of justice and injustice emerge in dynamic communities that may arise and disappear unpredictably. Moreover, one cannot start to know what attracts individuals into communities of interest and holds them there without addressing the nature of their judging activities wherein, as Arendt likes to say, individuals decide how the world is to look and who belongs together in it. In this respect, something I appreciate greatly in Arendt is how she thinks about the problem of politics from the ground up, as it were, as highly dynamic, local, and context-dependent conversations and actions rather than as expressions of large institutional structures, instruments, or forces of history. I think of this as a molecular rather than molar view of the constantly renewed formation of political communities. To evaluate judgment and artful conversation as an intersubjective activity that brings individuals into communities, no matter how dynamic and fragile, is a separate question from what I think of as sociological and historical accounts of given communities and their histories and ideologies. This is a fascinating question for political philosophy and history, which Arendt herself addresses in works like *The Origins of Totalitarianism*, though no doubt outside of my remit here.

I have been writing this book in the midst of one of the most dangerous and divisive political and constitutional crises that has ever arisen in the history of this country. Likewise, I could never have imagined that this book would emerge in an era where politics has profoundly deformed the public possibilities for discerning between truth and opinion, as well as between historical facts and strategic and dishonorable deception. Readers may then be surprised or disappointed that I refer to so few specific examples, whether from present or past history. Right or wrong, this choice is intentional. I am not offering a book of historical analysis, policy, pedagogy, or even methodology, nor am I able to do so. I am neither a political scientist or historian nor a sociologist, and I fear my reflections on those honorable disciplines may not be worthy of their prestige. I think of my work as something more like an *essai*, a thought experiment or "exercise" inspired by Arendt's own characterization of her essays as exercises in political thought. Therefore, I am inclined to maintain a certain distance and generality in my arguments about judgment, meaning, and evaluation. If they have any power to persuade, my readers will be drawn to their own examples, which will change according to their own historical circumstances and perspectives. In other words, any example or examples that seem deeply relevant today may have less of a hold on our attention in just a few years, or our understanding of their consequences may shift to greater or lesser degrees. A specific application of my ideas to a given discipline might, in its very specificity, seem inconsequential or irrelevant for another. And so I insist again that the power of judgment for framing our arguments about culture and politics is more deeply revealed when readers and critics apply their own examples drawn from the time and context of their reading, which I, of course, cannot foresee.

Nevertheless, it is also the case that exemplarity or the appeal to examples in judgment are fundamentally important to any understanding of the powers of judgment and its place in education. Throughout Arendt's postwar writings the figure of Socrates continually reappears as the exemplar of what I call the performative art of thinking and of a critical needling of his fellow citizens through the exercise of the elenchus as an open and inconclusive circle of questions and answers. Socrates has nothing to teach, but in the often disorienting to-and-fro of Socratic conversation something important happens nonetheless: one discovers what one thinks and values, and those thoughts and values are made apparent and open to criticism and revision, which in best cases leads to new and better opinions, if the whole process does not fall apart, which is a standing risk. I turn to the exemplarity of Socratic conversation and dialectic in the first section of the book, and in the fifth section I return to the exemplarity of the elenchus as a model for education in judgment in the humanities, if we should need one.

Nevertheless, I am a citizen whose responsibilities for exercising good judgment, especially in times of crisis, are no more nor less powerful and needed than those of any of my fellows and peers. If judgment is a political faculty as Arendt insists, examples will always be forthcoming, and if my arguments have any power to persuade, they will apply to any example or situation that readers find important enough to address on their own or in the company of like minds. To fully understand the power of judgment in art, culture, ethics, and politics requires acknowledging that it applies everywhere and in all human circumstances, whether or not we choose to exercise this faculty in critical and constructive ways. In other words, I have chosen to follow faithfully Kant's maxims and ask you to do the same: think for yourself, and judge for yourself.

I. THE ART OF THINKING

Any undergraduate student of philosophy can recount the three questions that Immanuel Kant posed as fundamental to human thought and life: What can I know? What ought I to do? What may I hope for? Less often considered is a fourth question, which appears in later writings and remarks on anthropology—What are humans (*Was ist der Mensch?*)?[2] The more subtle orientation of Kant's question might be better understood as: What does it mean to be human or to become more fully human, or to know that one can become so?

In a strong sense, Kant invented anthropology as a philosophical subject, which two hundred years later should still be considered as distinct from the better-known modern social scientific discipline. I ask first that you consider how strange it is that Kant should project the human as a subject or object of philosophical inquiry, which means placing the human in the sphere of metaphysical intangibles such as the possibilities and limits of reason, the imperative to self-consistent moral action, or the desire to overcome human finitude. Kant's lectures on anthropology are concerned with many dimensions of psychology, biology, and other matters open to scientific description. But if the fourth question is as fundamental to critical philosophy as the first three, then whatever might define the human is distinct from automatic

2. Kant added the fourth, and for him, culminating question with his lectures on logic from the year 1762. See, for example, *Immanuel Kant's Logik: Ein handbuch zu vorlesungen*, ed. Gottlob Benjamin Jäsche (Königsberg: Friedrich Nicolovius, 1800), 25. Trans. J. Michael Young as *Lectures on Logic* (Cambridge: Cambridge University Press, 1992), 538.

species belonging to *Homo sapiens*, and this is so by just the same criteria that Kant evokes to distinguish, for example, the senses from reason in the first Critique. What does it mean to qualify the "human" in the same terms as reason or morality, or to place it on a plane of abstraction more appropriate to concepts such as reason, virtue, beauty, or taste? The strange and difficult assumption here is that one is born into species life, but this unusual and talented though flawed animal may not yet be or have become human. Or even that for every individual born to history, the potential and possibility for becoming human is universal but also a path that might be only rarely taken or never finally or completely achieved.

With these thoughts, I am trying to address again questions left unanswered and thoughts left unfinished at the end of *Philosophy's Artful Conversation* (Cambridge, MA: Harvard University Press, 2015), all of which converge on my imagination of what a philosophy of the humanities might look like. A philosophy of the humanities, I will now add, is not guided by the search for a system or program of interpretation or evaluation. Its results, should there be any, will produce nothing that could be consistently applied in the form of methods or normative criteria guiding the interpretation of texts, objects, or experiences. In this way, I want to speak of a philosophical education in the humanities not in terms of canons, methods, or disciplines to be mastered, nor even knowledges and skills to be acquired, but rather as something deeper and more fundamental—the forging of a revisable moral life guided by reason in open and contingent intersubjective conversations with others or, in other words, the humanities in its deepest sense conceived as an education in judgment. (Later I will suggest that while good judgment cannot be taught, it can be practiced, and it should be practiced in company. In this situation, there are no teachers but rather only students.) Here critical philosophy has a role to play in both clarifying and valuing human powers of criticism and judgment but without making any final claims on either their limits or their possible expansiveness. Perhaps the question can be turned in another direction: What would a culture of thinking look like? Or what might it mean to practice thinking as a public and performative art?

Hannah Arendt ranks high among twentieth-century philosophers who cared most deeply about these questions. Education in judgment, in fact, might be considered a central theme of her last decade of writing as exemplified in essays like "The Crisis in Culture" (1960), "Thinking and Moral Considerations" (1971), and her late *Lectures on Kant's Political Philosophy* (first delivered at the New School in autumn 1970), as well as other important works like *The Life of the Mind* (1971). Following Kant, Arendt argues that our capacity for exercising judgment is one measure and means for achieving the human and for fully exploring, examining, and exercising the possibilities of human freedom in ways both enlivened and constrained by our intersubjective encounters with others. No human is without the capacity for judgment; it is part of our *sensus communis*. However, judgment can be exercised poorly, well, or not at all, which is one reason why defining and describing criteria for evaluating judgments, whether criticizing or affirming them, is a directive aim of the humanities. In other words, education in judgment, whether good or bad, is part and parcel of what a philosophy of the humanities hopes to achieve for the liberal arts. Even more crucially, as Arendt demonstrates in "Thinking and Moral Considerations" and other writing where her analyses of Adolph Eichmann's atrophied capacities for thinking and moral reasoning appear, a diminished capacity for judgment can lead to moral evil. Poor judgments, or worse, lack of judgment, are not only failures of reason; they are also routes to moral failure.

The relation of judgment to thinking thus provides another important context for understanding why an education in judgment is a central concern for a philosophy of the humanities. In a cultural and historical world of increasing violence and complexity, one reflexive quality of the human is to insulate oneself in thought and action with clichés, habits, conventions, and other standardized codes of expression and behavior. The unthinking reliance on habit and unreflective opinions is not an antisocial behavior per se but rather, according to Arendt, a human strategy for making communities cohere with a minimum expense of energy. To fall back on opinion and conventional beliefs is a socially sanctioned way of protecting oneself against the variety and intensity of occasions that lay claim to critical thought and attention. If individuals and communities were continually responsive to these claims, they would soon be exhausted by them. And as Arendt observes, Eichmann's nearly inhuman indifference was only that he knew of no such claim at all.

With the negative example of Eichmann in mind, Arendt's main concern in "Thinking and Moral Considerations" is to understand and to assess in what degree the ability to judge is dependent on the faculty of thought. This is where reasoning and moral reasoning coincide, with the capacity for one being dependent on the possibility of the other. Her precise question is the now well known: "Do the inability to think and a disastrous failure of what we commonly call conscience coincide? The question that imposed itself was: Could the activity of thinking as such, the habit of examining and reflecting upon whatever happens to come to pass, regardless of specific content and quite independent of results, could this activity be of such a nature that it 'conditions' men against evil-doing?"[3] Arendt points out that the Latin etymology of "*con-science*" refers to activities of knowing within and by oneself and as such suggests a kind of knowledge actualized internally in the process of thinking. Thinking and judgment are connected here, and the inability or refusal to think is directly proportional to the human capacity or incapacity to engage in moral reasoning as an activity of self-consciousness.

Here I pause to note that where Arendt's earlier accounts of judgment were motivated by her perceived crisis in culture in the context of a mass society, the urgency of "Thinking and Moral Considerations" is fueled by a crisis in philosophy as expressed, as in other examples, by Rudolf Carnap's attack on Heidegger.[4] In asserting that metaphysics is no more meaningful than poetry, Carnap wanted to exclude both poetry and metaphysics from the primary concerns of modern philosophy. Moreover, the desire of Carnap and other logical positivists was to bring an end to philosophy as such to the extent that metaphysics aims at questions that were unsolvable, indeed unaddressable, by logical analysis and empirical verification, such as What is thinking? or What is evil?

From the perspective of Carnap's scientism, it is tempting to sweep all of the humanities under the rug of metaphysics. (The term "scientism" was coined by P. M. S. Hacker to describe the illicit extension of the methods and forms of explanation of the natural sciences into the

3. Hannah Arendt, "Thinking and Moral Considerations: A Lecture," *Social Research* 38:3 (Autumn 1971): 418. These arguments, of course, take on a much more expansive form in Arendt, *The Life of the Mind: Thinking* (New York: Harcourt, 1978).

4. Rudolf Carnap, "The Elimination of Metaphysics through Logical Analysis of Language," in *Logical Positivism*, ed. A. J. Ayer (Glencoe, IL: Free Press, 1959), 60–81.

humanities.)⁵ Arendt does not shy away from "metaphysics," however, but rather redirects these questions through Kant to map out a new space for examining what she calls the modern crisis in knowledge. One of the remarkable arguments in the introduction to *The Life of the Mind: Thinking* is that in trying to erase or overcome the distinction between the sensory and the supersensory worlds, or perhaps, matter and spirit, the modern crisis in knowledge marks a decline of faith in positivism no less than the fading of belief in transcendental categories. Turning to Heidegger's reading of Nietzsche's *Twilight of the Idols*, Arendt reminds her readers that if "God is dead," it is not so much a personified authoritative deity that has disappeared from the world as what "God" stands for as symbol: the appeal to a supersensory world as understood by metaphysics. "We have abolished the true world," writes Nietzsche. "What has remained? The apparent one perhaps? Oh no! With the true world we have also abolished the apparent one."⁶ The crisis of knowledge is not that positivism eliminates belief in a supersensory world from which value and meaning can be drawn from immaterial sources but rather that the collapse of the opposition between matter and thought has also eliminated any grounds for certainty. Each needs the other to maintain the ground of their antagonism. Humans are adrift in a world of technology and mechanistic logic no less than one defined by the intangibles of faith. For good or ill, only belief can fill that void. But is there an alternative to belief?

Arendt's way of thinking through this problem is to reconsider what Kant called "the scandal of reason," which is that reason is continually drawn to questions of existential import that cannot be known through the senses or finalistically resolved by reason. What is at stake here is not the human ability to think as much as the human need "to think beyond the limitations of knowledge, to do more with this ability than use it as an instrument for knowing and doing" (*Life of the Mind: Thinking* 11–12). In other words, thinking is constantly drawn to matters that

5. See Hacker's essay "Wittgenstein and the Autonomy of Human Understanding," in *Wittgenstein, Theory and the Arts*, ed. Richard Allen and Malcolm Turvey (New York: Routledge, 2001), 39–74.

6. See *Life of the Mind: Thinking*, 10–11. The citation is from the section of *Twilight of the Idols* entitled "How the 'True World' Finally Became a Fable." Arendt is appealing here to Heidegger's argument in *Holzwege* (Frankfurt am Main: Vittorio Klostermann, 1963). See "Nietzsches Wort 'Gott Ist Tot,'" 193.

are not given to sense perception and that also transcend commonsense reasoning and its reliance on sense data and empirical testing. Fundamental to this argument is Arendt's reading of Kant's distinction in the first Critique between *Vernunft* and *Verstand*, or between reason and intellect, in her preferred translation. The urgent need of reason, she argues, is very different from the quest for certainty in knowledge so characteristic of scientism, for reason is continually pursuing questions of human existential import that are irresolvable, or more positively, continually open to question, to reconsideration, and to revision and reevaluation. The fundamental fallacy here is to interpret meaning on the model of truth. The distinction between the faculties of reason and those of intellect correspond to activities of thinking and knowing whose aims are very different—intellect is concerned with cognition, while reason is concerned with meaning. This is one of Arendt's key insights.

Arendt's turn to Kant also reorients his arguments in another direction. The aim of the Kantian critique of reason was to "purify" reason and in so doing to delimit those topics or questions that were indeed unknowable, though no less important for that, so as to clear the way to defining what fundamental aims and activities lie within the domain of human reason. But in so doing, Arendt feels that Kant neglects both the ordinariness of reason as well as its fundamental existential import, or "the fact that man's need to reflect encompasses nearly everything that happens to him, things he knows as well as things he can never know" (*Life of the Mind: Thinking* 14). Kant argues from the side of intellect here, but at the same time, Arendt feels that applying globally the results and criteria for cognition clouds our human existential interest in reason. In philosophy no less than the humanities, thinking and reason have aims and concerns that are entirely separate from those of the intellect and cognition: "To anticipate, and put it in a nutshell: *The need of reason is not inspired by the quest for truth but by the quest for meaning. And truth and meaning are not the same.* The basic fallacy, taking precedence over all specific metaphysical fallacies, is to interpret meaning on the model of truth" (*Life of the Mind: Thinking* 15; Arendt's italics). Thinking back to my book *Philosophy's Artful Conversation*, I note here the implicit yet strong alliance between Arendt and G. H. von Wright—both argue that the basic fallacy of modern philosophy is to interpret or even value meaning according to criteria of certainty. Arendt might well agree with von Wright's insistence that the humanities study phenomena of human culture or expression that may and should be distinguished logically from methods and objects of study in the natural sciences, and in this respect, von Wright insists that "the phenomena which the humanities study have features of their own which distinguish them logically from the typical objects of study in the natural sciences. A primary task of a philosophy of the humanities is to try to capture and do justice to those features."[7] Perhaps one can understand those phenomena better by more precisely delineating between the intellect and reason, and this is why von Wright insists upon remapping the grammar of reason for the humanities independently from scientism and the quest for certainty. The humanities have their own special forms of reasoning, interpreting, and valuing, which remain, perhaps, still to be discovered or recovered and valued.

The implied charge here against Carnap and other logical positivists is that in making intellect the whole of thought they lose sight of human reason and powers of judgment. Kant's defense of metaphysics is guided by his recognition of the human need to ponder intangible questions of God, freedom, and the immortality of the soul that are beyond the reach of immediate experience. Yet in Arendt's view Kant's own belief in the importance of such metaphysical questions blinded him to a more radical insight, namely, that his critical philosophy did not simply pause before these questions, leaving them to future generations of thinkers, but rather that his mode of critique effectively eroded the foundations of all possible philosophical and metaphysical systems. In this respect, Kant's real revolution was to assert that the capacity and the necessity of thinking are in no way restricted to specific subjects, such as questions of freedom or the immortality of the soul, which reason offers itself in full knowledge that it will never give final or even stable answers. In turn, critique is redirected to a picture of thinking as an open process without finality: where intellect demands unshakable conviction in the complete acquisition of knowledge, thinking requires only the standing possibility of its own activity as recurrence. Moreover, in separating intellect from reason Kant has not made room for faith, as he believed, but rather reaffirmed thought's critical capacity in all domains.

Arendt also notes that Kant understood philosophy as a fundamen-

7. G. H. von Wright, "Humanism and the Humanities," in *The Tree of Knowledge and Other Essays* (New York: E. J. Brill, 1993), 163–164.

tal human need and not as an elite activity of specialists. Indeed, a basic criterion of the human is the capacity to exercise critical judgment in the context of reason. This is why the distinction between thinking and knowing is crucial, or conversely, why the recurrent capacity for thought must be distinguished from the claim to possess knowledge and certainty. "If the ability to tell right from wrong should have anything to do with the ability to think," Arendt writes, "then we must be able to 'demand' its exercise in every sane person no matter how erudite or ignorant, how intelligent or stupid he may prove to be. Kant, in this respect almost alone among the philosophers, was much bothered by the common opinion that philosophy is only for the few precisely because of this opinion's moral implications" ("Thinking" 422). In Kantian terms, one needs philosophy, or the exercise of reason as the faculty of thought, in order to curtail and prevent the capacity for moral evil. Once again, this is a question of our powers of judgment, whether weak or strong.

The distinction between reason and intellect means that in its ordinary activity thinking must be something more than an instrument for knowing or doing. Thinking is not a practical matter, which leads to the view, whether humorous or scandalous, that it is somehow otherworldly. (Picture here the image of Socrates as *atopos*, as someone curiously out of phase with respect to other humans.) And at the same time, thinking is also full of risks and uncertainties. Arendt observes that one recurring characteristic of human thought is the intramural conflict that routinely arises between "common sense" (that is, the habitual sensory activity through which humans engage with the outer world and orient themselves in it) and the activity of thinking, which involves a withdrawal of self from world. And to the extent that in its critical capacities reason is in conflict with conviction and certainty, Arendt notes that Kant pictures the business of thinking like the veil of Penelope, undoing every morning what it accomplished the night before. Unguided by final aims, the open and recurrent process of thinking erodes conviction rather than sustaining it. Kant himself avers that the human mind has a natural aversion to conviction and a natural susceptibility to doubt.[8] For all these reasons, the human need for thinking can find no satisfaction apart from its own continuous and unending exercise.

---

8. See Kant, *Akademie Ausgabe* (Berlin: Königlich Preußische Akademie der Wissenschaften, 1900), vol. 18, nos. 5019 and 5036.

Thinking not only stops us short in our practical activities; it also removes us from the activities of life and community. This is another version of the antagonism between thinking and common sense, where to fall into thought is not only to withdraw into solitude but also to remove oneself from society. (In section V, I will address how the isolation of thinking informs the conflict between philosophy and politics.) Thinking risks isolation just as sociality impedes thinking, leading Arendt to observe that "it is true that the moment we start thinking on no matter what issue we stop everything else, and this everything else, again whatever it may happen to be, interrupts the thinking process; it is as though we moved into a different world. Doing and living in the most general sense of *inter homines esse,* 'being among my fellow-men'—the Latin equivalent for being alive—positively prevents thinking. As Valery once put it: 'Tantôt je suis, tantôt je pense,' now I am, now I think" ("Thinking" 423). Note the internal division or differentiation of the self in thought that Valery so beautifully expresses—the strange assertion here is that somehow thinking and being are discontinuous. One seems not to be present to oneself when thinking, or perhaps one is present to a different self. In thinking, one withdraws from the external world defined by sociability into an internal dimension where one is only occupied with one's thoughts. (Later I will argue that the exercise of judgment is what brings us from the isolation of thought into a community of critical conversation.) In Arendt's Kantian perspective, thinking is thus characterized by a redirection of perception, or perhaps it is better to say, a redirection of attention from the external world of physical objects to an internal sense of (re)imagined objects. Thinking directs itself toward objects that are removed from direct sense perception, where an object of thought is always a re-presentation open to remodeling. Arendt describes this as "something or somebody that is actually absent and present only to the mind which, by virtue of imagination, can make it present in the form of an image. . . . These remarks may indicate why thinking, the quest for meaning—rather than the scientist's thirst for knowledge for its own sake—can be felt to be 'unnatural,' as though men, when they begin to think, engage in some activity contrary to the human condition" ("Thinking" 423–24).

To recapitulate, Arendt proposes three main propositions concerning the inner connection between the ability or inability to think and the problem of evil. First, the faculty of thinking must be ascribed to everyone. Or as I have put it, it must be a defining possibility of the human even if only unevenly and incompletely achieved. Second, if Kant's view that thought has a natural aversion to conviction is accepted, then one cannot expect from reason any compulsory or doctrinal moral axioms or codes of conduct, or indeed any stable criteria for defining what is good and what is evil. Third, whatever one's feelings about the relation of thought to metaphysics, the internal relation of thought to imagination demonstrates that thinking is out of sync with the world of external appearances in which humans normally move and act. As Kant never tired of asserting, the powers of thinking are driven by those questions that reason itself cannot help asking and to which it will find no stable replies. These questions are supersensory, and in their relation to imagination fuel the energy of thought's restless and unceasing movements, which are all that thought claims for itself.

As I have already suggested, this all means that thought is by definition "impracticable." And here comes the charge that is often leveled at the humanities that only philosophy can respond to. If knowledge only achieves value through certainty or, indeed, becomes a commodity with measurable exchange value that can be transferred from one mind to another, then humanistic reason falls prey to criticisms of "uselessness," as if one could find no value in the capacity to reason and to revise one's thoughts and understanding. But this response, no matter how powerful, cannot satisfy a world dominated by quantitative measures and metrics and the expectation of defined practical results, for thinking is in principle without end and without aim. One might enhance or impede one's powers of thought, amplify or reduce their intensity, but never make of them an aim or a transmissible "knowledge." There is no measure of thinking apart from the act or performance of thinking itself, which means, Arendt says, "that we have to trace experiences rather than doctrines" ("Thinking" 426). Who can report this experience to us? The ordinary aspiring humans from whom one also expects thinking, and who do in fact think, also have the urgent business of life to attend to, as do we all. And those who Kant called "professional thinkers" (who I suppose are all humanists), and who are therefore aware that thinking is without result, are not anxious to make this knowledge public, even if it were possible.

There are, however, exemplars for making philosophy a business of public life. Here is where I like to think of Socrates as the first ordinary-language philosopher, even if quite extraordinary language and concepts are often deployed in Plato's writing. A remarkable stylist and perhaps even a competitor in composition with the dramatists of his day, Plato the philosopher held a deeply ironic view of writing.[9] As he recounts in the *Seventh Letter*, "On the subjects that concern me nothing is known since there exists nothing in writing on them nor will there ever exist anything in the future. People who write about such things know nothing; they don't even know themselves. For there is no way of putting it in words like other things which one can learn. Hence, no one who possesses the very faculty of thinking (*nous*) and therefore knows the weakness of words, will ever risk putting down thoughts in discourse, let alone fixing them into so unflexible a form as written letters" (cited in "Thinking" 426–27).

Of course, the first irony in these lines is that Plato is committing this argument to letters. A second irony is that the Platonic Socrates is a dramatic character—a written figure whose only claim is that he has no knowledge to transmit, much less to commit to writing. One might say, then, that what is most important in Plato's dialogues is the picture of thought for which Socrates is the agent, and again like Penelope's veil, this is a picture that is continually unwoven as soon as its texture begins to reveal itself. What the image of Socratic activity offers is an example of one who thinks without claiming to be a philosopher or even to have a doctrine that can be taught and learned. Socrates is only "a citizen among citizens," Arendt writes, "doing nothing, claiming nothing that, in his view, every citizen should do and had a right to claim" ("Thinking" 427). As few thinkers have cared to describe and examine the experience of thinking, Socrates becomes the image of thought without specific aim and the expression of an incessant desire for reasoned conversation that cannot arrive at knowledge but can only show itself in its time of deployment. In Stanley Cavell's terms, one might say that Socrates acknowledges the condition of philosophy as a fact of the human. And if Plato does know something, this claim can only be expressed indirectly. Thought only emerges in writing ironically as a space and time where thinking is ever present but cannot show

9. See, for example, Alexander Nehamas on Platonic or Socratic irony in *The Art of Living: Socratic Reflections from Plato to Foucault* (Berkeley: University of California Press, 1998), especially part 1. Among others, Martin Puchner has also noted how Plato's dialogues brought him into direct competition with the Athenian theater. See his essay "Theater, Philosophy, Pedagogy," *PMLA* 131:2 (March 2016): 423–29.

itself or give itself directly to external representation, especially to a spectator who is not prepared to apprehend it.[10]

By what criteria can the presence of thought in the Platonic writing of Socrates be recognized? Thought is the absent dramatic character in the Socratic dialogue or elenchus whose very movements of question and response, assertion and criticism, thrust and parry, blockage and release, make (nonvisible) thinking present like the wind that moves the water. As a picture of thought the Socratic elenchus is aporetic: the argument either leads nowhere or goes around in circles. In every dialogue, the arguments fly off in all directions, digress, and turn around themselves. Their very motor is Socrates's only claim: that he does not know anything. The fact that he has no answers as to what it means to know, to be just, or to be pious, makes of his discourse and his thinking a perpetual-motion machine. Once the elenchus comes full circle, it is Socrates who cheerfully proposes to start over because nothing has been resolved and nothing is finally known. You can stick with him, or like Euthyphro, run for cover.

The dialogues also ordinarily deal with familiar everyday concepts relating to experiences that every human undergoes and indeed wants to think or talk about. The trouble starts, Arendt suggests, when attention is focused on the habit of describing moral actions and qualities, as humans often perceive them, with nouns derived from adjectives—an action is just or unjust; a person is happy, pious, courageous, wise, or their contraries. An almost imperceptible transition occurs in this usage, where from within the judgment of a singular act or event comes the need to generalize and to subsume it under imagined comparable categories. Here concrete and descriptive nouns become abstract and general concepts. In its appeal to concepts and definitions, everyday speech has the disarming quality of grouping together seen and manifest qualities and experiences in the world with internal and unseen criteria that are fluid, contingent, and open ended. These orbits of expressed nouns into invisible concepts "are part and parcel of our

10. The inverse ratio between perceiving and reasoning is one of the most striking features of Platonic epistemology, whose most thorough explication appears in the *Republic* in the distinction between *eikāsia* and *noēsis* as the passage from an unreliable visibility to the nonvisible ideality of Form. See especially book 7 and the analogy of the divided line. I will return to these arguments later in discussion of Arendt's difficult concept of beauty and its role in judgments of taste.

everyday speech," Arendt writes, "and still we can give no account of them; when we try to define them, they get slippery; when we talk about their meaning, nothing stays put anymore, everything begins to move" ("Thinking" 429).

A particular difficulty is raised in the fact that nestled within every concept expressed as a noun is what Solon called a "non-appearing measure," which at the same time must refer to singular and particular things in the world. The converse is also true. To be capable of describing someone's particular dwelling as a /house/ means that one is in possession of the concept "house" defined by a limited yet open set of implicit and explicit criteria. Neither word nor concept would exist without the presence of unseen and perhaps unspoken measures such as the thought of dwelling, of being housed, or having a home. The noun is shorthand for all these things without which thinking would not be possible. To fix a concept with a noun is akin to pinning a thought to a word like a butterfly in a box. However, thinking must be unpinned and liberated to flight if it wants to set out, expand, revise, and deepen the criteria by which house and home can be recognized and newly qualified. So what is Socrates doing when he spins out concepts in ordinary language through the unending process of the elenchus?

This is where thought becomes what might properly be called *theōria*, and which Arendt characterizes as meditation—an ongoing process that does not and cannot arrive at definitive consensus and meaning, and in this sense, is entirely without results. Meditation is distinct in meaning and practice from contemplation and deliberation in that, as I argued before, it is impracticable: it has no specific aim, end, or terminus. What kind of praxis can thought lead to, then? Socrates wanted his fellow citizens to become more pious, more courageous, more just, and indeed more thoughtful. But the only thing he claimed to know was that no closed definition or determined qualification of these things could define and direct their conduct or meaning. In the dialogue named for him, Meno calls Socrates an electric ray, a fish that in paralyzing others paralyzes itself. In turn Socrates admits, "It isn't that, knowing the answers myself I perplex other people. The truth is rather that I infect them also with the perplexity I feel myself."[11] And perhaps this is the

---

11. See for example, Plato's *Meno*, in *Five Dialogues*, trans., G. M. A. Grube (Indianapolis: Hackett, 2002), 80d, 70.

only definition of teaching and thinking that humanists could really settle on. But there is something else, which perhaps makes Socrates the first ordinary-language philosopher. If there is a particular aim to the elenchus, it comes from Socrates's thoughtful need to find out if his perplexity was shared and shareable with his fellow humans. This need amounts again to what Cavell calls acknowledging—to bring criteria forth, to check them with others, to seek out patterns of agreement and disagreement, and this process is without end.

The practice of meditation or aimless thought can be further enlarged by examining three similes that were used to describe Socrates: as gadfly, midwife, and, again, electric eel. Socrates is a gadfly in that through the elenchus he wants to awaken citizens to thought—without his incessant and stinging dialectic, they will sleep on undisturbed for the rest of their lives. This is an awakening to thinking, to examining matters and activities that make a life worth living and without which one is not fully and humanly alive. One might also consider this pestering as awakening thought to change, to being open to change, and to making oneself more self-aware, indeed more fully human. Socrates also calls himself a midwife, but like the midwives of ancient Greece, he is past the age of "childbearing"; he cannot teach because he has no particular knowledge to impart. As midwife, Socrates only "teaches" by helping others bring forth whatever thoughts and opinions they are capable of bearing and communicating. And in this manner, as Arendt puts it, "he purged people of their 'opinions,' that is, of those unexamined prejudgments which prevent thinking by suggesting that we know where we not only don't know but cannot know, helping them, as Plato remarks, to get rid of what was bad in them, their opinions, without however making them good, giving them truth" ("Thinking" 432–33, with reference to *Sophist* line 258).[12]

Socrates's elenchus aims at emptying his interlocutors of all their

12. In her lecture "Philosophy and Politics," Arendt characterizes Socrates's "sterility" as his lack of *doxa*, which is perhaps his acknowledgment of both the partiality of each individual's perspective—their *dokei moi* or it seems to me—and the value of that perspective, which situates actors in a common world. The absence that marks Socrates's sterility is to be without opinion, or perhaps, to withdraw or withhold his *doxa* as a tactic for encouraging others to bring their unexamined assumptions into the light of criticism and self-criticism. The dialogue between friends here becomes the basic condition for self-knowledge and self-revision. See Arendt, "Philosophy and Politics," *Social Research* 57:1 (Spring 1990): 91. I will return to these arguments in section V.

unfounded and unexamined beliefs and opinions. The elenchus is among the first arts of critique in the Kantian sense, where critique means assessing the limits of the faculty of reason itself. Arendt describes this activity as an art of discrimination—a *techne diakritikē* that sorts, separates, and distinguishes among our beliefs and opinions. However, no final knowledge follows dialectical examination. In circling about the possibilities and limits of knowledge, the elenchus encourages reflexive examination of the process of reasoning itself. Here one must take seriously the idea that Socrates practiced thinking as an art and that there is no art that is not a public art. Therefore, in Arendt's account, "Socrates' uniqueness lies in this concentration on thinking itself, regardless of results. There is no ulterior motive or ulterior purpose for the whole enterprise. An unexamined life is not worth living. That is all there is to it. What he actually did was to make public, in discourse, the thinking process—that dialogue that soundlessly goes on within me, between me and myself; he performed in the marketplace the way the flute-player performed at a banquet. It is sheer performance, sheer activity."[13]

Here is another reason why I consider Socrates to be the first ordinary-language philosopher. His performance of the elenchus is an expert performance, but dialectical conversation is not something beyond the capacity of ordinary citizens. Moreover, Socrates draws others into the practice of philosophy in an entirely public way. He founded no schools and belonged to no sects but rather engaged any willing citizen in the open forum of the marketplace and other public spaces. As a public figure, Arendt notes, he was entirely unprotected and open to all questioners and to all demands that he stand by his thought and live up to what he argued. There can be no appeal to doctrine or authority here; one's only defense is the public demonstration of what and how one thinks in an open forum.

In similar ways, Kant was also ideally committed to placing philosophy in the public discourse of the polis in that he defined political freedom as the universal right and obligation to the public use of reason. In the *Reflexionen über Anthropologie*, for example, Kant writes that

13. Hannah Arendt, *Lectures on Kant's Political Philosophy* (Chicago: University of Chicago Press, 1992), 37. A deeper and more expansive account is given in Arendt's section on "Invisibility and Withdrawal" in *Life of the Mind: Thinking*, 69–80.

the faculty of thinking is dependent upon its public use—this is a key bridge between Kant's critique of judgment and the earlier critiques of pure and practical reason. Neither reasoning nor judging are possible without "the test of free and open examination," which means that the greater the participation in a public discourse, the wider the appeal of critical reason. In this respect, Kant says that reason is not made "to isolate itself but to get into community with others."[14] There is something counterintuitive about this insistence on the public performance of thinking as Arendt is well aware. In her *Lectures on Kant's Political Philosophy* Arendt writes,

> Thinking, as Kant agreed with Plato, is the silent dialogue of myself with myself (*das Reden mit sich selbst*), and that thinking is a "solitary business" (as Hegel once remarked) is one of the few things on which all thinkers were agreed. Also, it is of course by no means true that you need or can even bear the company of others when you happen to be busy thinking; yet, unless you can somehow communicate and expose to the test of others, either orally or in writing, whatever you may have found out when you were alone, this faculty exerted in solitude will disappear. In the words of Jaspers, truth is what I can communicate. Truth in the sciences is dependent on the experiment that can be repeated by others; it requires general validity. Philosophic truth has no such general validity. What it must have, what Kant demanded in the *Critique of Judgment* of judgments of taste, is "general communicability." "For it is a natural vocation of mankind to communicate and speak one's mind, especially in all matters concerning man as such."[15]

Though no doubt a solitary business, Kant nonetheless asserts that thinking depends on others for its possibility and potentiality—Arendt calls this the criterion of "publicity," where the political implications of critical thinking are defined by its communicability. This is why I have characterized the Socratic elenchus as a making present of thought, or perhaps better, making perspicuous the process of thinking with

14. Immanuel Kant, *Reflexionen über Anthropologie*, no. 897, in *Gesammelte Schriften* (Prussian Academy ed.), 15:392; cited in Arendt, *Lectures on Kant*, 40.

15. Arendt, *Lectures*, 40, citing Kant, "On the Common Saying: That May Be True in Theory, but It Does Not Apply in Practice," in *Kant: Political Writings*, ed. H. S. Reiss (Cambridge: Cambridge University Press, 1991), 85–86. I will turn again to Kant's arguments concerning human sociability and what Kant calls the transcendental principle of publicity in section IV.

all of its false starts, fumbles, detours, and digressions. The aim of the elenchus is to extract from every statement its hidden or latent implications and its unacknowledged assumptions. However, submitting to this kind of critical examination also presupposes that everyone is willing and able to give account of what he or she thinks and says. To give an account is to retrace critically one's steps, as it were, not to give proof but rather to offer reasons—to acknowledge and recount how one came to express a given idea or argument—hence Socrates's demand to hold oneself and indeed everyone else responsible and answerable for their thoughts and opinions. *Quaestio facti*, or questions of intellect in which one claims possession of a fact or concept, are of little use here. More fundamental are questions of judgment, *quaestio juris*, that examine whether one has earned the right to use and deploy a concept. And so Arendt concludes that "it is precisely by applying critical standards to one's own thought that one learns the art of critical thought. And this application one cannot learn without publicity, without the testing that arises from contact with other people's thinking" (*Lectures* 42). The problem here, which all of Socrates's interlocutors come to realize if they choose not to avoid the fact, is that thinking is a difficult, uncertain, and unsettling business, which can affect humans in their practical and political lives as much as in the domain of pure reason.

Socrates knows that he knows nothing but is unwilling to let it go at that. His perplexities are paralyzing like the sting of an eel in the sense that they seem to lead nowhere, and contact with Socrates induces this state in others. But what looks from the outside like confusion and paralysis, a diversion of practical activity, might also be felt as becoming more fully human and committing more fully to human life both internally and externally. Here Arendt notes that "Socrates himself, very much aware that thinking deals with invisibles and is itself invisible, lacking all the outside manifestation of other activities, seems to have used the metaphor of the wind for it: 'The winds themselves are invisible, yet what they do is manifest to us and we somehow feel their approach'" ("Thinking" 433, citing Xenophon's *Memorabilia*, IV. iii. 14). The force of being caught up in the elenchus is paralyzing but also storm driven, and if one considers thinking as an invisible wind that carries us into thought, it is also a force that can sweep thought away. Nothing is given in advance, nor can thinking be taken for granted. Considered in this way, thinking has the capacity to destroy, undermine, or cast doubt upon normative values and criteria for judging good and evil or other actions and beliefs. Or more positively, Socrates is not asking his interlocutors to cast aside the customs and rules by which moral behavior is judged and evaluated but rather to make them present to view, that is, open to examination, assessment, critique, reevaluation, and revision; otherwise, we sleepwalk through lives guided by unexamined beliefs, and while the shock of the elenchus rouses you from your sleep, it also makes you more fully alive. The cost is discovering that your most cherished criteria and concepts, and your normative routines, have dissolved into perplexities; the most you can do is to share them with others.

Arendt characterizes the paralysis of thought as, on one hand, an interruption or immobilization of habitual thought and action and, on the other, as a hesitancy or uncertainty of direction that arises when you emerge out of thought "no longer sure of what had seemed to you beyond doubt while you were unthinkingly engaged in whatever you were doing" ("Thinking" 434). In both cases, one finds suddenly that whatever general rules are in use to conduct particular cases in ordinary life are dispersed by the wind, and there is no guarantee that these rules will be immediately replaced. This is why critical thinking is a dangerous and disorienting business. If one is unwilling or unable to restart the elenchus, the nonresults of Socratic thinking may turn into the negative result of nihilism—if there is no doctrine to guide us into piety, let us be impious.

Another way to put this is to say that nihilism is a danger inherent to the activity of thinking. If thinking is capable of overturning and dissolving doctrines and rules, then it can also at every moment turn against itself. Nothing shelters thought from thought, and no reversal of old values assures the creation of new values, which is why critique must be measured by judgment. As Arendt puts it, the negative results of thought may be applied as indolently as any habit, routine, or *doxa*, and in this respect, it is important to understand that nihilism is an inversion of *doxa*, not its replacement or destruction. "There are no dangerous thoughts," Arendt writes,

> thinking is itself dangerous, but nihilism is not its product. Nihilism is but the other side of conventionalism; its creed consists of negations of the current, so-called positive values to which it remains bound. All

critical examinations must go through a stage of at least hypothetically negating accepted opinions and "values" by finding out their implications and tacit assumptions, and in this sense, nihilism may be seen as an ever-present danger of thinking. But this danger does not arise out of the Socratic conviction that an unexamined life is not worth living but, on the contrary, out of the desire to find results which would make further thinking unnecessary. Thinking is equally dangerous to all creeds and, by itself, does not bring forth any new creed. ("Thinking" 435)

This is why judgment is so important: in bringing thinking out of oneself it opens thought not only to communication but also to debate with others capable of challenging and modifying it. Judgment makes thought public and offers it to evaluation, critique, and revision. I will return to this.

Even worse than nihilism is the danger of not thinking at all. From her mid-twentieth-century perspective, Arendt was well aware that conformity and adherence to power discourages people from critical examination or self-examination, and to hold fast to prescribed rules of conduct: "What people then get used to is not so much the content of the rules, a close examination of which would always lead them into perplexity, as the [unthinking] possession of rules under which to subsume particulars" ("Thinking" 436). What makes the examined life worth living, then? Thinking accompanies living when it aims to acknowledge those qualities that enhance individual and collective life such as justice, happiness, loyalty, wisdom, or pleasure, which Arendt states are all "words for invisible things which language has offered us to express the meaning of whatever happens in life and occurs to us while we are alive" ("Thinking" 436–37). Thought withdraws within itself to examine these "non-appearing measures" not because of duty, but rather out of desire, which is another reason why thinking might be considered a fundamental human impulse. This is the important Socratic theme of the immanent relation between thought and *erōs*, to which I will return presently. Thinking is driven by *erōs* in that it desires what it cannot possess or contain. Philosophers seek wisdom and are in love with it because it is something they desire and cannot finally or fully possess. But in desiring what is not there, *erōs* directs us to thought's intangible absence. In the Platonic sense, objects of thought—concepts—can only be lovable things: wisdom, justice, virtue, or beauty; thus evil becomes privation, an absence of love and an absence of thought.

In noting Plato's claim in *Protagoras* that no one commits evil voluntarily, Arendt asks, "Where does this leave us with respect to our problem—inability or refusal to think and the capacity of doing evil? We are left with the conclusion that only people filled with this *erōs*, this desiring love of wisdom, beauty, and justice, are capable of thought— that is, we are left with Plato's 'noble nature' as a prerequisite for thinking. And this was precisely what we were *not* looking for when we raised the question whether the thinking activity, the very performance itself—as distinguished from and regardless of whatever qualities a man's nature, his soul, may possess—conditions him in such a way that he is incapable of evil" ("Thinking" 438). "Not looking for" because Arendt is concerned with our ordinary human capacities of reasoning and judgment, whether exercised well or poorly, or even exercised at all.

The criterion of publicity returns here in important ways, not only as the context for performing or externalizing thought but also as a bridge between pure and practical reason, that is, thinking and moral consideration. The elenchus would seem to produce little but perplexity and thoughts that circle in loops. But in making thought a public performance, one might say that it also brings thoughts *out* such that arguments become present to themselves and expressible in a public space. In bringing forth positive assertions, no matter how compelling or problematic, the public dimension of the performance of the elenchus also makes opinions or ideas examinable and thus intersubjectively revisable. Arendt notes that for his own part, Socrates is known only to have made two positive philosophical statements, both of which occur in a late dialogue, *Gorgias*.[16] The first states, "It is better to be wronged than to do wrong"; the second avers, "It would be better for me that my lyre or a chorus I directed should be out of tune and loud with discord, and that multitudes of men should disagree with me rather than that I, being one, should be out of harmony with myself and contradict me" ("Thinking" 439). The second statement is in fact the prerequisite for the first one, which demands that one not act contrary

16. Arendt's claim that Plato's Socrates makes few positive claims is surely not wholly accurate. The *Republic* in particular differs from the earlier works both dramaturgically and logically, especially in its design of building more or less systematically a picture of the city and its laws through a progressive series of interlocking assertions.

to virtue, or in Kantian terms, that moral acts be self-consistent. And it is curious that the second assertion is expressed in analogy with musical performance or direction, for like a good artist and improviser, Socrates performs according to a persistent theme, which in the *Critique of Judgment* Kant calls the maxim of consistency. This maxim of consistency has both logical and ethical commands for the thinker: do not talk or think nonsense—that is, let your thought be consistent with itself, and let your thought be consistent with your *self* (it is better to be at odds with multitudes than, being one, to be at odds with yourself). One of Kant's great accomplishments was to insist in this way on the intimate connection between reason and ethics as embodied in the categorical imperative. As Arendt explains in her *Lectures*, "Act so that the maxim of your action can be willed by you to become a general law, that is, a law to which you yourself would be subject. It is, again, the same general rule—Do not contradict yourself (not your self but your thinking ego)—that determines both thinking and acting" (37).[17]

The Socratic insistence on internal consistency is apparently paradoxical in the sense that a being identical with itself cannot be internally divided and out of sync with itself—it takes a relation of two or more to produce either discord or harmony. What relation of self to self is Socrates suggesting here? What the elenchus aims to produce, if it produces anything, is a presence of self to consciousness by making us suddenly aware of our relation to thinking, as if our thoughts could be separate from our selves or brought out of ourselves into the light of rational examination. From the external perspective of others, I appear singular and whole, and when barely conscious of myself in the midst of habitual actions, I may not be thinking. However, the picture is changed by the emergence of consciousness in this special sense as active thinking. Arendt observes that consciousness means literally "to know with myself," which she defines as "the curious fact that in a sense I also am for myself, though I hardly appear to me, which indicates that the Socratic 'being-one' is not so unproblematic as it seems; I am not only for others but for myself, and in this latter case, I clearly am not just one. A difference is inserted into my Oneness" ("Thinking" 441).

This observation is an important logical and dramatic feature of the Socratic dialogues. The dialogues, no less than the structure of the elen-

17. For a deeper discussion of these issues, see *Life of the Mind: Thinking*, 180–83.

chus itself, require the active presence of two or more as the basis for active thinking and a coming to consciousness of one's thoughts, both in relation to oneself and to others. Perhaps this is a recognition that each singular thing exists within and with respect to a plurality of other things. In other words, every singularity is also defined by alterity and by its differential relation within a contingent and variable community of other singularities—whenever thought wants to grasp the One, it must also take into account difference, alterity, and otherness. And here is the paradox that Arendt explains in Socrates's "being one": "This curious thing that I am needs no plurality in order to establish difference; it carries the difference within itself when it says: 'I am I.' So long as I am conscious, that is, conscious of myself, I am identical with myself only for others to whom I appear as one and the same. For myself, articulating this being-conscious-of-myself, I am inevitably two-in-one—which incidentally is the reason why the fashionable search for identity is futile and our modern identity crisis could be resolved only by losing consciousness" ("Thinking" 442). Difference and otherness are an external relation in the world of appearance—every singular thing is defined in relation to difference and otherness, but internal difference and otherness are also constitutive of the human capacity for self-examination and internal reflection: "For this ego, the I-am-I, experiences difference in identity precisely when it is not related to the things that appear but only to itself. Without this original split, which Plato later used in his definition of thinking as the soundless dialogue (*eme emautô*) between me and myself, the two-in-one, which Socrates presupposes in his statement about harmony with myself, would not be possible. Consciousness is not the same as thinking; but without it thinking would be impossible. What thinking actualizes in its process is the difference given in consciousness" ("Thinking" 442). Herein also lies the theme of the philosophical friend, even if that friend is only an internal relation with oneself. The Socratic two-in-one of thinking means that if you want to carry out thinking in the elenchus, then the participants should be friends, that is, seeking out harmony even if it proves to be impossible, perplexing, and paralyzing. On one hand, the elenchus is diagnostic—it forces us to recognize that we are out of tune with our own beliefs or thoughts—but it is also aims to assure, shall we say, a wellness program for thought.

Review for a moment those qualities or dimensions of reason, or its absence, that Arendt has presented to her readers: habit, *doxa*, thought-lessness, thinking, destructive or disorienting thought, meditation, active thought, and finally the active internal difference of consciousness, which will all finally lead to "action" or politics. To complete this list will require turning more assiduously to the activity of judgment. One starting point will be the active internal difference of consciousness as something like internal judgment as moral self-assessment, that is, judgment of and within one's self where consciousness is informed by conscience. In this respect, self-judgment is a genetic element or motor of judgment per se, which must become a public and discursive act. To reconnect thinking to moral reasoning, then, Arendt pursues this line in order finally to examine the relation of conscience to consciousness. Conscience is also ordinarily considered to be an internal relation of self to self. But to the extent that conscience is pictured as the presence of a moral imperative from within or above, whether Kant's practical reason or God's commandments, the relation of thinking to conscience is passive. The Socratic characterization of conscience is something other. In *Hippias Major*, Socrates tells the rather dull Hippias that he is a fortunate fellow because when he returns home, he is alone with his thoughts, if he has any. Alternatively, Socrates recounts that he is always awaited by an obnoxious relative ever present in his home who relentlessly cross-examines him. Conscience, then, is this unrelenting inner dialogue and critical examination of one's self and one's relation to thought that is no more powerful than when one is alone with one's thoughts in meditation. Or as Arendt puts it, "He who does not know the intercourse between me and myself (in which we examine what we say and what we do) will not mind contradicting himself, and this means he will never be either able or willing to give account of what he says or does; nor will he mind committing any crime, since he can be sure that it will be forgotten the next moment" ("Thinking" 444–45).[18]

18. In her 1967 essay "Truth and Politics," Arendt discusses the relation between self-consistency in thought and moral reasoning in the following terms: "Everything that can be said in its defense we find in the various Platonic dialogues. The chief argument states that for man, *being one*, it is better to be at odds with the whole world than to be at odds with and contradicted by himself—an argument that is compelling indeed for the philosopher, whose thinking is characterized by Plato as a silent dialogue with himself, and whose existence therefore depends upon a constantly articulated intercourse with himself, a splitting-into-two of the one he nevertheless is; for a basic contradiction between the two partners who carry on the thinking dialogue would destroy the very conditions of philosophizing. In other words, since

I want to insist again that the capacity for thinking is an ordinary human capacity, as is the actualization of internal difference given in the relation of conscience to consciousness. Alternatively, the inability to think, or the avoidance of this internal dialogue with oneself or with others, is not the special province of the "uneducated." This possibility is equally present in knowledge specialists like humanists and scientists, and for Arendt it defines the evil of nonthinking in "the non-wicked everybody who has no special motives and for this reason is capable of *infinite* evil" ("Thinking" 445). This claim is the basis for Arendt's arguments about the ethico-political force or power of thinking, and her claim that the faculty of judgment is the most political of human faculties. There are moments of history, as Arendt well knew, when the faculties of thought, reasoning, and judgment are swept away by ideology and thoughtlessness. When the mass is subsumed by the tides of opinion and unexamined belief, those still capable of reason, judgment, and criticism become conspicuous in their refusal to succumb to nonthinking, and this refusal itself becomes a kind of active resistance. What Arendt calls the purging quality of reflexive critical thought brings forward the implications of unexamined opinions, values, doctrines, and convictions with the aim not only of exposing them but also of demolishing them. Here thought is political by implication. As Arendt insisted, "Unlike speculative thought, which rarely bothers anyone, critical thought is in principle antiauthoritarian. And, as far as the authorities are concerned, the worst thing is that you cannot catch it, cannot seize it" (*Lectures* 38). This destruction has the power to liberate judgment and to put thoughts into action.

I will turn to a deeper account of judgment in relation to thinking in the next section. By way of transition, I will just note for the moment that Arendt defines judgment as the faculty of evaluating particulars without subsuming them under general rules, especially rules that have become normative in the sense of an ingrained habit through repetition. Therefore, judgment carries within it the power to challenge normative opinions, no matter how deeply held, just as thought carries

---

man contains within himself a partner from whom he can never win release, he will be better off not to live in company with a murderer or a liar. Or, since thought is the silent dialogue carried on between me and myself; I must be careful to keep the integrity of this partner intact; for otherwise I shall surely lose the capacity for thought altogether." "Truth and Politics," in *Between Past and Future: Eight Exercises in Political Thought* (New York: Penguin Books, 1977): 240–41. I will return to this essay in greater depth in section V.

within itself a destructive capacity. However, Arendt is clear in stating that judging is not the same as thinking, and vice versa:

> The faculty of judging particulars (as Kant discovered it), the ability to say, "this is wrong," "this is beautiful," etc., is not the same as the faculty of thinking. Thinking deals with invisibles, with representations of things that are absent; judging always concerns particulars and things close at hand. But the two are interrelated in a way similar to the way consciousness and conscience are interconnected. If thinking, the two-in-one of the soundless dialogue, actualizes the difference within our identity as given in *consciousness* and thereby results in conscience as its by-product, then judging, the by-product of the liberating effect of thinking, realizes thinking, makes it manifest in the world of appearances, where I am never alone and always much too busy to be able to think. The manifestation of the wind of thought [as judgment] is no knowledge; it is the ability to tell right from wrong, beautiful from ugly. And this indeed may prevent catastrophes, at least for myself, in the rare moments when the chips are down. ("Thinking" 446)

These are the last lines of "Thinking and Moral Considerations," and the historical and political stakes they evoke should be clear to anyone. For Arendt, acts of judgment are political by implication because, first of all, they are *acts*. They bring us out of the solitude of thought; they are the very medium through which we disclose ourselves and our thoughts by performing them publicly like Socrates, as a citizen among citizens, doing nothing, claiming nothing other than what every citizen should do and has a right to claim. And again, like Socrates, in this public space we are entirely unprotected and open to all questioners and to all demands that we stand by our thoughts and live up to our arguments. In other words, acts of judgment bring thought into the space of the polis.

II. JUDGMENT AND CULTURE

I began the last section with the question, What does it mean to be human or to become more fully human, or to know that one can become so? Before continuing, I want both to review and anticipate some possible routes of response to these questions, all of which should

be considered less as pathways to conviction than as vectors on a map
that both cross and branch out from one another. Whether these assertions persuade or not requires a test of experience.

1. Becoming human requires more than species belonging to the cat-
   egory *Homo sapiens*. One is not born human; one must strive to
   become human.
2. Becoming human is an ethical, not a biological process, and it
   requires ethical evaluations, decisions, and actions. These routes
   to becoming human pass through the operations of judgment.
3. Becoming human is a continuous ethical exercise without finality,
   which assumes the possibility of human revisability.
4. Humans are intentional beings, pursuing actions and thoughts pur-
   posively, and thus cannot help asking questions relating to existential purpose.
5. If the necessity of thinking, and to think beyond the limitations of
   empirical knowledge, is a basic condition of the human, then philosophy is not an elite activity but rather an always present human
   potentiality, even if it is exercised infrequently and unevenly.
6. To become human is to exercise a capacity for judgment in an
   intersubjective context, which Kant calls representative thinking,
   or thinking from the standpoint of others.
7. The expression of taste (call this the acknowledgment and expression of meaningfulness and value) is exemplary of the exercise of
   judgment whose domain is artful conversation. To communicate
   freely one's taste is to find one's place in a community of others,
   where communicability and sociability are defining criteria of the
   human.
8. Plurality is another fact of the human. Becoming human is not
   becoming one, but rather learning how to navigate one's life in
   common community. The most fundamental fact that associates
   plurality with politics is that living together with others means living
   together with one's self. It is as if that internal relation of self to self
   that Arendt calls conscience makes of every human a polis in microcosm. Perhaps this is another way of asserting that every being who
   aspires to be human carries that possibility within him- or herself
   as a shared community sense, or what Stanley Cavell characterizes
   as the internal relation of each human being with all others.

If any single aim is capable of uniting these otherwise diverse and multiform activities within the humanities, it could only be described as encouraging an education in judgment. Many will recognize the perfectionist orientation of these "compass points." To examine the operations of judgment in intersubjective conversations about taste or, better, in disagreements about meaning and value in literature, art, or philosophy can help us better understand how daily rehearsals of judgment and the public performance of thinking (call this teaching) can expand our powers of critical reason. My assertion here is that judgment is the core activity of humanistic study and that only through the practice of judgment—with its activation and externalization of thought, its conflicts and intersubjective testing of reason, and its encouragement to revise one's opinions and values in open communication with others—does one come to recognize the potentials and possibilities for becoming human. Through judgment we discover, express, and reconsider both old and new criteria for defining what it means to be a thoughtful and responsible citizen in local and global communities of human existence, and for better or worse, these criteria are endlessly revisable.[19]

I hope to have given some depth of response to the first five propositions in the previous section of this essay. However, the last three propositions, in what is no doubt an open and revisable list, need to be addressed more completely.

The example of Socrates—as gadfly, midwife, and electric eel—presents a picture of thought emerging from its solitary exercise into the public space of performance. What remains to be discovered is how thinking relates to judgment and how judgment relates to the formation of critical communities no matter how fragile or contingent. Here lines must be traced that lead out from the internal, private, solitary, and invisible relation of thought to itself, to the external, public, sociable,

19. As one of my thoughtful readers remarked, "On this perfectionist account, the humanity of human beings is not merely a property we all possess, but a *possibility* we all possess of self-realization through an education in judgment—that is, an education in the practice of working out together, in open and contingent intersubjective conversations with others, how we want our world to look, how we want our lives together to go, and what our situation means in light of the histories and possible futures of our world. In effect, . . . a defense of the humanities on the grounds that the very things that make humanistic education seem of doubtful value from the point of view of the ends-directed and utilitarian demands of corporate capitalism are actually central to what it means to be human."

and visible activity of judgment in community with others. The path from thinking to judgment must be better understood, as well as the activity of judgment itself in relation to the formation of contingent polities at variable scales. Only in this way can a bridge be raised between art and politics in relation to culture, broadly conceived.

In her long philosophical career, Arendt wrote relatively little on aesthetics, nor did she seem overly concerned with the criticism of art.[20] At the same time, she was deeply concerned about the humanities and its connection to politics. In this respect, there is a complexly designed bridge that connects the 1960 essay "The Crisis in Culture" to her later lecture "Thinking and Moral Considerations," as well as, inter alia, works like *The Human Condition, The Life of the Mind*, and her posthumous *Lectures on Kant's Political Philosophy*. Arendt's bridge is fashioned out of her compelling and original account of Kant's critique of the human powers of judgment, a project that was supposed to lead to her final contribution to *The Life of the Mind*, where judgment was to complete the activities of thinking and willing. The problem of judgment in fact dominated the last decades of her philosophical life. Arendt's guiding idea, strange on the face of it, is that the third Critique should be read as Kant's contribution to a political philosophy whose fundamental elements and actions are grounded in judgments of taste. The place and power of the formation and communication of aesthetic experience is not neglected here but rather reframed with respect to a particular concern: care of the polis and its attendant cultures, and how the power of a singular experience—aesthetic experience expressed as a judgment of taste—may be woven into communities of shared taste and moral concern. The question of freedom of action is also of special significance. As singular judgments, which are made in perfect freedom out of a disinterested relation to the object, form and pass into contingent critical communities, the question now is valuing how the freely expressed singular judgment is conditioned (and potentially transformed and revised) intersubjectively, in contrast to the silent and solitary exercise of thought. Expressive critical freedom is the *energeia* of the polis. A care for culture entails preserving and perpetuating

20. Of course, Arendt's many occasional essays on poetry, literature, and art show a lively and lifelong interest in these activities. See, for example, the collection of Arendt's criticism in *Reflections on Literature and Culture*.

enduring aesthetic experiences, of course, but even more fundamental is cultivating the kinds of free relations, for ourselves and for others, that are open to transformation by our encounters with others. In this manner, the power of judgment extends judgments of taste into an ever-widening fabric of intersubjective moral consideration, which for Arendt is the basis of any polity. The humanities' care for culture, or if one still dares to use these terms, its cultivation of taste and powers of judgment, here becomes the basis of both a politics and an ethics.

Arendt's 1960 essay "The Crisis in Culture" is a sprawling and erudite manifesto that offers in a condensed way the main arguments of her magisterial book, *The Human Condition*, first published in 1958. Many interrelated factors are at play in Arendt's sense of crisis in postwar American and European culture. One familiar theme, addressed in varied and contradictory ways by other authors, is raised in the persistent critique in contemporary art criticism of the devaluation of aesthetic experience in general, whether with respect to the leveling effects of mass culture and mass entertainment or, relatedly, the fabrication and distribution of aesthetic experience for circuits of commodity exchange.[21] Arendt will have some surprising and counterintuitive things to say here that countervail her otherwise ostensible cultural conservatism. But the question remains: How can philosophy reassert and revalue aesthetic experience and, in turn, reassert its connection to political action?

Arendt responds to this question by asking another related one in the second half of her essay: What are the proper terms for intercourse with art? This is another way of addressing the principal theme of my larger argument: How might judgment as artful conversation be considered as both a critical and an ethical practice? Much like the late Adorno, at her time of writing Arendt is concerned with the emergence of an American mass society in contrast to what one might call "high society"—that is, forms of European culture historically linked to the disappearance of court patronage and the rise of the mercantile classes.

21. For a fascinating account of the intellectual and artistic context in which Arendt's essay was written, see Patchen Markell's "Arendt, Aesthetics, and 'The Crisis in Culture,'" in *The Aesthetic Turn in Political Thought*, ed. Nikolas Kompridis (New York: Bloomsbury, 2014), 61–88.

For the latter, art is a form of investment, and for the former, culture is an object of consumption and social status. This dialectic is unfinished today, and in fact it has achieved a point of intensity where investment and consumption are inextricably bound together. Of this there is little doubt. Arendt herself asserts that there are definitely two misuses of intercourse with art, leading to one definition of her crisis in culture. Think of these as misdirected encounters with art, both of which are compromised by self-interest, and both of which contaminate with necessity our potentially free relations with art objects. The first misuse engages art only for purposes of self-education or self-improvement; the second values art only in terms of its exchange value, whether as capital or social investment. In either case, these attitudes lead to philistinism, which Arendt defines as something like self-investment independent of community or, alternatively, investing oneself with unshared cultural capital. The philistine defines himself only by self-interest, independent of community and the polis, and his interest in art is purely selfish. Cultural values are leveled out here to a form of evaluation where culture is reduced to signs of personal wealth and social status—culture becomes currency.[22]

The more intercourse with art is framed by exchange value as capital or personal investment, the more one loses touch with a power that Arendt suggests "is originally peculiar to all cultural things, the faculty of arresting our attention and moving us."[23] Aesthetic experience is close to thinking here. Recall again how thinking not only sweeps us up in its currents but also stops us in our tracks. Related forces of aesthetic experience might hold or reorient thinking, directing it toward criticism. I should also add another fundamental area of concern for Arendt: the devaluation of aesthetic experience involves a

22. In her lecture "Culture and Politics," which may be read as an early version of "The Crisis in Culture," Arendt provides a brief genealogy of the phenomenon of cultural philistinism (*Bildungsphilisterium*) as characterized by Clemens Brentano in his 1811 pamphlet "Philistines before, in, and after History." Among other themes, Arendt examines the socialization of culture on the model of the eighteenth-century salons and "good" society as the origin of mass culture. The psychology of this particular kind of social response to art or culture is characterized by the following qualities: a loosening of one's rootedness in a local, national, or religious culture (*Verlassenheit*) along with a new kind of adaptability close to conformism, an extraordinary capacity for consumption, the utter inability to judge or make discernments, and an egocentrism expressed as a fatal alienation from the world mistaken as self-alienation. See *Reflections on Literature and Culture*, 179–202.

23. Hannah Arendt, "The Crisis in Culture: Its Social and Political Significance," in *Between Past and Future*, 201.

loss of freedom in our intercourse with art or, rather, absorbs freedom into necessity. Ultimately, Arendt will argue that works of art must be defended as the one area of human action whose value and meaning cannot fully or finally be absorbed by use value or exchange value. I will come back to this.

Before turning to questions of criticism and judgment in the second half of her essay, in the first section of "The Crisis in Culture," Arendt introduces a somewhat mysterious criterion in asking: What is art's relation to life, or what is the relation of culture to life? By life she means something quite literal—that which sustains biological existence such as food, shelter, and security, indeed what serves the immediate animal need for survival and reproduction. There is no freedom from these needs, but more importantly, understanding the relation of culture to life sets the context for evaluating artifacts of art and culture in relation to time and history. It will be important to understand that Arendt values art at two radically different time scales: one is immediate, intensive, affective, and sociable; the other is transgenerational, autonomous or "objective," and worldly. You will soon understand that in Arendt's arguments, these two dimensions are irreconcilable in many respects, though both will invoke the capacity for judgment, as should soon be clear. On the larger historical time scale, objects are judged to be art or to belong to culture because they endure, and they endure for a culture beyond the lifetime of individuals. You are thinking that this is the old problem of canon formation, and you are correct. But it is important to understand this question as always conflicted and unfinished, though this is more my position than Arendt's. There can be no final agreement on which artifacts belong to culture or not, nor will there finally be agreed-upon common criteria for belonging; otherwise, judgment could not be tied to thinking by the fact of its recurrent, unfinished character. Moreover, if Arendt is right about this criterion, individuals are never around to really know if any artifacts of their own contemporary culture will become integrated into future human cultures. At the same time, from our own historical standpoint, ideally, we are constantly assessing and reassessing, evaluating, and debating the terms for judging which artifacts of the past are worth engaging with and in what ways they might remain relevant to contemporary problems and concepts. This is one way in which we come to define our presence in critical communities at various scales. For whatever else we think we're doing, humanists are constantly and generally engaged with this critical activity. And in this respect, for better or worse, we are agents of and for culture.

In this context, questions of impermanence and the temporality of present and immediate uses are also raised. For Arendt, the question of culture is always suspended between investment and entertainment. The investment classes consider art as a currency that can rise and diminish in value. Their aim is not to enjoy art in Kant's sense, for example, but rather to assure its cultural permanence in terms of maintaining exchange value and cultural capital. Alternatively, mass society wants entertainment, not culture, and entertainment is defined by the impermanence of consumption. This is another tendency that has only intensified since Arendt's time. Arendt says that entertainment products do not serve "life" in the same way that food or shelter materially sustain the *bios*. The role they serve is filling up time. But this is not leisure time or free time, but rather "leftover" time, that is, time that remains after the activities of labor and sleep have been served. (And remember that this time was only difficultly won by the working classes of the late nineteenth and early twentieth centuries.) Arendt calls this vacant time where entertainment fills in the gaps and hiatuses of the biologically conditioned cycle of labor and reproduction. I note here that it is neither Arendt's position nor mine that art or culture disappears into an antimony defined by investment and entertainment. Nor do I consider investment and entertainment to be inherently undesirable or immoral activities. Choose at random for yourself any two examples. Are *Westworld* or Jeff Koons's balloon dogs entertainment or art? In either case, this question can only be posed and (temporarily) decided in recurrent acts of judgment.

Ironically, in our own information-addled era, there is less and less leftover time, which perhaps makes the activity of judgment more urgent. Or more precisely, this vacant time is no longer available in extended and continuous blocks. Rather, it is thinned out, fragmented, and multiplied into discontinuous segments of shorter and shorter duration as access to labor time is amplified and overrun by electronic communications and social media. Or worse, it is expanded into the dead time of unemployment and precarious labor. (As those who survived the 2020 pandemic well know, an abundance of vacant time can itself be a curse, especially in the absence of social life.) At the same time, entertainment expands exponentially to fill the fragmented intervals of contemporary vacant time. While the inventory of vacant time may be continually eroded by new forms of labor and communication, the human need for entertainment (and for Arendt it is a human need) will not disappear. Entertainment in Arendt's sense of the term is linked to the *bios* as one of the constituents of the human life process. Like the need for nourishment and shelter, leisure and entertainment are necessary for life's preservation and recuperation. But in similar terms, entertainment disappears as it is consumed, and so must be continually reproduced in order to sustain the process. In this respect, entertainment is ordinarily judged by its freshness and novelty. In my view, this does not mean that other terms of judgment cannot be applied to "entertainment"; the products of entertainment might indeed be newly considered as belonging to culture in new acts of criticism and judgment. One lesson to be learned here, as I will discuss later, is that the power of judgment has no *necessary* link with the objects that provoke aesthetic experience and judgments of taste. Interest and value do not reside in the work, either formally or essentially, but only arise in the intersubjective context of judgment.

For a late modern European cosmopolitan and refugee like Arendt, there is nevertheless a dangerous antimony that runs between investment and culture, society and mass society. On one hand, Arendt writes, "The commodities the entertainment industry offers are not 'things,' cultural objects, whose excellence is measured by their ability to withstand the life process and become permanent appurtenances of the world, and they should not be judged according to these standards; nor are they values which exist to be used and exchanged; they are consumer goods destined to be used up, just like any other consumer goods" ("Crisis" 202). Entertainment has an oddly paradoxical status in her view. To the extent that it exists only to be immediately consumed, entertainment is not culture but rather a commodity. Yet from the standpoint of the consumer, entertainment objects are not evaluated from the standpoint of their exchange value, or at least, not in the same way as the investors and producers of cultural capital. The investing classes are a greater threat to culture than the consumers of mass entertainment, since ultimately all cultural objects are only considered in terms of their value as commodities and social investments.[24]

24. Arendt notes that despite the perceived crisis in culture, the arts and sciences are flourishing even in a mass society dominated by the need for mass entertainment. In this respect, the need of mass society for entertainment is "probably less of a threat to culture than the philistinism of good society" ("Crisis" 203). She continues this thought with the judgment that "at

On the other hand, Arendt worries that mass entertainment erodes the historical context in which judgments about culture can be made. The entertainment industry must respond to enormous and insatiable appetites that consume its artifacts evermore rapidly and intensively. And since entertainment's products vanish in acts of consumption, it must constantly produce new and novel commodities. Here the risk for Arendt is that the entire "inventory" of culture, past and present, is continually ransacked for new raw material. However, this material cannot be offered up unaltered; like processed food, it must be prepared and packaged to be made readily consumable. Mass culture comes into being through those processes in which mass society feeds upon culture to produce entertainment, and through the consumption of entertainment, Arendt worries that culture threatens to become exhausted or overrun by the scale and velocity of overproduction.

It should be clear from these remarks that the question of time, whether on the personal scale of life and work or the transgenerational span of history, inflects in important ways how Arendt assesses the modalities of human intercourse with objects as either investment, functional use, consumer good, or culture. In fact, what is most deeply at stake in Arendt's crisis in culture is how, in her words, the

> objective status of the culture world, insofar as it contains tangible things—books and paintings, statues, buildings, and music—comprehends, and gives testimony to, the entire recorded past of countries, nations, and ultimately mankind. As such, the only nonsocial and authentic criterion for judging these specifically cultural things is their relative permanence and even eventual immortality. . . . The point of the matter is that, as soon as the immortal works of the past became the object of social and individual refinement and the status accorded to it, they lost their most important and elemental quality, which is to grasp and move the reader or the spectator over the centuries. ("Crisis" 199)

---

any event, as long as the entertainment industry produces its own consumer goods, we can no more reproach it for the non-durability of its articles than we can reproach a bakery because it produces goods which, if they are not to spoil, must be consumed as soon as they are made. It has always been the mark of educated philistinism to despise entertainment and amusement, because no 'value' could be derived from it. The truth is we all stand in need of entertainment and amusement in some form or other, because we are all subject to life's great cycle, and it is sheer hypocrisy or social snobbery to deny that we can be amused and entertained by exactly the same things which amuse and entertain the masses of our fellow men" ("Crisis" 203).

Our postmodern sensibility no doubt balks at Arendt's evocation of "immortality" as a normative term for valuing art and defining culture. But perhaps one also recoils from the idea that our own mortality sets limits to our judgments of art—within a singular and finite life, there can be no certainty that our valuations, interpretations, or judgments will themselves endure. For Arendt, history will be our only judge.

Of deeper interest to me, however, is how Arendt's modalities of intercourse with cultural objects play out at different time scales. The valuations of life are conditioned by the immediacy of individual consumption in the present time of maintaining existence and of reproducing all necessary means for immediate survival. This is a time of pure repetition where the conditions of life are extended without either deepening or undergoing change. At the other end of the spectrum, the valuations of culture appeal to an extended transsubjective sense of time. For an artifact to be understood as belonging to cultural inheritance, it must be judged retrospectively in a historical framework defined by the ongoing accumulation of critical and evaluative conversations both past and present. The valuations of investment also take a multigenerational perspective, but only with the goal of preserving capital over the long term. The valuations of inheritance differ here. Investment is evaluated in terms of the mechanisms of commodities and exchange value—this is one form of "intercourse" with art, and it is closely related to Arendt's sense of philistinism as a mentality that judges everything in terms of immediate usefulness and economic value. (Think again here of Arendt's critique of self-interest in the form of self-perfection and self-education where in both cases "the art object has been used for ulterior purposes" ["Crisis" 200].) Along these lines, Arendt concludes,

> Culture relates to objects and is a phenomenon of the world; entertainment relates to people and is a phenomenon of life. An object is cultural to the extent that it can endure; its durability is the very opposite of functionality, which is the quality which makes it disappear again from the phenomenal world by being used and used up. The great user and consumer of objects is life itself, the life of the individual and the life of society as a whole. Life is indifferent to the thingness of an object; it insists that every thing must be functional, fulfill some needs. Culture is being threatened when all worldly objects and things, produced by the

present or the past, are treated as mere functions for the life process of society, as though they are there only to fulfill some need and for this functionalization it is almost irrelevant whether the needs in question are of a high or a low order. (204–5)

By just these criteria one might also think of culture as inviting perception across two radically distinctive time scales as if suspended between the collective and transgenerational historical conversation of culture, on one hand, and on the other, local and singular intensive sensory experiences with potential cultural objects. Cultural history requires participation in an expansive and multigenerational conversation about aesthetic value. But what Kant calls judgments of taste arise out of an immediate slow and thick engagement with objects in a singular aesthetic experience—an experience of aesthetic duration, as it were, in a time that cannot be fully used up, which is also an interruption in our functional, quotidian lifetime. Value does not inhere in a shape or form here, but perhaps rather in unmeasured time.

I noted above that Arendt values art for arresting our attention and moving us, perhaps to think and then to judge. This suggests that among other activities aesthetic judgment requires discernment, or the capacity for recognizing aesthetic "qualities" and of being drawn to and into objects and events that could count as aesthetic experiences. The question thus arises: By what criteria—whether formal, perceptual, or durational—may things provoke aesthetic experience and so solicit judgment? This question is important, because only through singular acts of judgment can objects be lifted out of the immediacy of the stream of life and into a potentially enduring cultural world. In this respect, individual acts of judgment are the first steps toward assessing whether an object or experience belongs to culture or not, and therefore whether they will be incorporated into the narrative of history or not. Arendt's key criteria involve qualities of appearance. In her account, whether it is a functional object, a consumer good, or a work of art, every thing possesses a shape through which it appears. And with respect to things fabricated, and thus shaped by human creative intentions and actions, one can further distinguish between the ordinary durability (and relative impermanence) of functional objects and what Arendt calls the "potential immortality" of works of art ("Crisis" 205). Shape and time are thus both related to appearance, and where duration is concerned, one of Arendt's strongest terms of positive evaluation, as I have noted, is the criterion of (relative) permanence. "From the viewpoint of sheer durability," Arendt writes,

> art works clearly are superior to all other things; since they stay longer in the world than anything else, they are the worldliest of all things. Moreover, they are the only things without any function in the life process of society; strictly speaking, they are fabricated not for men, but for the world which is meant to outlast the life-span of mortals, the coming and going of the generations. Not only are they not consumed like consumer goods and not used up like use objects; they are deliberately removed from the processes of consumption and usage and isolated against the sphere of human life necessities. This removal can be achieved in a great variety of ways; and only where it is done does culture, in the specific sense, come into being. (206)

It seems that artworks are considered to be world making or coming to belong to a world or the world, and this world is distinguished from "life" in two senses. First, it does not serve the immediate needs of human existence—it is neither used up nor consumed, and most importantly, it is free from the force of necessity. Furthermore, in order for a work of art to be judged as belonging to culture, it must be removed from the time of individual human existence. Like history, its temporality is supra-individual and multigenerational. For Arendt, then, the creation of works of art contributes to the creation of a culture. And the creation of a culture is the creation of a human or cultural world distinct from the natural world that takes place in a series of "removals": a removal from nature by human fabrication; removal from individual use and consumption, which is removal from "the life process of society"; and finally, removal from the finite time of individual existence. (These "removals" also link judgment to acts of curation, which will be the subject of the next section.)

The worldliness of culture is distinct from both life and nature. And if worldliness is distinct from the time and needs of individual existence, how or to what extent is it a human world? Arendt's response is,

> The question here is not whether worldliness, the capacity to fabricate and create a world, is part and parcel of human "nature." . . . This earthly home becomes a world in the proper sense of the word only when

the totality of fabricated things is so organized that it can resist the consuming life process of the people dwelling in it, and thus outlast them. Only where such survival is assured do we speak of culture, and only where we are confronted with things which exist independently of all utilitarian and functional references, and whose quality remains always the same, do we speak of works of art. ("Crisis" 206)

To become part of a culture, it would seem, artworks must outlast individual existence and become part of historical time. Alternatively, to assess and evaluate the powers of judgment requires a return to the more immediate and significant encounters with art and aesthetic experience. Culture achieves its worldliness, which is to say, its autonomy, by transcending or outlasting the finitude of individual existence. (One can also say in Arendt's terms that cultural objects claim their autonomy with respect to life.) In some of the best-known pages of his *Critique of the Powers of Judgment*, Kant argues in the "Analytic of the Beautiful" that objects of aesthetic experience must also assert their autonomy with respect to human needs and interests. In other words, the experience of art must be relieved of all necessity. Otherwise, aesthetic judgment cannot function as a space of action for human freedom. Any discussion of culture must therefore take the local and singular experience of art as a starting point.

For Arendt, to undergo and to judge aesthetic experiences are preconditions for the longer-term construction of a cultural world. In this respect, judgment is the first step toward curating culture, that is, of assessing whether objects and experiences will become part of culture and how they are to be valued and what they might mean. Looking forward, it seems to me that this experience begins with discernment focused by individual apperception and tempered by insight, which is then enlarged into social conversation. Acts of apperception are initiated when one becomes aware of appearances through the activities of discernment and self-aware looking or listening—call this viewing in the company of thinking—but what does discernment aim at or distinguish? I have noted Arendt's assertion that all things have "shapes," but she also insists that only works of art are made for the sole purpose of appearance and that artful appearance is to be judged according to the quality of beauty. Beauty is a quality that attends all aesthetically shaped objects, which can pass or have passed into the enduring world of culture.

Postmodern ears may again rise up skeptically at the evocation of such terms, and perhaps with good reason. The qualities of appearance in cultural objects that Arendt so insists upon are intimately tied to her sense of beauty as the attractive force that draws humans to potential sites of aesthetic experience and occasions of intensified perception. As aesthetic experience is tied ineluctably to the perception of beauty, one needs discernment to know which sites might provide these occasions or not. At the same time, despite the centrality of the term for her argument, Arendt's sense of what beauty is and how it is linked to appearance is somewhat mysterious and taken for granted. This observation demands deeper investigation of the centrality of beauty to Arendt's and Kant's accounts of the powers of judgment.

A first point of interrogation is raised around the unshakable immanence of beauty to a free appearance unshaped by necessity, which I imagine as connected by Arendt to the multiple senses of *Erscheinung* in German, not only as appearance but also apparition, manifestation, or phenomenon. Alternatively, the linking of appearance to shape suggests materiality, substance, and extension in space. If beautiful appearance is considered as *Erscheinung*, it could then be distinguished from shape as an experience of intelligibility rather than of visibility; in other words, beauty appears in shape as the apparition of nonvisible form—it is given to the interiority of the mind and not to the externality of the eye.

Other candidate terms arise in Arendt's frequent appeals to classical philosophy and ancient Greek sources, where the distinction of visible and material shape from nonvisible and immaterial appearing is expressed by distinguishing *kallos* from *erōs*.[25] Plato's dialogues *Symposium* and *Phaedrus* are among the most important sources here. The more ordinary senses of *erōs* arise out of worldly and temporal desires such as the bodily attractions of beautiful youth for the lover. But in both dialogues, Socrates directs his interlocutors to look beyond the attractions of physical manifestations of beautiful shape, or *kallos*, which are temporal and transient, to where the power of *erōs* really directs us. In Plato's account, *erōs* is the most powerful manifestation of the beautiful because it is the most unattainable. Ultimately, it is a force of desire that does not belong to this world, because true beauty is an

---

25. These themes recur with renewed intensity in *The Life of the Mind: Thinking*. See in particular Arendt's account of the immortalizing qualities of beauty and appearance on pages 130–32 and the links between beauty, wonder, and admiration on pages 143–44.

intuition of the divine and the immortal that shines forth in material attractions, even if it is not often recognized as such. The most powerful manifestations of beauty thus arise in ways that are only truly receivable through intellection or *noēsis*, not perception. Ultimately, in its true attractive power shape is only a transient and material conduit to time-less and changeless Being, which is *eidos* or Form in the Platonic sense. In Plato's view, *erōs* directs us from ignorance to wisdom (*sophia*) to the extent that vision is recognized as a lure. In F. E. Peter's account, "The lover weans himself away from a single body and becomes a lover of all beautiful bodies ..., thence to beautiful souls, laws and observances, and knowledge (*episteme*), always freeing himself of bondage to the particular, until 'suddenly' there is revealed to him the vision of Beauty itself.... This is immortality."[26] And indeed, what has appeared here in all of its suddenness is an intuition of what has been lost to the memory of human souls incarnated in temporal matter—the transcendent *eide* that convey Form and intelligibility to all things and beings.

The point of this digression is to ask how and in what degree Arendt's coupling of shape with beauty, and indeed her implicit though unstated definition of beauty, is only sustained by Plato's grounding of knowl-edge and *erōs* in the transcendent Forms. (Grappling with this question will be important for deepening my account of the powers of judgment, and the relation of judgment to politics and history.) Some key pas-sages in *The Human Condition* are more informative here than in "The Crisis in Culture" itself. With respect to shape, appearance, and beauty, Arendt's gloss on Plato characterizes *eidos* as a variation of the beautiful in "'what shines forth most' (*ekphanestaton*)."[27] This is the true essence

26. F. E. Peters, *Greek Philosophical Terms: A Historical Lexicon* (New York: New York University Press, 1967), 64.

27. Hannah Arendt, *The Human Condition* (Chicago: University of Chicago Press, 1958), 225. Much later, in her remarks on "imagination" in her seminar on Kant, fall 1970, Arendt pro-vides a clearer presentation of this perspective. "What Kant calls the faculty of imagination," she explains, "to make present to the mind what is absent from sense perception, has less to do with memory than with another faculty, one that has been known since the beginnings of philosophy. Parmenides (fragment 4) called it *nous* (that faculty 'through which you look steadfastly at things which are present though they are absent'), and by this he meant that Being is never present, does not present itself to the senses. What is not present in the perception of things is the *it-is*; and the *it-is*, absent from the senses, is nevertheless present to the mind. Or Anaxagoras: *Opsis tōn adēlōn ta phainomena*, 'A glimpse of the nonvisible are the appearances.' To put this differently: by looking at appearances (given to intuition in Kant) one becomes aware of, gets a glimpse of, something that does not appear. This something is Being as such.

of Being, the nonvisible, immaterial, and unchanging Form that guides the possibility of knowing any contingent and worldly thing. In a note, Arendt also explains that the word *ekphanestaton* occurs in *Phaedrus* as the main quality of the beautiful, and "in the *Republic* (518) a similar quality is claimed for the idea of the good, which is called *phanotaton*. Both words derive from *phainesthai* ('to appear' and 'to shine forth'), and in both cases the superlative is used" (*Human Condition* 226).[28]

The point of Arendt's gloss on *eide* in *The Human Condition* is to contrast her philosophy of action with Plato's insistence in the *Republic* and elsewhere that societies can be formed or fabricated through the assiduous application of ideal models. But herein lies a difficult problem concerning beauty. The only basis for accepting Arendt's otherwise weakly defended claims concerning the enduring quality of beautiful appearance—its timelessness and transcendence of human finitude, and its consistency, or being everywhere and always the same—is to recognize Arendt's unacknowledged metaphysical debt to Plato. The contradiction lies in the fact that while in *The Human Condition* Arendt criticizes the Platonic *eidos* as a regulative idea for modeling the formation of a polis, it returns no less powerfully to haunt "The Crisis in Culture" as a normative concept for the formation of culture. And to the extent that Arendt appeals to Kant's third Critique as a political philosophy where judgments of taste become the basis for intersubjective assessments guiding the emergence of a polity, this contradiction must be accounted for.

Arendt's account of beauty is suspended between Plato and Kant in ways that are informative though ultimately irreconcilable. It might equally be the case that Arendt takes for granted Kant's own appeal to the criterion of beauty in his analysis of judgments of taste or, worse, endows it with a Platonism foreign to Kant's late thinking. The problem here is that Arendt risks confusing her criterion of "immortality" with Kant's assertion of the subjective necessity of universal assent

---

Hence, metaphysics, the discipline that treats of what lies beyond physical reality and still, in a mysterious way, is given to the mind as the nonappearance in the appearances, becomes ontology, the science of Being" (*Lectures* 80).

28. Perhaps one might also find echoes of the late Heidegger here? For example, in the lectures collected as *What Is Called Thinking?*, Heidegger writes that "Beauty is a fateful gift of the essence of truth." *What Is Called Thinking?*, trans. J Glenn Gray (New York: Harper Perennial, 2004), 19.

in aesthetic judgments. Recall how Kant characterizes the demand for universal assent in judgments of taste as unreasonable, or at least not subject to regulation by concepts. The unreasonable demand for universality in aesthetic judgments could be considered as the claim of a singular experience to submit itself immediately to the judgment of history. But what universality lays claim to here, without reason, is an appeal to qualities that are everywhere and always the same, in spite of their subjectivity and in the absence of determinate concepts. In presenting a concept of beauty underwritten by the Platonic *eidos*, Arendt makes it into a determinate and regulative principle, which is something that Kant unambiguously warns against. Here Arendt would do well to reconsider Kant's argument that "to seek a principle of taste that would provide the universal criterion of the beautiful through determinate concepts is a fruitless undertaking, because what is sought is impossible and intrinsically self-contradictory."[29]

Is there a reasonable context in which the connection of beauty to appearance can be defended as the basis of aesthetic judgments? Kant's own account of judgments of taste provides one alternative. It must be said that Kant himself has no clear concept of beauty, because in his account there cannot be one. Judgments of taste are without concept and, moreover, they are ungrounded by empirical criteria. To call something beautiful in judgments of taste is less a persuasive description of an object than an agent's account of its own internal sensation or affect. While logically and psychologically judgments of taste ask for universal assent, once expressed publicly they are open to context-dependent debates whose terms are both qualitative and existential. Beauty is linked here to the powers of the imagination rather than any cognitive content, which means that there are no transcendental terms that could ground a concept of beauty, thus assuring its immortality and consistency. And if this were not the case, there would be no reason to express a judgment and to submit it to intersubjective testing; that is, there would be no reason to entertain artful conversations.

Therefore, if as Kant asserts judgments of taste are without concept, then it does not matter that the apprehension of beauty is without conceptual or transcendental justification. In both Kant and Arendt,

---

29. Immanuel Kant, *Critique of the Power of Judgment*, ed. Paul Guyer, trans. Paul Guyer and Eric Matthews (Cambridge: Cambridge University Press, 2000): §17, 116.

"beauty" is deployed as a strong term yet one that is strangely undefined or even undefinable. For Arendt, this is the intuition of qualities of durability, permanence, or even immortality that once expressed as judgments must suffer the test of history. One might not be able to define certain criteria for qualifying beauty, but in Arendt's view it will always be recognized across the span of time by discerning individuals, no matter how many or few, who will continue to preserve and defend those artworks that have passed into culture.

In these terms, Arendt commits implicitly to a Platonic account of beauty to defend the imperishability of culture's monuments and the human capacity to discern beauty. But Arendt's appeal to beauty is indefensible in Kantian terms and indeed is contrary to her own account of the importance of judgments of taste for the formation of a polis, as will soon be seen. It should be said that in Kant's "Analytic of the Beautiful," beauty also functions as something like an empty placeholder for an experience with an uncertain ground. However, Kant does not need beauty as a regulative term. All that Kant requires is recognition that everyone is capable of undergoing experiences of intensified perception, which they feel compelled to express and to share, and that this capability is a defining criterion for belonging to the human community.

Kant's notion of beauty is "without concept," or perhaps one could say it is another instance of Solon's nonappearing measures where beauty is a term no different in principle from the good, virtue, wisdom, justice, and so on. Its exemplarity has to do with the condition of its unreasonable appeal to universality and its grounding in what Kant calls a "community sense" (*eines gemeinschaftlichen Sinnes*) and the desire to share freely this experience in discourse. To call something beautiful is a term of judgment like good or bad, like or dislike, pleasurable or unpleasurable, tasteful or distasteful. These are terms used to describe and evaluate experiences for which no quantitative and context-independent measures are appropriate. In this respect, Kant is less concerned with what grounds or qualifies the beautiful than the nature of judgments provoked by it. After all, his concern is with the modality of judgments of taste and not the beautiful itself. Perhaps Arendt or Kant focus on beauty because of its intuitive relationship to appearance? But the most important thing here is to account for those kinds of experience that invariably elicit subjective responses, which in turn demand both publicity and universal assent. And in so doing, these responses test our presence in a community or not. The major difference between Kant and Arendt here, and it is key for my own argument, is that for Arendt beauty is an unchanging quality that inheres in artful form or shape, which is everywhere and at all times recognizable by discerning individuals, who are endowed with what she calls, after Cicero, a *cultura animi*. For Kant, the curious fact of judgments of taste is that they demand public universal assent, yet Kant's analytic recognizes that there are no grounds for compelling agreement. This means that the value and peril of judgment is that one must operate without certain or stable criteria, just as in "Thinking and Moral Considerations" Arendt acknowledges that critical thinking can assure no normative or doctrinal distinctions between good and evil. Alternatively, because beauty is without concept in judgments of taste, it serves as the motor of artful conversation with its dilemmas of dissent and agreement, no matter how partial or contingent. Here judgment is the bridge that brings us out of solitary thought into a local space of sociability, where a testing of one's thoughts or opinions is a form of self-disclosure in a public space that is as capable of contradicting those thoughts as affirming them.

I have still not fully answered my question: Is there a reasonable context in which the connection of beauty to appearance can be defended as the basis of aesthetic judgments? Certainly, Kant and Arendt agree that beauty points to a particular experience of intensified perception, which is more closely linked to imagination than to an empirical perception, and that the activity of apperception or becoming self-consciously aware of appearance leads to public acts of judgment and criticism. Channeling Kant, Arendt argues that in order to apprehend appearance, the engaged viewer must be free to establish a certain distance between herself and the object—the object will not be consumed and digested, one might say, but must preserve its autonomy, "and the more important the sheer appearance of a thing is, the more distance it requires for its proper appreciation" ("Crisis" 207). This distance can only come about where and when the viewer can "forget herself," that is, distance herself and her relation to an aesthetic object from any consideration of self-interest or necessity.[30] There can be no hunger,

---

30. This idea is connected in powerful ways to Arendt's account of thinking's withdrawal from the commonsense world of external appearances. This withdrawal is one way that thinking

desire, or need for the object—it must be left to itself as appearance. Here Arendt invokes Kant's well-known condition for aesthetic judgments, that of *uninteressiertes Wohlgefallen,* which she translates as disinterested joy, claiming that it "can be experienced only after the needs of the living organism have been provided for, so that, released from life's necessity, men may be free for the world" (207). Another way of thinking about this condition is to consider the experience of aesthetic pleasure in terms of whatever sensation or force releases one from one's self or self-absorption, thus bringing the viewer out of the solitude of thought and into the realm of discourse through public acts of judging.

According to this criterion, the potential autonomy of art and of aesthetic experience is endangered in contemporary society. For Arendt, the problem with mass society is not with the number of humans in it, who historically speaking have more and more leisure time at their disposal and are thus, as she puts it, "released from life's necessity," but rather that this society is increasingly dominated by the activities of consumption and entertainment. Mass culture is an oxymoron, then; there is only mass entertainment that feeds voraciously on culture and its history. For Arendt, a society of mass entertainment will not become more cultured through education alone: "The point is that a consumers' society cannot possibly know how to take care of a world and the things which belong exclusively to the space of worldly appearances, because its central attitude toward all objects, the attitude of consumption, spells ruin to everything it touches" ("Crisis" 208). Things that could become objects of aesthetic experience, and thus become possible constituents of a culture-world, are degraded by impermanence and utility. There is no thinking forward from the time of consumption to the time of history.

III. CULTURE AND CURATION

This is the crisis in culture of which Arendt writes. But what alternative sense of culture does she advocate for? And in turn, how does judgment lead to politics, or to the formation of a polis?

---

prepares for judgment. See, for example, *Life of the Mind: Thinking,* section 10, "The Intramural Warfare between Thought and Commonsense."

Any discussion of culture must aim at, identify, and argue for exemplary works of art that will constitute this culture, even if in present time they may be recurrently, even violently, contested, or in future times be forgotten. In my view, criteria for defining exemplarity are obviously dynamic and sensitive to cultural and historical context. Moreover, critical conversations about exemplarity are inevitably connected to questions about evaluation, that is, which works matter to a culture and why. The problem here is not to set out definitive criteria for evaluation—there are none, or at least none that are not local and contingent despite the demand that exemplary works prove themselves "universally" to have enduring value. Rather, what exemplarity points to is the persistent demand for critically informed curation as one of the key activities in caring for culture or cultivating culture, if you will. While this term is absent from Arendt's writing, the activity of curation is implicit in her views on how a culture is formed and memorialized and by whom. Call this a form of action in culture that is closely related to thinking and judging.

In his indispensable *Keywords*, Raymond Williams remarks that culture is one of the most complicated words in the English language because of its conceptual linkages to "several distinct intellectual disciplines and in several distinct and incompatible systems of thought."[31] In ways similar to Williams, Arendt turns to Latin and Roman roots to locate more precisely the fundamental activities of culture, where *colere* means to cultivate, to dwell within or upon, to care for, tend to, and preserve. Originally, cultivation indicated humanity's stewardship of nature, tending and cultivating it until it becomes fit for habitation. Nature here becomes a kind of world for humans, a world cultivated with love and care in contrast to subjugation and exploitation. As humans cultivate nature into a place for dwelling—indeed a place to sustain life—this human life only becomes a culture in caring for what humans make in excess of life, and in excess of human finitude itself. There is both curation and cultivation in the sense that, as Arendt puts it, care must be taken for the monuments of the past. (In like terms, one might ask, What makes monuments appear and persist within or fade from a common world? I will return to this.) For Arendt, "monuments"

31. Raymond Williams, *Keywords: A Vocabulary of Culture and Society* (New York: Oxford University Press, 1976), 76–77.

include all works of art and literature that endure or have endured. But more important than cultural things themselves are the kinds of thoughtful and social interaction they inspire. "In this sense," Arendt writes, "we understand by culture the attitude toward, or better, the mode of intercourse prescribed by civilizations with respect to the least useful and most worldly of things, the works of artists, poets, musicians, philosophers, and so forth" ("Crisis" 210). This mode of intercourse— judging—will play an important role in how Arendt's "monuments" mediate a culture's sense of history and memory, that is, how a culture gives sense and value to its history through its forms and modalities of memorialization.

To tend to culture is to have the capacity, again, for discernment—to be able to perceive, recognize, and identify those kinds of objects that might pass into a culture, or fade from it if not protected and preserved. Arendt appeals here to something she refers to as a "humanistic faculty" adapted from Cicero's account of a *cultura animi*, a cultured mind, that can exercise taste and is sensitive to beauty. Importantly, this *cultura animi* is not necessarily a faculty of artists and makers but rather of spectators or observers, who make judgments of taste out of the experience of disinterested pleasure. As a first response to her question, What is the proper mode of intercourse with art? Arendt replies that these activities of discerning, judging, and curating define culture as the mode of intercourse prescribed by civilizations as the attitude to take toward the most worldly of things, which is the achieved works of artists and philosophers—in other words, those who make and who think free of necessity.

At this point, Arendt raises the question that will consume her for the rest of her philosophical life: "Could it be that taste belongs among the political faculties?" However, the lead-up to this question is complex, and it deserves detailed consideration. Read, then, the full text, which follows her account of Greek attitudes toward culture as presented in a Pericles's funeral oration as reported by Thucydides in his *History of the Peloponnesian War*:

Could it be that philosophy in the Greek sense—which begins with "wonder," with θαυμάζειν [*thaumazein*], and ends (at least in Plato and Aristotle) in the speechless beholding of some unveiled truth—is more likely to lead into inactivity than love of beauty? Could it be, on the

other hand, that love of beauty remains barbarous unless it is accompanied by εὐτελεία [*euteleia*], by the faculty to take aim in judgment, discernment, and discrimination, in brief, by that curious and ill-defined
capacity we commonly call taste? And finally, could it be that this right
love of beauty, the proper kind of intercourse with beautiful things—
the *cultura animi* which makes man fit to take care of the things of the
world and which Cicero, in contradistinction of the Greeks, ascribed
to philosophy—has something to do with politics? Could it be that
taste belongs among the political faculties? ("Crisis" 211)[32]

The relation between art and politics, so present to contemporary
debates in the humanities, and indeed the role of philosophy in mediat-
ing that relation, is in my view one of the trickiest yet most interesting
arguments in Arendt's essay. Matters are clarified, however, by insisting on the central role that Kant's *Critique of the Powers of Judgment*,
and also his late writings on anthropology, will play in the last decades
of Arendt's philosophical life. The problem here is not so much what
counts as art, now or for history, and who has the right to say so (we
all do), but rather the modalities of discourse or intercourse that arise
out of aesthetic experience as judgments of taste. What connects art
to politics here are the questions of what is a polis and what activities encourage a polis to take shape and to sustain itself in the actions,

32. As should be clear later, Arendt reads Pericles's oration as critiquing philosophy for
undermining citizens' capacity for active life in the polis. For example, in her 1954 lecture
"Philosophy and Politics," she writes, "The reproach that philosophy can deprive citizens of
their personal fitness is implicitly contained in Pericles' famous statement: *philokaloumen met'
euteleias kai philosophoumen aneu malakias* (we love the beautiful without exaggeration and we
love wisdom without softness or unmanliness)" (76). After trying several versions in "The Crisis
in Culture," Arendt retranslates the central though difficult line in Pericles's oration, which is
the subject of her discussion here, as "We love beauty within the limits of political judgment,
and we philosophize without the barbarian vice of effeminacy" ("Crisis" 210). I will return to
this strange assertion presently. However, note for the moment the odd use that Arendt makes
of the controversial term *euteleia* from Pericles's oration. In ordinary language *euteleia* can mean
"cheapness" or, more kindly, "frugality," "thrift," or "economical." Considering the context of
Pericles's speech, it may be that what Arendt characterizes as the right love of beauty is a lack
of extravagance or excessiveness—in other words, taste as moderation. Her larger argument is
that while judgments of pure taste are something like the active foundation of political speech,
assertions about beauty must be moderated by a consensus among those educated in right
judgment. Soon Arendt will call this capacity insight, her translation of *phronēsis*. I am grateful
to Richard McKirahan for conversations about the meaning of this difficult passage.

words, and memories of its participants. "The *polis*," Arendt explains in *The Human Condition*,

> is not the city-state in its physical location; it is the organization of the people as it arises out of acting and speaking together, and its true space lies between people living together for this purpose, no matter where they happen to be. "Wherever you go, you will be a polis": these famous words became not merely the watchword of Greek colonization, they expressed the conviction that action and speech create a space between the participants which can find its proper location almost any time and anywhere. It is the space of appearance in the widest sense of the word, namely, the space where I appear to others as others appear to me, where men exist not merely like other living or inanimate things but make their appearance explicitly. (198)

The space of the polis is dynamic, contingent, fleeting, and responsive to local circumstances, and in these respects, is analogous to the aesthetic conditions leading to judgments of taste. And even though every human is capable of words and actions, this does not mean that everyone will exercise them collectively and freely and so form a polis. Arendt reaches two important conclusions here: the space of the polis does not always exist, and "No man, moreover, can live in it all the time. To be deprived of it means to be deprived of reality, which, humanly and politically speaking, is the same as appearance. To men the reality of the world is guaranteed by the presence of others, by its appearing to all" (*Human Condition* 199).

The polis is not the sum total of individuals that populate a given collective but rather the ephemeral space that appears contingently and dynamically in the network of intersubjective relations that emerges as people act and speak together in community. I am reminded here of Arendt's characterization of the Socratic dialectic as the public performance of thought—the elenchus is what makes thought appear, publicly and among friends, as a kind of ambulant and temporary polis. Arendt's criterion of appearance through action and speech also links the space of politics to the emanation of the beautiful in objects that solicit judgments of taste. Here is where judgment might raise a bridge between art and politics: judgment has no critical or historical force, which is to say no social reality, until it is made to appear, that is, is brought out of the solitude of thought and into public acts of self-disclosure and critical conversation. This is a common element between art and politics—judgments of taste and judgments of self-disclosure in moral consideration partake of the same modality.

But a crucial element is missing here. In her lectures on Kant's political philosophy, Arendt closely links the formation of a polis as a shared space of appearance, which has both existential and ethical qualities, to what Kant calls "community sense," which is also the assumed ground for judgments of taste. Indeed, here she confronts directly the surprising fact of Kant's idea that the faculty of judgment, and of discriminating between right and wrong, should be based on something so subjective and idiosyncratic as a "sense of taste" (*Lectures* 64).

Kant himself clearly distinguishes between what is habitually called "common sense" and what he refers to as community sense (*gemeinschaftlichen Sinnes*), or sensus communis. Ordinarily, "common sense" is characterized as a sense like any other and is assumed to be the same for each human in his or her privacy. But Kant means something different by sensus communis. In using the Latin, Arendt argues, Kant is postulating "an extra sense—like an extra mental capability or *Menschenverstand* that fits us into a community. The 'common understanding of men . . . is the very least to be expected from anyone claiming the name of man'" (*Lectures* 70, citing Kant, *Critique of the Powers of Judgment* §40).

For Kant, the humanity of humans (does one yet say a fact of the human?) manifests itself in terms of communicability and sociability. We become human, perhaps, through our uses of language in relation to others in the context of specific forms of life. Communal sense is thus distinguished from private sense or private reflection. Sensus communis is what judgment appeals to in every individual in his or her collective communications; it is what gives judgments their special validity in the form of an appeal to universal agreement. Feelings of pleasure or displeasure are ordinarily thought of as internal and noncommunicative, or at least as uncommunicated except to oneself. But Kant portrays these feelings as rooted in a human community sense that aims for external assertion once transformed by a mode of reflection that takes the feelings and thoughts of others into account: "By 'sensus communis,'" Kant writes, "must be understood the idea of a communal sense [*eines gemeinschaftlichen Sinnes*], i.e., a faculty for judging that in its reflection takes account (a priori) of everyone else's way of representing in thought, in order as it were to hold its judgment up to human reason as a whole." (*Critique of the Powers of Judgment* §40, 173).

The appeal to communal sense fends off the illusion that our subjective private conditions could be held to be objective and thus adversely influence judgment. This occurs by holding one's judgment up to the possible as much as actual judgments of others and by projecting ourselves into the perspective of others. At stake here is abstracting ourselves from the contingent limitation of our own aesthetic judgments, which means setting aside as far as possible any external and empirical sensations. Only in this way can we attend solely to our representations of the object and our own representational states. Another way of putting this is to say that we must abstract ourselves internally from subjective feelings of charm and emotion to assert a judgment that could serve as a universal rule. (This may yet be another form of "withdrawal.") It should be apparent that the presumption of a sensus communis functions for Kant as the universal ground for the human capacity for judgment. And in the same way that the Socratic elenchus is presented as an example of the capability of any ordinary human to perform critical thinking, Arendt insists on Cicero's observation that there is little difference between the learned and ignorant in the capacity for judgment. What is the source of the subjective need to assert that one's judgments of taste be accepted as universal? Perhaps from the intuition that the capacity to judge is distributed universally across the whole of humanity. Ordinariness links thinking and judging as a shared or common power of any human being in his or her daily existence, should he or she choose to exercise these powers.

Other questions are opened by this line of inquiry. Why in fact should taste be the vehicle for the faculty of judgment, or why should judgment be based on a subjective, private, and internal "sense"? Arendt suggests that the answer to this question resides in Kant's appeal to the imagination in relation to the operation of reflection in §40 of the third Critique. Imagination is the mental capacity for making present what is absent in space and time; imagination translates externally received forms into "objects" of inner sense. Reflection is the activity of mentally considering an internal presentation, but it is also an active remaking of our perceptions. Judgments of taste arise only by reflecting on these imaginative representations rather than their external forms, and this is why judgment must be freed from empirical necessity. Through the operation of reflection, the aesthetic object is internalized as an image that no longer confronts me directly; what was outward and empirical becomes inward and imaginative, and the subject can no longer be affected by the object as though it were given by her external senses. For this reason, in reflection it is not important that the object pleases in perception. Remember that only disinterested and free satisfaction can be the object of pure judgments of taste; interest of neither the senses nor of reasons demands approval here. Imagination prepares judgment, then, as a kind of internal distancing, or another removal of the object from the external world. For Kant, only what affects one internally in representation, and where one can no longer be affected by immediate presence (criterion of disinterestedness) can be judged right or wrong, important or irrelevant, beautiful or ugly, or something in-between. "One then speaks of judgment and no longer of taste," Arendt asserts, "because, though it still affects one like a matter of taste, one now has, by means of representation, established the proper distance, the remoteness or uninvolvedness or disinterestedness, that is requisite for approbation and disapprobation, for evaluating something at its proper worth. By removing the object, one has established the conditions for impartiality" (*Lectures* 67).

It should be made clear that the conditions of impartiality are not conditions for objectivity. Rather, impartiality refers to judgment's appeal to intersubjective testing and consideration, of modifying one's judgment by projecting oneself into the place or perspective (whether aesthetic or moral) of others. And while I doubt that reflection establishes the conditions for true impartiality, it does enable the conditions for considering a representation in perfect freedom. But this freedom is itself imperfect—it is only too human, that is, freed by the imagination but limited by its one-sidedness and subjectivity. These considerations need to be returned to the world and to be tested against the judgment of others. If not, one could not entertain possibilities for revising the sense and value of representations as measures of taste or moral consideration. Therefore, what Kant calls the operation of reflection in relation to the imagination also establishes the conditions for revisions of the sense and value of the object. Imagination reframes and recontextualizes the sense of the object in ways Wittgenstein might characterize as shifts in aspect. Through imagination and the operation of reflection, the sense and value of the object become malleable and modifiable. This remaking also involves a revision of meaning and value according to one's own sense of history, a personal context of learning and knowledge that in turn wants to be shared.

The potential in aesthetic experience for revisions of sense and value is an important capacity of imagination, though not completely self-evident in Kant or Arendt. Nevertheless, it would be one way of assessing what Kant considers to be the most valued quality of the apprehension of beauty, which is the free play of mental powers unleashed from the restriction of determinate concepts so that the imagination and the understanding may freely associate concepts with intuitions and intuitions with concepts. (To refer back to my previous book, this is yet another power that philosophy seeks in art.) In this manner, pleasure arises as consciousness of formal purposiveness in the free play of the subject's own cognitive powers in relation to the representation in imagination of the aesthetic object. Acknowledging this formal purposiveness is the first step to discovering and communicating how and what one values, and to do so freely.

One of the most surprising yet most essential qualities of judgments of taste returns again here in Kant's awareness that there is something nonsubjective or impartial in what seems to be the most private and subjective sense, which is our apprehension of the beautiful. The beautiful, writes Kant, is that which, without concepts, is represented as the object of a *universal* satisfaction. (Recall again that the "beautiful" is only the placeholder for many qualitative judgments that demand universal agreement, and to the extent that this demand is unreasonable, it calls for reasons to justify it intersubjectively.) The odd thing about judgments concerning the beautiful is that the condition of being made "without interest" also contains an appeal to universality: the judgment "must contain a ground of satisfaction for everyone," Kant writes in the third Critique (§ 6, 96). The judgment is not grounded in any inclination of the subject nor in any explicit or implicit interest in the object. It is rather the case that the judging subject feels himself entirely free with respect to the apprehension of the beautiful. But because he cannot discover any private conditions grounding his satisfaction, he must presuppose that the conditions for satisfaction are universally shared and that a similar pleasure will be shared by everyone. For these reasons, the subject speaks of the beautiful *as if* it were a *property* of the object, and *as if* the judgment were *logical*, that is, as a cognition of the object through concepts. Nevertheless, the sentiment of the beautiful is only aesthetic, not logical. The framework of sensus communis, or of common human understanding, returns here as the condition of necessity alleged, reasonably or not, by judgments of taste. "The judgment of taste ascribes assent to everyone," Kant again asserts, "and whoever declares something to be beautiful wishes that everyone should approve of the object in question and similarly declare it to be beautiful. The 'should' in aesthetic judgments of taste is thus pronounced only conditionally even given all the data that are required for the judging. One solicits assent from everyone else because one has a ground for it that is common to all; one could even count on this assent if only one were always sure that the case were correctly subsumed under that ground as the rule of approval" (121–22). But of course, for Kant, one cannot count on this assent; otherwise, judgments of taste would not be arguable, that is, open to contest and revision.

The other curious fact about this appeal to universality is that it is a *spoken* appeal, as if the operation of reflection internally in the imagination instinctively required outward exclamation and expression. More importantly, for both Kant and Arendt, this is never a solitary assertion but rather a social and intersubjective expression—it is an appeal to sociality and conversation. One might also say that it makes of criticism a public performance. This is why Kant attributes the operation of reflection to a communal sense, which is perhaps also a sense of community. Kant's community sense, then, is the ground for accepting that our private subjective conditions and apprehensions might be shared as a form of acknowledgment that wards off solipsism or skepticism and connects us back to a human world. In this manner, holding judgment up to reason as a whole is also a way of asserting one's aspiration to form a polis and to share in the human community, and to forge a polis through shared judgments is also to form a culture in community. Arendt makes this point directly in stating that the nonsubjective element in the otherwise "nonobjective senses" of taste is intersubjectivity. In her reading, judgments of taste make us "considerate" in the sense that our own special subjective conditions are overcome for the sake of intercourse with others. In other words, the volubility of judgments of taste is also an acknowledgment of their foundation in human sociality and an expression of belonging to the community of humans through a shared capacity for common human understanding, or *gemeines Men-*

schenverstand. "I judge as a member of this community," Arendt writes, "and not as a member of a supersensible world, perhaps inhabited with beings endowed with reason but not with the same sense apparatus; as such, I obey a law given to myself regardless of what others may think of the matter. This law is self-evident and compelling in and by itself" (*Lectures* 67–68). And at the same time, the fundamental other-directedness of judgment and taste stands in opposition to the absolutely subjective and idiosyncratic nature of the sense of taste itself. Could it be, then, that this other-directedness, the intersubjective conditioning of artful conversation by a shared community sense, is what "humanizes" us, brings us out of our selves and into world and community; in short, what "acculturates" us? By the same token, the refusal to listen or to participate, to enter into community, or to barricade oneself within a community that refuses the possibilities of ethical self-examination and revision in relation to others, may token a lapse into barbarism.

The appeal to intersubjectivity in judgments of taste aims not only to define the shape of a shared world but also the terms and frameworks of cultural kinship and common experience in that world. Assessing qualities and conditions of intersubjectivity is the basis for constructing a common culture and for understanding how one inhabits a world shared with others. "From the viewpoint of this common experience," Arendt says, "it is as though taste decides not only how the world is to look, but also who belongs together in it" ("Crisis" 220). Intersubjectivity is forged in the fact that every individual judgment of taste enacts a disclosure, that is, an expression or affirmation that is intended to be shared. Through acting and speaking in a given public or polis, one discovers and discloses who one is, what one thinks, and in this manner manifests and thus discovers one's taste, by making it apparent and shareable as part of a world of social appearance. Arendt believes such disclosures are to a certain extent involuntary. Be that as it may, ideally, judgments of taste are acts of self-disclosure where one discovers and tests to what degree one's tastes and beliefs are idiosyncratic, or whether they belong in or to a community in formation. In sharing our responses to the objects and events of this world, we not only reveal ourselves; we also declare ourselves members of a community of fellow appreciators, that we belong together in a kind of polis. We fashion a solidarity of sensibility, a company of critics.

The example of taste and judgments concerning the beautiful bring forward the fundamental dilemmas of exercising insight in a shared life. Taste is contrary to private feelings and opinions because it is subject to dispute and open to discussion. It is not a private experience by definition, for judgments of taste are expressed externally through the impossible desire of soliciting universal agreement. Judgments of taste always arise on that shared frontier where external sensations and internal perceptions meet—there is a collision here between the world as an objective datum common to all of its local inhabitants and the subjective perspective and framework from which a given agent observes and interprets, judges, and evaluates. When I express a judgment, what do I want from others? Importantly, I want to know in what degree and to what extent my understanding of the shape and value of this world is shared locally—that others somehow see, understand, and value the world as I do. And if they do not, to what degree must I partially or wholly modify my own perspective, and therefore sense of self, if I want to reach agreement—and thus share this world—with others? Or alternatively, how far am I willing to go to persuade others to modify their perspective and to come in line with my judgments? This is why Arendt claims that "the activity of [judgments of] taste decides how this world, independent of its utility and our vital interests in it, is to look and sound, what men will see and what they will hear in it. Taste judges the world in its appearance and in its worldliness; its interest in the world is purely 'disinterested,' and that means that neither the life interests of the individual nor the moral interests of the self are involved here. For judgments of taste, the world is the primary thing, not man, neither man's life nor his self" ("Crisis" 219). And for Arendt, this world is culture and history in formation.

Judgments of taste are disinterested because they are concerned neither with the functionality of objects in the world nor with conditions for sustaining life. Something more fundamental to human sociality is at stake. Call this the need to assert that despite subjective differences and conflicting needs we do share a world in common—that it looks more or less the same to all of us, and that in our local communities we value objects and activities in it for more or less similar and comparable reasons, even if we have not chosen the same objects and activities to value. When building a house together, arguments concerning construction and design may be resolved by appealing to common measurements. If there is disagreement about whether a patient suffers from the onset of cardiac arrest or from an acute case of acid reflux, new data can be acquired to resolve the nature of the symptom, and its disappearance will prove whose diagnosis is correct. Nevertheless, humans engage in many common activities, world-building activities, where no such quantitative measurements apply, and these are some of our most important cultural and political activities. Taste is subject to dispute because it expects agreement from everyone else. This is where aesthetic and moral judgments are linked. We also expect assent on questions of good and bad, right or wrong, or justice and injustice. The difference between the two is that moral judgments routinely appeal to regulative concepts or transcendental principles though of course, in "Thinking and Moral Considerations" Arendt finds this idea to be without support. In this respect, judgments of taste share an important framework with moral reasoning and political argument: both are exercised through criticism and persuasion. Standards of proof will not settle a disagreement in these domains, only a testing of conviction. Persuasion rules the polis because it asks that conflicts be resolved without violence or coercion. In like manner, the powerful example of the Socratic elenchus is a demonstration of the process and value of testing conviction without the coercion of the finality of "truth." There is simply no final truth to be arrived at or transmitted, which continually turns the dialogue back onto terms and frameworks for testing conviction. (Socrates's deepest lesson is this: to persuade his interlocutors that they have no secure knowledge, that in fact, like him they know nothing.) Arendt notes that in Aristotle persuasion, or *peithein*, is offered in contrast to *dialegesthai*, or dialectic, because dialectic is concerned with an acquisition of knowledge that aims for truth—it therefore demands a process of compelling truth. Alternatively, Arendt argues that "culture and politics . . . belong together because it is not knowledge or truth which is at stake, but rather judgment and decision, the judicious exchange of opinion about the sphere of public life and the common world, and the decision what manner of action is to be taken in it, as well as to how it is to look henceforth, what kind of things are to appear in it" ("Crisis" 223). It seems to me that these activities define a kind of common "curation" of the world whose terms of appearance, and of potential and possible actions, are both forged and revised in conversations arising from judgments of taste, that is, value. Yet, there is also a strong link here to moral reasoning where judgment takes on ethical dimensions whose evaluative assertions involve descriptions of modes of existence, where I must decide whether this world is one I can live in with others or not.

I return here to Arendt's commitment to the idea that judgments of taste be considered as political rather than merely theoretical actions. Arendt claims repeatedly in her later works that Kant's critique of aesthetic judgment is his greatest and most original contribution to an otherwise unwritten political philosophy. In the *Critique of Practical Reason*, the categorical imperative insists upon the necessity for rational thought to agree with itself—the self-giving of a maxim that should apply universally as a principle of rational agreement with oneself and serve as a guide to practical moral actions. However, the direction of judgment changes in the third Critique. It is no longer sufficient to be in agreement only with one's self. The test of *phronēsis*, or insight, is that one must also be able to think in the place of others through the exercise of an enlarged mentality (*eine erweiterte Denkungsart*). "The power of judgment rests on a potential agreement with others," Arendt writes, "and the thinking process which is active in judging something is not, like the thought process of pure reasoning, a dialogue between me and myself, but finds itself always and primarily, even if I am quite alone in making up my mind, in an anticipated communication with others with whom I know I must finally come to some agreement" ("Crisis" 217).

Aesthetic judgment aims toward agreement, or at least a fragile consensus. And to do so, judgment must liberate itself from "subjective private conditions." These are individual and private idiosyncrasies and idiolects that would lack validity in the public realm. The appeal to taste as the outward manifestation of a sensus communis asks that one hold one's judgments up to the possible as much as actual judgments of others, which is another way of saying that it requires judging subjects to project their selves imaginatively into the position of everyone else, to see and to judge from the perspective of the other, and to be open to revising one's own judgments and actions with respect to the claims of the other. This representative thinking presents a fundamentally ethical situation where Kant's enlarged mentality becomes the condition sine qua non of right judgment. Private conditions and circumstances limit and inhibit the exercise of judgment. However, imagination and reflection liberate us from our solitary internal worlds to attain the relative impartiality that Arendt calls "the specific virtue of judgment"

(*Lectures* 73). The enlarged mentality of aesthetic judgment must direct the subject toward a revision of self where one's individual limitations of perspective and sense are overcome and transcended. Importantly, this enlargement cannot function in isolation or solitude, for it needs the presence of others for its space of operation and expression. In other words, in judgment the subject must engage with a polis (whether possible or actual), become part of it, and negotiate its place within the polis through public acts of criticism. To think in the place of others is to know how to project oneself into the perspective of others. Judgment is what brings my self out of myself and into intercourse with others, without whom judgments have no value. "Hence judgment is endowed with a certain specific validity but is never universally valid," Arendt writes in "Crisis in Culture." "Its claims to validity can never extend further than the others in whose place the judging person has put himself for his considerations. Judgment, Kant says, is valid 'for every single judging person,' but the emphasis in the sentence is on 'judging'; it is not valid for those who do not judge or for those who are not members of the public realm where the objects of judgment appear" (217, citing Kant, *Critique of the Powers of Judgment*, introduction, part VII).

One might wonder why Arendt defines the exercise of judgment as a political capability rather than a moral or ethical one. I think this is because of her commitment to the idea of the polis as a self-governing community and to the implicit idea that when the judging subject undertakes self-revision, it is in response to one's understanding of a shared world and one's desire to assume a place in the community defined by the actions and values of that world. Because action and speech, which define their own space of appearance, are so ephemeral, revision is key to this process. The auto-constitution of the polis is ongoing and without finality—if it is not open to continuous revision through the exercise of judgment, it stagnates, fails, and disappears. As the second Critique is a work of moral reasoning and not political theory, there is an interesting recharacterization of Kant here. Arendt considers judgment as a political capacity in the sense of exercising a power to see from one's own limited perspective and at the same time to take the perspective of all present into account in a given conversation or deliberation. To exercise judgment is to orient oneself in the public realm and the common world. As I remark above, Arendt notes that the Greeks called this ability "insight" (*phronēsis*) and used it to qualify excellence in *politikous*, statesmen or citizens, in contrast to the wisdom of the philosopher as a sort of practical intelligence in social life that is distinct from the solitary theoretical intelligence of philosophy. How is the insight of judgment, then, different from the speculative and critical thought presented in "Thinking and Moral Considerations"?

In this context, one might think of insight as the exercise of public character that aims at intersubjective transformation in contrast to the solitary meditations of the philosopher. Recall Arendt's reading of the line from Pericles's oration in which the statesman or public citizen asks of philosophers to overcome their inwardness by providing examples of right judgment, which is also an appeal to the philosopher to come out of the solitude of thought to be an active contributor to the polis. Pericles contrasts love of wisdom with that of beauty in stating that the philosopher's solitary meditation is more likely to lead to inactivity than the aesthete's expressed love of beauty. Moreover, both love of wisdom and love of beauty are "barbarous" or excessive if not moderated by insight. With the example of Kant's arguments in mind, I believe that Arendt interprets barbarity to mean being uncultured, uncivilized, being uncivil, or not open to conversation and the revision of belief and moral attitudes—in other words, of being impervious to both self-examination and persuasion. The question thus raised in Arendt's interpretation is, Does the right love of beauty—which is discerning, moderate, or moderated by consensus through persuasion—have something to do with politics? Or from my perspective the question might be, What is the relation of artful conversation to ethical revisability and political debate or discussion? In this context, one might understand that the "right love of beauty" is not about beauty per se, which is an empty concept, as I have argued after Kant. To say that beauty is an empty concept turns the argument from beauty to the modality of judgment itself as a means for self-disclosure and self-revision, of persuading and dissuading, expressing and challenging conviction or belief, and of coming to agreement within an enlarged and revised perspective—in other words, as the means for building a shared life or culture with others. This assertion also brings attention to qualities analogous to "beauty" that require qualitative evaluation rather than measurement, experiences or beliefs that inspire aesthetic as well as moral consideration in terms of contingent and dynamic assessments of good or bad, right and wrong, healthy or destructive, just and unjust.

What moderates excessive love of beauty, then, are procedures of dissensus and consensus legislated dynamically and contingently by the exercise of insight and right judgment, meaning, in Arendt's terms, "taste." The exercise of judgments of taste models in the most local ways the possible formation of a polis as a self-governing and self-regulating space of action and discourse. In turn, however, philosophy is tasked with education in judgment. Rather than presenting a conflict between the insight of the statesman, or *politikos*, and the contemplation of the philosopher, Arendt seems to suggest after Pericles that they are the two integrated sides of an active public citizenship mediated by judgment. On one hand, judgment is the bridge leading from the solitary exercise of contemplation or meditation to the activity of shared life in the polis. On the other, excessive or uncivil judgments need the moderation of intersubjective critique, where the insight of the *politikos* might regulate the perimeters of right judgment and where the philosopher's wisdom might provide an education in good judgment. Socrates the citizen-philosopher and public thinker is here again the model educator and citizen. Referring to Cicero, Arendt will later give a name to this model citizen: the humanist, who exhibits the qualities of a *cultura animi* in the free exercise of taste. I will come back to this.

As I have already suggested, the role of insight arises from Kant's *gemeines Menschenverstand*, which Arendt depicts as the "good sense" that discloses to the human community the nature of the world insofar as it is a world lived in common, and in which every individual's thoughts and actions must be worked out in a dynamic and open network of interactions with others. As exercised in the context of human community sense, insight is a means for actively recalibrating our internal thoughts and internally received sense data with this external and objective world shared with others. Judging is the most important activity in which this sharing the world with others comes to pass.

However, another question of culture and curation is left unresolved here. If the philosopher and the public citizen are two sides of every judging subject as a potential member of a polis, wherein lies the role of art and the artist? Recall that Arendt defines culture as a mode of intercourse engaging "the least useful and most worldly of things, the works of artists, poets, musicians, philosophers, and so forth" ("Crisis" 210) and thus relates art and philosophy as distinct in some ways from statesmanship and public civic discourse. Here Arendt insists that a

clear distinction should be maintained between the activity of making art (utilitarian and ends-directed fabrication) and the viewing and
judging of art (free and disinterested spectatorship). Arendt has some
difficult things to say about the place of artists as distinct from their
works in the polis. As I am concerned here principally with her late
emphasis on acts of judgment, let it just be said that unlike Kant she
often seems to confuse the artist and the craftsperson; or at least she
considers the artist a craftsperson until that moment when a work of
art is released to the world and becomes an element of world making
to be judged as such. (The same might be said for the philosopher's
thoughts and concepts, of course, which must be exposed to the world
as discourse.) *Homo faber* is ends-directed and concerned with acts of
fabrication. Only when creative works are released into the world and
become publicly available for judgment do they potentially become
works of art and elements of a culture. Indeed, to belong to culture, the
work of art must transcend and outlast the artist, as must the expressed
thought of the philosopher—again, a criterion marked against human
finitude.[33]

Perhaps the critique of taste suggests another way of addressing this
problem? Whether artist, public citizen, or philosopher, every single
person in his or her solitude has the capacity, perhaps even the right,
to exercise taste and to call a thing beautiful or to make a moral judgment in calling an action right or wrong, just or unjust. But these acts
are meaningless without public tests of conviction. By the same token,
art, it would seem, has no content, at least no aesthetic content, until
it is complimented by judgments of taste that bestow meaning and
value, no matter how contradictory and contested or ephemeral, onto
works of art. What aesthetic judgment shares with both art and political activity is the necessity of public display and conversation. Art and
politics are both phenomena of the public world, and both require
presentation in a public space where they can be examined and discussed: "They can fulfill their own being, which is appearance, only in a
world which is common to all" ("Crisis" 215). Arendt calls this common
world "culture," and in order to enter into public culture, works of art

---

33. Arendt works through these questions in greater depth in section 23 of *The Human
Condition*, "The Permanence of the World and the Work of Art" (167–74), which along with
her lecture "Culture and Politics" should be considered as forming the basis of her arguments
in "The Crisis in Culture."

must be protected against the possessiveness and self-interest of private individuals and institutions, no less than the solitary work of the artist. Here is one area where art and politics are interrelated and mutually dependent in spite of their inherent conflicts—the formation of culture requires policy, and thus politics, as a bulwark against the withdrawal of art from the public sphere into private life and possession, which is equally a removal of art from the space of public conversation. Bringing works back into a space of public conversation is one role of curation.

At this point in Arendt's argument, roles are shuffled once again. Or rather, Arendt brings another framework of interpretation to Pericles's oration in its gesture toward achieving balance in the intertwined concerns of art, philosophy, and citizenship or politics. The crisis in culture arises from the global spread of philistinism and ends-directed evaluation throughout public life, which might also be considered a restriction or reduction in the free exercise of thought and judgment, which are concerns of philosophy. This is also a concern about the absence of philosophy—meaning critical thinking and right judgment—in public life. Who thinks most freely? Invoking Cicero once more, Arendt argues that the conflict between the ends-directed aims of the artist and the free exercise of political life should be mediated by *cultura animi*—minds trained and cultivated to curate and care for the world of artful appearances. This training is one aim of philosophy, for only philosophers approach things as spectators or attentive observers. Here Arendt relates a well-known story about Pythagoras recounted in Diogenes Laertius's *Lives of the Eminent Philosophers*. When Leon, the tyrant of Phlius, asked Pythagoras who he was, he responded, a philosopher, "and that he compared life to the Great Games, where some went to compete for the prize and others went with wares to sell, but the best as spectators [θεαταί]; for similarly, in life, some grow up with servile natures, greedy for fame and gain, but the philosopher seeks for truth."[34] Philosophy is disinterested in ends and means, winning and losing, or buying and selling, and so preserves its capacity to judge independently of either life's necessities, the will to fabrication, or the expediencies of politics. Philosophers are therefore the best viewers,

---

34. See Diogenes Laertius, *Lives of the Eminent Philosophers*, vol. 2, trans. R. D. Hicks (Cambridge, MA: Harvard University Press, 2000), 328–29. Arendt returns to this anecdote with similar arguments in both *The Life of the Mind: Thinking* and her *Lectures on Kant's Political Philosophy*.

the ones most attentive to the spectacle because of their independence from it. "Cicero calls them *maxime ingenuum*," Arendt writes, "the most noble group of the free-born men, for what they were doing: to look for the sake of seeing only was the freest, *liberalissimum*, of all pursuits" ("Crisis" 216). Whether in politics, art, or any other social domain, the exercise of freely observing and judging is framed as a philosophically informed activity. Likewise, among all human activities directed toward the formation of a polis at whatever scale, aesthetic judgment is most independent from necessity, and thus entails the greatest exercise of freedom. This is where philosophy makes a bridge between art and politics in relation to culture. But perhaps there is also an ethical question here: What qualities and activities does the philosophical mode of existence wish to preserve and perpetuate for the polis in the idea of a *cultura animi*? Arendt credits Cicero as being among the first thinkers to extend the human world-building sense of cultivation to matters of spirit or mind—that is, of cultivating a cultured mind—and suggests the Greek term *paideia*, or educator, as the best description for what I have been calling an education in judgment.

Here I return yet again to Arendt's free translation of the line from Pericles's oration as recorded by Thucydides: "We love beauty within the limits of political judgment, and we philosophize without the barbarian vice of effeminacy." This line is something like a maxim indicating the role judgments of taste play in the intersecting domains of art and politics. Both instances want to set limits to an uninformed or immoderate attraction to beauty or wisdom. In Arendt's gloss, she claims that for the Greeks the polis or community set limits to the love of wisdom and beauty, "and since we know that the Greeks thought it was the polis and 'politics' (and by no means superior artistic achievements) which distinguished them from the barbarians, we must conclude that this difference was a 'cultural' difference as well, a difference in their mode of intercourse with 'cultural' things, a different attitude toward beauty and wisdom, which could be loved only within the limits set by the institution of the polis" ("Crisis" 210–11). The self-regulating formation of the polis is here linked to the formation of a culture, where both beauty and wisdom must find their proper place and appropriate modes of intercourse. In this context, the vice of "effeminacy" attributed to barbarians is less a question of aestheticism than it is "an indiscriminate sensitivity which did *not know how to choose*" (211; my emphasis), and in this respect, an immoderate love of wisdom in philosophy is judged politically as harshly as an excessive love of beauty. In the first case, one withdraws from the world, in the latter, one is too much in love with the world; for the former, the distance is too great, and for the latter, distance is annihilated. Politics and philosophy come into relation here precisely through an assessment of the powers of judgment, where the aim of a philosophy that serves the polis is not to reach for and to convey transcendental truth (Plato) but rather to educate potential members of the polis to discern, to curate, and to make judgments in the public domains of both art and politics in a state of freedom whose only constraint is intersubjective assessment and decision as exercised through conversation and persuasion. There is a tyranny of philosophy, which is to seek or to impose conviction through "dialectics." There is a tyranny of art through being "enslaved" by love of beauty. Right judgment lies, then, in discrimination, in maintaining the freedom to choose, and in the ability to persuade and to be persuaded. Taste functions here as a limit to excessive evaluations and reactions to the beautiful, which Arendt associates with the ends-directed quality of artfully fabricated works. Again, the aim here is to free judgment from the necessity imposed by an overvaluation of the beautiful as a telos—in other words, to leave the human agent free to judge and to decide in the absence of any transcendental standard.

You may have remarked that while the action and discourse of politics is always a public business, the creative work of the artist and the thought of the philosopher are linked by their solitude. (Solitude, it would seem, is an affront to political life.) What Arendt calls publicity is required for art or philosophy to enter culture or become elements for building and caring for culture. But there is also an interesting link here between art and politics. Creative work enters the cultural world by giving form to appearance and making it endure. The public action and discourse of politics also define a space of appearance, which is dynamic, situational, and above all, unlike achieved works of art, ephemeral. Here culture relates to politics artfully as the retroactive recording or narrating of events that otherwise risk being lost to time—in other words, writing into history the deeds and words of human events. Both art and history "memorialize" politics, as it were, by giving form, significance, and permanence to its ephemeral appearance. Arendt calls such works monuments. And in this respect, judgments of taste are not only the genetic core of the public formation of a polis; they are also acts of curation——the preliminary steps to discerning whether works of art or philosophy are candidates for culture and whether memorialized events and works have withstood recurring tests of time and judgment.

What Arendt calls monuments are the means for maintaining and preserving the historical memory of a polis and of perpetuating that memory across generations in the enduring works of "artists, poets, musicians, philosophers, and so forth." There is an explicit connection between monuments and beauty in Arendt's argument because some powerful quality must inspire and attract pure judgments of taste into those discursive processes of discernment and distinction that are the first steps of curating culture—that is, of deciding whether creative and formative acts will be able to endure monumentally, as it were. That Arendt takes for granted the immanent relation between beauty and monumentality is a residue of her implicit Platonism, as I argued above. Moreover, Arendt also assumes that the capacity of a *cultura animi* to recognize and proclaim that beauty in judgments of taste is something like an anthropological universal. While she draws powerful support from Kant in this regard, I have also argued that there is a stark contradiction in their positions with respect to their claims concerning beauty.

An unexamined foundation of Arendt's account of culture and its crisis links the permanence of beauty to the timelessness of monuments and the recurring appearance of a *cultura animi* prepared to recognize, value, and preserve them. At stake here are Arendt's justifications for asserting that monuments sustain and perpetuate a long-term or even permanent historical memory and that criteria for valuing monuments remain consistent and invariable over time. I ended the previous section by observing that Arendt's crisis in culture is defined by the incapacity to think forward from the time of consumption to the time of history. That beauty endures in formal appearance and that the potential for discerning beauty is an anthropological universal both suggest, paradoxically, that culture and history are timeless. The crisis of culture, then, is not a failure to create new works of art or to elicit new and transformative human actions. It is a failure, rather, of understanding, of making sense of culture, of making new sense of culture, and of being open to the potential revisability of the terms and protocols through which the meaning and value of a culture are addressed both singly and collectively. The crisis of culture is a failure of education and, indeed, judgment, as an erosion of human capacities for discernment and decision. These capacities are diminished by historical forces of capitalism, consumerism, and philistinism against which "authentic" monuments would themselves appear to be impervious, at least so long as discerning individuals trained in the proper mode of intercourse with beautiful things keep being reborn to human culture. Arendt thus gives an optimistic edge to her account of the crisis in culture—just as authentic monuments cannot fade from history, a *cultura animi* will also persist, no matter how rare and vulnerable, in new human communities.

Such ideas are strange coming from one of the most powerful and discerning historical and political intellects of the twentieth century. What indeed is the relation of *history* to culture and curation?

Arendt's crisis in culture is defined by the erosion of our modes of intercourse with monuments and artworks, which is in fact a worry about a decline in our powers of judgment as well as our ability to educate new citizens in judgment. But monuments and the enduring appeal of beauty are not so buffeted by the winds of history in Arendt's 1960 account, which is her one hope of perpetuating the culture she values and believes in. Such arguments are culturally conservative at best. For me, the central problem is that if beauty is a transcendental force, and every civilization produces without fail cultured minds, no matter how few in number, then there is no possibility for imagining new and unprecedented creative strategies and philosophical ideas or for contesting and revising our senses of history, community, or aesthetic experience.

I asserted above that there can be no final agreement on what artifacts belong to culture or not, nor will there finally be agreed-upon common criteria for belonging; otherwise, judgment could not be related to thinking by the fact of its recurrent, unfinished character. Yet Arendt's argument rests on her conviction that beauty is timeless and immortal. For her, an education in judgment involves enhancing and reproducing the capacities of citizens for discernment, insight, and judgment. But if beauty is without content, there is no aim or anchor for judgments of taste. The power of judgment has no *necessary* link with the objects that provoke aesthetic experience and judgments of taste. Interest and value do not reside in the work, either formally or essentially, but only in the intersubjective context of judgment. Pleasure in judgment refers only to imagination and internal affect, and perhaps the revisability of conce. Like moral considerations, judgments of taste cannot rely on transcendental principles. One of the most difficult lessons for education in judgment, then, is that like the process of thinking, it is without finality. It cannot be accomplished once and for all, but rather only practiced, rehearsed, revised, and refined, widened and deepened, but without the satisfaction of final consensus or permanent results.

Here Arendt's fascinating concept of natality, the ever-recurrent human capacity for beginning anew, is in conflict with history, and the place of beauty in Arendt's argument must be contested because it undermines her arguments about history.[35] If beauty is everywhere and at all times recognizable by those prepared with taste, in what sense is one free to apprehend it, much less to make persuasive judgments that might revise our understanding of the sense and value of aesthetic experiences and historical events? A stark contradiction also emerges between Arendt's assertion of the ordinariness of thought as a fact of the human and her defense of a cultural elite tasked with the assessment and preservation of culture.[36] I have argued that her account of beauty in relation to judgments of taste conflicts in nontrivial ways with Kant's own account. What Kant calls beauty (without a determining concept), I have redescribed as experiences of "intensified perception" characterized, perhaps, by what classical philosophy called *thaumazein*, and there are innumerable occasions, both creative and historical, that give rise unpredictably to such elusive experiences. Nothing is more ordinary, or extraordinary. However, there are neither empirical cri-

35. One of Arendt's most striking definitions of natality occurs in her essay "What Is Authority?," which is also included in *Between Past and Future*. Here Arendt writes, "It is in the very nature of every new beginning that it breaks into the world as an 'infinite improbability,' and yet it is precisely this infinitely improbable which actually constitutes the very texture of everything we call real. . . . The very impact of an event is never wholly explicable; its factuality transcends in principle all anticipation" (168). I will return to the concept of natality in relation to history in the next section.

36. As Arendt writes in "The Crisis in Culture," "Taste as the activity of a truly cultivated mind—*cultura animi*—comes into play only where quality-consciousness is widely disseminated, the truly beautiful easily recognized; for taste discriminates and decides among qualities. As such, taste and its ever-alert judgment of things of the world sets its own limits to an indiscriminate, immoderate love of the merely beautiful; into the realm of fabrication and of quality it introduces the personal factor, that is, gives it a humanistic meaning. Taste de-barbarizes the world of the beautiful by not being overwhelmed by it; it takes care of the beautiful in its own 'personal' way and thus produces a 'culture'" (220–21).

teria nor determinative concepts for defining "beauty"—it is only an experience, an internal reflection on one's imaginative response, that one may attest to and report on, and these experiences are open to everyone in the human community. Indeed, in making judgments of taste, or in a public airing of opinion, I declare and test my presence in a community, and I invite others to a conversation about whether our ways of understanding and valuing experience, whether aesthetic or historical, is shareable or not. For Kant, every human endowed with reason (and this is one fact of the human) is capable of undergoing these experiences and sharing them in acts of judgment. Perhaps only a human being endowed with a *cultura animi* is capable of discerning beauty, but every being endowed with what Kant calls common human understanding is affected by the desire to express and share publicly his or her judgments concerning experiences in art and politics. There is indeed a kind of anthropological universalism in Kant, but its ground lies in our *sensus communis*, not in beauty, and the felt need to make judgments arises, in any experience, moral or aesthetic, where we feel compelled to make and defend qualitative distinctions.

Make no mistake. My criticisms here are not meant to disarm completely Arendt's idea that monuments, in her very broad sense of the term, serve to define and preserve human cultures by maintaining the historical memory of a polis. Monuments are certainly a very powerful bridge between history and memory, and art and politics, but this memory has no claim to permanence. In fact, the retraction of this permanence is what gives the faculty of judgment its attractions and powers.

By the same token, culture is not an achieved state, nor is it an archive preserved for history, as Arendt seems to believe or suggest, but rather a dynamic mode of discourse modeled by judgment that requires its own forms of natality fueled by imagination and revisability. Culture is not a state, mentality, or archive but rather a mode of conversation that, like politics, forges its own space of appearance. Moreover, the formation of culture is intrinsically linked to the space of appearance of the polis, and if properly memorialized, a culture may endure longer than a polis, yet it is no less subject to forces of critique, destruction, and natality. Its meaning and durability are, or should be, continually open to challenge and revision—this is what history means in relation to the assumption of monumentality. The question that Arendt

consistently wrestles with in "The Crisis in Culture," often unsuccess-
fully, is how culture can really be forged in ways that are preserved in
history. The works of artists made public, and the action and speech
of intersubjective judgments about art and historical experience, need
to be monumentalized for a culture to maintain publicly its historical
memory. The problem here is that Arendt's attention to the dynamism
and transitoriness of judgment and its recurrent activities of interpretation and evaluation does not translate into the transsubjective time
of history except through metaphysical appeals to the timelessness of
beauty and the capacity of cultured individuals to recognize it and to
preserve it in all times and places. This observation raises questions
about the durability of artworks. How do monuments *stay* in the world,
or more importantly, sustain any continuity of sense *for* the world? They
must be judged, evaluated, and curated, and this process is continuous
and interminable. Durability makes no sense apart from the context
of the open and unfinished character of judgment. Present-time judgment is the first step toward curation, of a collective decision about
what kinds of things and experiences belong in and to a culture, but
judgment also informs retroactive assessments, at whatever temporal
scale, no matter how far or distant from the origins of a monument in
time. The immediacy of imaginative responses to a work are always
informed by historical imagination as well. The broad-mindedness of
an enlarged mentality includes not only taking the perspective of others into account but also accounting for and assessing our collective
historical imagination in terms of its sense, value, affect, and relevance
for our judgments in and of the present.

I can agree with Arendt that the appearance of memory and its
inscription in monuments or historical writing are tied to the space
of appearance of a polis. Yet Arendt is equally aware that the polis is a
dynamic, variable, and contingent appearance, so historical memory,
too, must be equally variable and impermanent. It is also clearly the
case that monuments are subject to natality and destruction—that
they come to ruin over time or are destroyed, that new monuments
are erected in their place, and in fact, the sense and value of existing
monuments are continually being dismantled and remade. The erection and destruction of monuments, and the continuous contestation
and revision of their sense and value, are all decided through acts of
judgment, and education in judgment is a recurring problem for every
polity because there is no end to it. One must always begin again.

I wrote earlier that Arendt values art at two radically different time scales: one is immediate, intensive, affective, and sociable and finds its expression in judgment (if not immediately consumed as entertainment); the other is transgenerational, autonomous or "objective," worldly, and is related through history. For Arendt, there is no culture without history, that is, without conveying some permanence to appearance. At the same time, judging is crucial in marking out the first steps of appearance becoming history—perceiving, discerning, selecting, interpreting, evaluating, and above all, preserving. Every human being endowed with community sense has the capacity to judge. But just as the artist is trained expertly in fabrication and the *politikos* in the art of insight and legislation, the critical thought of the philosopher exemplifies the activity of spectatorship, of viewing and judging. How, then, might these philosophical acts of viewing and judging be enlarged to consider the full spectrum of history as a contingent, dynamic, and conflictual process arising from the complexly interconnected actions of human plurality?

IV. THE WORLD-OBSERVER

All culture and art that adorn humanity, and the most
beautiful social order, are the fruits of unsociability.

IMMANUEL KANT, "Idea for a Universal
History with a Cosmopolitan Aim"

L'acte est vierge, même répété.

RENÉ CHAR, *Feuillets d'Hypnos*

I began the first section of this book by rephrasing Kant's anthropological question: What does it mean to be human or to become more fully human, or to know that one can become so, and so engage more fully in a revisable ethical and political life? My revision is a perfectionist reading of Kant, which frankly is not entirely supported by his political writings. There is in fact a strange gap or dislocation in Kant's philosophy between the demands of practical reason, where an individual moral life is actively forged in reason, and Kant's conception of human history as a teleological drive that guides the progressive evolution of *Homo sapiens* as a whole from a creaturely instinctual life toward an enlightened cosmopolitan existence. For Kant, the end of human history, should there be one, would result in the peaceful coexistence of all individuals on the planet in civil societies governed freely through the exercise of rational deliberation. This idea is stated most directly in the eighth proposition of Kant's "Idea for a Universal History with a Cosmopolitan Aim" (1784): "*One can regard the history of the human species in the large as the completion of a hidden plan of nature to bring about an inwardly and, to this end, also an externally perfect state constitution, as the only condition in which [nature] can fully develop all its predispositions in humanity.*"[37] Humankind's humanity will only be achieved when humans enter into a self-perpetuating state of peaceful coexistence where the absence of violent conflict amplifies possibilities for exercising a freely chosen existence guided by reason. For Kant, the achievement of a perfect political constitution would be the monument that celebrates finally the achievement of a political culture in which each individual might pursue moral perfection as guided freely by reason. Nevertheless, Kant knows full well that achieving the ends of human history might not nor even could not eliminate human conflict tout court. Herein lies the irony of the Dutch innkeeper's joke that inspires the title of Kant's essay "Toward Perpetual Peace" ("Zum ewigen Frieden")—the only sure road to eternal peace leads to the graveyard.

However, the contradiction in Kant's political philosophy does not

37. In *Anthropology, History, and Education*, ed. Günter Zöller and Robert B. Louden, trans. Alan W. Wood (Cambridge: Cambridge University Press, 2007), 50; the emphasis is Kant's. In her *Lectures on Kant's Political Philosophy*, Arendt notes how in Kant's anticipatory picture of history, the predispositions nature has seeded in humanity develop progressively across generations as a process whose product "is sometimes called *culture*, [*Critique of the Power of Judgment* §83] sometimes *freedom* ("from the tutelage of nature to the state of freedom") ["Conjectures on the Beginning of Human History"]; and only once, almost in passing, in a parenthesis, does Kant state that it is a question of bringing about 'the highest end intended for man, namely, *sociability* [*Geselligkeit*]' ["Conjectures on the Beginning of Human History,"]" (*Lectures* 8; my emphasis). The realization of a universal cosmopolitan existence would thus enhance the following potentialities for becoming human: the capacity to choose and to act freely according to the limits of reason, to impose upon oneself universally applicable moral laws, and to acquire the capacity to exercise right judgment in the company of others. This is why the critique of the powers of judgment is so important. In Kant's antagonistic world, judgments of pure taste exemplify the "natural" sociability of humans and in turn propose a model for the amical expression of conflict as a desire to seek consensus. In this, Arendt is not far wrong to see in the third Critique Kant's unwritten political philosophy.

lie in recognition that human conflict is unavoidable even if the aim of perpetual peace is to eliminate war. Indeed, conflict is the very motor of history in Kant's account—without conflict, there is neither human culture nor history. Rather, the contradiction lies in the argument that the history of humankind's becoming human is directed by an inhuman providential hand whose reasons are hidden from the collective agents of history. For Kant, progress toward perpetual peace is guaranteed by no less an authority than Nature herself, a great artist whose eventual goal is to produce the cultural and political conditions wherein a fully realizable human existence becomes possible in an imaginable future no matter how distant. To an attentive observer, however, there may appear in nature's inhuman mechanistic processes the image of a purposive plan that will one day produce concord among men, even against their will and indeed by means of their very discord.[38]

If the development of humanity in humankind as a whole is guided by a hidden plan of nature, how do individuals come to recognize the ideal of a cosmopolitan existence as the best ethical framework for building a life in common? Paradoxically, in Kant's view they cannot, or at least they cannot to the extent that they are occupied as history's collective actors. Busily engaged in the local and global conflicts that drive human history ineluctably forward, individuals are completely

---

38. Kant writes that the philosophical assumption of a hidden plan of nature "opens up the comforting prospect of a future in which we are shown from afar how the human race eventually works its way upward to a situation in which all the germs implanted by nature can be developed fully, and in which man's destiny can be fulfilled here on earth. Such a *justification* of nature—or rather perhaps of *providence*—is no mean motive for adopting a particular point of view in considering the world" ("Idea for a Universal History," 52–53; Kant's emphasis). Kant here as much admits that assuming a plan of nature is a speculative idea, that is, its inherent lawfulness cannot be proved. Enlightenment *needs* this utopian idea, however. Moreover, as the sense of history only reveals itself retroactively, and as a perfect civil constitution remains unachieved, no living spectator is in a position to really judge whether humans are collectively progressing or not. The assumed plan of nature is the utopian idea of Enlightenment, which exists even in Hegel and Marx as transposed into history, whether idealist or materialist. (Nature has no plans for humans—we are on our own.) Yet, crucially, one will see here the importance for Arendt of creating the concept of the "world-observer" out of her reading of Kant. This is the *historical* sensitivity and sensibility of an "enlarged mentality," one that attains at least a limited capacity for framing and understanding collective human actions with a view toward projecting how future progressive actions can emerge. Hence the interest of the bloody French Revolution, which despite its violence projects the ideal of equality in a society governed by reason according to a commitment to universal human rights. In the French Revolution, Kant hopes for the first seeds of a "perfect civil union of mankind."

unaware that they are the agents of a larger hidden plan. It is as if consciousness, or at least historical self-consciousness, disappears in action, and along with it, any possibility of freely exercising judgment whether for the present or the future. Nevertheless, is there a position or perspective from which historical self-consciousness, and a power of historical judgment, can be achieved and put into action? In my view, this question is the compass point directing Arendt's reflections on judgment in late works like the exercises in political thought collected in *Between Past and Future* and especially the posthumous *Lectures on Kant's Political Philosophy*.

Arendt's lectures on Kant are built out of a close reading of his political and anthropological writings, yet the guiding question of her speculations is drawn from her earlier essay "The Crisis in Culture": "Could it be that taste belongs among the political faculties?" ("Crisis" 211). Given the number and variety of works that can be counted among Kant's political writings, why does Arendt insist here again that Kant's critique of pure judgments of taste is the basis of his unwritten political philosophy? What motivates Arendt to turn to Kant's critique of the power of judgment to define a "political faculty" and, moreover, to establish links between her own account of thinking and moral considerations and problems of judgment with respect to politics and history? Forging answers to these questions is the central project of her late lectures on Kant, which one assumes are the blueprint for the projected last volume of *The Life of the Mind* on judgment.

Recall again the key assertions that Arendt reads into Pericles's funeral oration, all of which lead to her picture of "right judgment." The philosopher's speechless attraction to otherworldly truths, no less than the aesthete's unbridled enthusiasm for beautiful appearance, place the polis at risk because they lead to solitude and inaction. (One might also add the isolation of the creator or fabricator in his or her workshop or studio.) These are two forms of spectatorship, as it were, as if two variations of enraptured and isolated contemplation, both of which are in stark contrast to the active public participation of citizens in a polis, whose emblematic figure is the *politikos*, or "statesman." Moreover, embedded within this picture is one of the most persistent questions in Arendt's postwar writing: Is there an inherent and irresolvable conflict between politics and philosophy, between actively participating in the auto-constitution of a community and the speechless beholding of unveiled truths? (I will return to this problem in the next section.) Indeed, the central concern of Arendt's gloss on Pericles's funeral oration is to return philosophy to politics. In this respect, Arendt expands the semantic range of that curious word "taste" in three stages. Taste begins with an attitude where guided by discernment the "right love of beauty" leads to a particular kind of action, which is the proper kind of intercourse with beautiful things; in other words, to have taste is to have the capacity to exercise good judgment. However, judgment must also be guided, which is to say, educated. It must be accompanied by another quality, *phronēsis*, or insight, exemplified by the perspective of the *politikos* who knows how to discern and discriminate, to orient himself in the world of public appearances, action, and discourse, and to participate freely in a public plurality. And here, in one of Arendt's most densely composed paragraphs, an open circle is drawn as insight must in turn be guided by a cultured mind, or a mind attentive to culture, which that Roman citizen and thinker Cicero, in contrast to the Greeks, ascribes to philosophy. What the character of Cicero exemplifies, here and elsewhere in Arendt's writing, is a particular kind of bridge in perspectives, where reconciling the attitudes—or if you will, the "taste"—of the aesthete, the statesman, and the philosopher defines the terrain for exercising good judgment and active public citizenship, indeed for acting in concert to build and maintain a culture.

One might conclude here that Arendt's fundamental concern is to imagine how a philosophical education can inform good citizenship, and this is not wrong. But why would she frame this problem with respect to a crisis in *culture*? (Such a question is of course of great interest for the humanities.) For Arendt, judgment is not only a modality for negotiating disputes about taste—that is, value conflicts that can be worked out only through persuasion because there is no external rule or authority to which one can appeal—judgment is also the basis for any claim to culture as the mode of intercourse most appropriate for discerning, assessing, and evaluating works of art and other elements of culture. Indeed, the quality of a culture is defined not by the artful and memorable things that populate its museums and libraries but rather by the human will and capacity for making judgments that can define, discern, assess, evaluate, and give meaning to those objects that will populate, construct, and maintain a "world," and this world is as much political in Arendt's sense of the term as it is cultural.

It should be clear at this point that in my reading of Arendt the exercise of judgment is an ethical activity bridging philosophy, culture, and politics. Ethics is defined here not in terms of morals or the exercise of practical reason but rather as a matter of existential choice—of freely choosing one's company in order to act in concert to make a world together.[39] Therefore, the public exercise of judgment is an ethical practice in the sense that it is a world-building activity, but also a world-revising and a self-revising activity—ethics and politics are inseparable in the building of a culture whose highest end is *Geselligkeit*, or sociability.[40] In Arendt's account the free exercise of judgment in the company of others is both a form of ethical self-disclosure and a request to forge a community and to discover one's place within that community. Arendt's model of judgment also deploys a concept of culture that is extremely elastic—it is a space and time that can equally emerge spontaneously in present-time conversations yet must also be extended and sustained across the transgenerational span of history. Arising out of immediate acts of discernment and curation, judgment defines a space of memory and memorialization where a culture's history is both made and transmitted across time. This idea will be the basis of Arendt's dual claims in the Kant lectures that judgment is both a political or world-building faculty and a historical faculty for assessing the past and how the future emerges out of the present. For Arendt, acts of judgment are political by implication because they are *acts*: they bring us out of the solitude of thought and they are the very medium through which

39. In my recent books *Elegy for Theory* and *Philosophy's Artful Conversation* (Harvard University Press, 2014 and 2015), I argue in greater depth that the practice of a philosophical ethics should be distinguished from morality. Morality involves sets of constraining rules that judge actions and intentions against transcendent or universal values. An ethics evaluates expression according to the immanent mode of existence or possibilities of life it implies. Morals refer ordinarily to a transcendental system of values to which we conform, or against which we are found lacking. An ethics is an immanent set of reasoned choices. In ethical expression, we evaluate our current mode of existence, seeking to expand, change, or abandon it in the effort to achieve another way of living and another form of community. Inspiring an individual to choose a mode of existence embodied in a community, real or imagined, philosophy thus entails the expression and justification of this existential choice and its representation of the world. See, for example, *Philosophy's Artful Conversation*, 162 *et passim*.

40. See for example Kant's essay "Conjectures on the Beginning of Human History," whose aim is to consider the evolution of human history from an ethical point of view, that is, seeking the true principles of man's education as human being and citizen as guides to a "*changed mode of living*" marked by the advantages of "mutual *exchange*." In *Kant: Political Writings*, 230; Kant's emphasis.

we disclose ourselves and our thoughts by performing them publicly in the space of the polis. The polis so conceived by Arendt is dynamic, flexible, and above all *scalable*. As a space of appearing modeled on the Socratic elenchus, the polis only needs two participants. But one of the important questions raised by the *Lectures on Kant's Political Philosophy* is how judgments of pure taste function as the genetic motor of critical communities that may emerge in a common public space and time of discourse and action, but as importantly, also frame a critical capacity for making judgments of and in the full scale of human history in its own space of appearance. After the aesthete, the public citizen, and the philosopher, in her *Lectures on Kant's Political Philosophy*, Arendt introduces a new dimension of spectatorship, the *Weltbetrachter*, the world-spectator or observer.

Arendt's *Lectures on Kant's Political Philosophy* provide a fulsome outline of what I have called the operations of judgment as described in the preceding sections, which include discernment, imagination and the operation of reflection, impartiality, and insight, all of which lead ideally through the practice of judgment to the exercise of what Kant calls an enlarged mentality, or as Arendt often describes it, a practice of representative thinking grounded in human community sense. There is no need to rehearse these arguments again. Nonetheless, I want to emphasize that in this picture of judgment there is a continual rotation between an inside and an outside, from external experience to internal thought and back again, from private imagination and reflection to public exclamations of value. Publicity is the key factor here if judgment is to have a political value, not only because Arendt's main concern is how a polis—communities of like minds and shared values—forges a space of appearance in discourse but also because judgment is a privileged mode for expressing and resolving dissensus in human communities without a priori limitations of freedom. A bridge is created here between culture and politics since the kinds of conversations that arise in exchanging and evaluating opinions, in expressing and defending one's taste, are the genetic core of what it means to form and maintain a polis.

However, we are called to judgment not only by our passions and enthusiasms but also by our disappointments and anger. This is what Kant means when he characterizes the history of the human as driven by humankind's "asocial sociability"—the continuous and unavoid-

able tension between individual and community interests, which
themselves scale up to internecine and international conflicts such as
wars and revolutions. When Kant suggests in his political and historical
writings that the potential achievement of a cosmopolitan existence
will not eliminate human conflict even if global peace becomes constitutionally assured, he is making two existential or even ontological claims. First, the specificity of judgment as a faculty arises in the
acknowledgment that sensus communis and asocial sociability are two
inextricable dimensions of the same fact of the human, which is that
the exercise of one's individual freedom will always be in tension with
the will of others with whom one must still live in community. The
question of disputes concerning taste are only the most ordinary and
widespread expression of a universal human tendency toward dissensus and conflict. The commonality of these disputes demonstrates in
one and the same gesture both the sociability and interdependency of
humans and their inescapable tendency to disagree. Humans are born
into this situation, as it were, but only achieve their humanity through
their capacity to exercise judgment in expressing and negotiating these
conflicts sociably through the persuasive use of critical reason. Second,
in reading Kant's political writings side by side with his *Critique of the
Power of Judgment*, Arendt foregrounds the idea that while conflict may
be the main driver of human history, one can only make judgments
about the cultural and political progress of humankind from the perspective of collective public actions rather individual efforts—hence
her emphasis on publicity, community, and the importance of the public use of one's reason. If judgment is the most fundamental modality
in which humans prepare to act politically, then the enlargement of
the powers of judgment and representative thinking to a world scale
becomes an urgent historical problem, which in turns requires philosophical modifications of how judgment and the perspectives from
which it takes place are understood.

    Arendt's claim in the second session of the lectures that beyond
matters of taste, judgment is also a faculty for dealing with the past,
is perhaps her most radical modification of Kant's thought.[41] Unlike

41. I note here that in the canon of Kant's political writings, most of which follow the
Critique of Pure Reason and are composed in parallel with the other two critiques, the term or
concept of judgment appears relatively infrequently, even though it might seem everywhere
suggested to an attentive reader. The most fundamental claim appears after the publication of

aesthetic experiences, where the artwork's "purposive purposeless-ness" produces pleasure without interest in the spectator, the world-observer is drawn to the drama of collective action in events like the French Revolution because of a certain political interest, which Kant calls "sympathy." Moreover, the enthusiasm of the world-observer for such events is excited by the discernment of a particular purpose in world events, which is the teleological unfolding of an Enlightenment ideal of human progress. In turning to history, neither Kant nor Arendt functions as a historian. Kant is interested neither in description nor in the analysis of the causes or the immediate consequences of events. This is why Arendt rightly argues in the fourth session that Kant's own interest in history is not an interest in the particular with respect to which one is usually called to judge. As set out in a variety of Kant's essays, progress is always the progress of the species, or perhaps better, the human community collectively; it is not a measure that applies to the individual. In this respect, in their aims, historical judgments differ significantly from judgments of taste in that "the thought of progress in history as a whole, and for mankind as a whole, implies disregard of the particular and directing one's attention, rather, to the 'universal' . . . in whose context the particular makes sense—to the whole for the existence of which the particular is necessary." (*Lectures* 26). Only in this way can a philosopher like Kant comprehend human conflict as a progressive force where war, catastrophe, or even plain human evil can be understood as necessary for the development and expansion of human culture.[42]

---

the third Critique when in his 1793 essay, "On the Common Saying: That May Be Correct in Theory, but It Is of No Use in Practice," Kant opens his argument in stating that the middle term between theory and practice is judgment—a process of discrimination in understanding. See Immanuel Kant, *Practical Philosophy*, trans. and ed. Mary J. Gregor (Cambridge: Cambridge University Press), 279.

42. Kant's nine propositions in his 1784 essay "Idea for a Universal History with a Cos-mopolitan Aim" set out with great clarity his view that the will's manifestations in the world of human actions are determined in accordance with natural laws, and in this respect, are no different from other events in nature. The aim of history is guided by the idea that if history "considers the play of the freedom of the human will *in the large*, it can discover within it a regular course; and that in this way what meets the eye in individual subjects as confused and irregular yet in the whole species can be recognized as a steadily progressing though slow development of its original predispositions. . . . Individual human beings and even whole nations think little about the fact, since while each pursues its own aim in its own way and one often contrary to another, they are proceeding unnoticed, as by a guiding thread, according to an aim of nature,

The fundamental question for Arendt, no less than for Kant, is understanding how the nature of judgment is transformed in this enlarged historical perspective, where comprehending the incalculable complexity of human affairs on a global scale is somehow connected to, and in conflict with, the demand for universal consensus in individual judgments of taste. If there is any design to the shape of historical events in their course of happening, it is hidden from actors who are immersed in the contingent flux of events and the spectacle of history as they pursue individually their myriad collective and conflictual interests. Only a spectator of history can perceive the design because she is not involved and therefore disinterested in the Kantian sense, and thus free to judge. Again, the emphasis shifts here from the representative thought of local evaluation in community to the impartial judgment at a distance of an observer of history who needs to decide, by having an idea of the whole, whether human progress is discernible in any single, particular event. And of course, some judgments will also set out for display and argument criteria for evaluating whether actions lead to collective progress or not.

Arendt's term *"Weltbetrachter"* is presented in German and first appears in the *Lectures* in the seventh session after a review of the concept of impartiality.[43] The appeal to German is curious, for Arendt seems desirous of attributing the concept to Kant even though the term as such appears nowhere in his writing. This is another Arendtian modification and extension of Kant's thought, and an important one. In the seventh session, Arendt begins laying out her argument for expanding Kant's appeal to the practice of an *erweiterte Denkungsart*, enlarged thinking or broad-mindedness, as a form of representative thinking that is both historical and critical. Impartiality and imagina-

---

which is unknown to them, and are laboring at its promotion, although even if it were to become known to them it would matter little to them" (108). At the same time, since humans neither pursue their aims governed only by instinct, like animals, nor do they act like rational cosmopolitans according to an integral and prearranged plan, how is it possible for the philosopher to assess the moral progress of the human species? Kant's response is that the only way out for the philosopher, since he cannot assume that mankind follows any rational purpose of its own in its collective actions, is for him to attempt to discover "an *aim of nature* in this nonsensical course of things human; from which aim a history in accordance with a determinate plan of nature might nevertheless be possible even of creatures who do not behave in accordance with their own plan" (109; Kant's emphasis).

43. I might note her that the concept of the world-observer is anticipated in *The Human Condition*, especially in Arendt's comments on what she calls "the human surveying capacity" (251).

tion remain key terms here. Arendt characterizes impartiality not as the attainment of some higher and more objective perspective but rather by the individual capacity to take the viewpoints of others into account as part of a common community. Arendt often insists that one can only judge from within a community of others and thus impartiality defines the capacity for broadening one's own thought by expanding and also modifying it. Imagination comes into play because this broad-mindedness must include the potential to anticipate and compare one's judgments with the possible as well as actual judgments of others who may be distributed elsewhere in space and time, and thus may be able to respond to us directly or not. The world-spectator judges not as an individual in the presence of others but rather as an aspirant for a community to come. Acts of imagination are also essential for developing a historical perspective that encourages a kind of mobility in critical thought. "Critical thinking," Arendt writes, "is possible only where the standpoints of all others are open to inspection. Hence, critical thinking, while still a solitary business, does not cut itself off from 'all others.' To be sure, it still goes on in isolation, but by the force of imagination it makes the others present and thus moves in a space that is potentially public, open to all sides; in other words, it adopts the position of Kant's world citizen. To think with an enlarged mentality means that one trains one's imagination to go visiting. (Compare the right to visit in *Perpetual Peace*.)" (*Lectures* 43). A cosmopolitan existence, it would seem, requires not only the right of hospitality, to welcome strangers and to be in turn welcomed by them, but also the imaginative flexibility to entertain other minds and perspectives and, consequently, to open one's mind and opinions to others. I will suggest later that what this kind of historical judgment requires is a cosmopolitan public sphere.

Arendt's first suggestion of the term *Weltbetrachter* follows the question, "Is the general standpoint merely the standpoint of the spectator?" (*Lectures* 44). By slipping in a German word, Arendt is linking herself to Kant's thought as well as modifying it. The *Weltbetrachter* is related to but not synonymous with the "world citizen," the rational cosmopolitan, or *vernünftige Weltbürger*, that appears in Kant's later political writing. Rather, she is working to identify a difficulty in Kant's argument from which she hopes to liberate herself with this new term. To the extent that the position of the *Weltbetrachter* is a *philosophical* perspective, to what degree does it find itself at a distance from politics—of tak-ing decision to act in concert—and how does one qualify or character-ize this "distance"? With the classical connection of *theōrein* to *philosofia* hovering in the background, Arendt assumes that the philosopher is a spectator and not an actor, thus suggesting once again the question of the degree to which politics and philosophy can be reconciled. The impartiality of the philosophical spectator, writes Arendt,

> is a viewpoint from which to look upon, to watch, to form judgments, or, as Kant himself says, to reflect upon human affairs. It does not tell one how *to act*. It does not even tell one how to apply the wisdom, found by virtue of occupying a "general standpoint," to the particulars of political life. (Kant had no experience of such action whatsoever and could have had none in the Prussia of Frederick II.) Kant does tell one how to take others into account; he does not tell one how to combine with them in order to act. (44; Arendt's emphasis)

In other words, neither judgment nor representative thinking can tell agents how to apply their will as political actors.

Along these lines, it is also clear that Arendt's world-spectator is not a world citizen. "To be a citizen," Arendt clarifies, "means among other things to have responsibilities, obligations, and rights, all of which make sense only if they are territorially limited. Kant's world citizen was actually a *Weltbetrachter*, a world-spectator. Kant knew quite well that a world government would be the worst tyranny imaginable" (*Lectures* 44). Here is another version of what Arendt means by impartiality. The world-observer should not be limited by territoriality or national interest of any kind, for ideally, she must through her judgments imagi-natively stand in for, indeed represent, the whole of humanity. In her judgments of any given conflict, the world-spectator does not inter-vene as a citizen with duties and obligations to exercise but rather as a diagnostician of world history in the making and as a representative of an idea of the human.

This last observation also informs Arendt's account of the appar-ent contradiction arising between Kant's boundless admiration for the French Revolution and his resolute condemnation of any violent action against authority. Here Arendt appeals to a long citation from part 2 of Kant's essay "The Contest of the Faculties," which sets out for the philosopher what is at stake in the observation and evaluation of such a momentous event.[44] Kant was well aware of the moral difficulties in evaluating revolution as a break in history. Revolutions may succeed or fail, partially or wholly, and the violence done to people and institutions may be judged, especially in the moment, to have not been worth the price of the destruction caused, whether physical, civic, or cultural. In these pages, Kant is clearly passing his own judgment on the French Revolution.

Yet despite his late interest in constitutional law, what concerns Kant philosophically is not the appearance of new institutions or forms of constitution, but rather the discernment and evaluation of a particular form of "taste," which Kant characterizes as a "disinterested sympathy," not for one side or the other, but for the event itself in the degree to which it could be interpreted as expressing a moral disposition in the human race, whose true enthusiasm is always inspired exclusively by an ideal, such as the concept of natural rights. As the passage comes to a close, Kant formulates directly what is at stake in a philosophical judgment of history, which is its prophetic or predictive insight that humanity as a whole is irreversibly progressing in spite of inevitable regressions and retrogressions. For all its violence and complexity, Kant views the French Revolution as something like a "monumental" event in which he discerns "from the aspects and signs of our times that the human race will achieve this end, and that it will henceforth progressively improve without any more total reversals. For a phenomenon of this kind which has taken place in human history can *never be forgotten*, since it has revealed in human nature an aptitude and power for improvement of a kind which no politician could have thought up by examining the course of events in the past" ("Contest of the Faculties" 184; Kant's emphasis). There is something like a moral or ethical meaning to the French Revolution, which in Kant's view now becomes indelible in human history as memory and as a force of progressive becoming that is always capable of returning: "For the occurrence in question is too momentous, too intimately interwoven with the interests of humanity and too widespread in its influence upon all parts of the world for

44. See "A Renewed Attempt to Answer the Question: 'Is the Human Race Continually Improving?,'" in "Contest of the Faculties," *Kant: Political Writings*, 177–90. This argument is set out most completely in the section entitled "An occurrence in our own times which proves this moral tendency in the human race" (182–83). Arendt's own citation from an older translation appears on page 46 of the *Lectures*.

nations not to be reminded of it when favourable circumstances present themselves, and to rise up and make renewed attempts of the same kind as before. . . . And if one considers not only the events which may happen within a particular nation, but also their repercussions upon all the nations of the earth which might gradually begin to participate in them, a view opens up into the unbounded future" (185).

Here arises another of the key themes of Arendt's *Lectures on Kant's Political Philosophy*, wherein the distinction between the engaged actor and the judging spectator is presented in her reading of the second appendix of "Toward Perpetual Peace" as a conflict of politics with morality. This conflict can only be assessed and resolved by appealing to what Kant called the transcendental principle of publicity (*das transzendentale Prinzip der Publizität*). Arendt begins the ninth session by observing that the potential significance and meaning of the French Revolution as occurrence or event is something to be judged, not interpreted. Its world-historical importance is only discernible "in the eye of the beholder, in the opinion of the onlookers who proclaim their attitude in public. Their reaction to the event proves the 'moral character' of mankind. Without this sympathetic participation, the 'meaning' of the occurrence would be altogether different or simply nonexistent. For it is this sympathy that aspired hope" (*Lectures* 46–47). This hope, of course, is expressed by Kant's prediction that in the wake of seemingly endless revolutions the highest purpose of nature will finally be realized in the creation of a cosmopolitan existence. Although it must be constitutionally constituted, this is an ethical domain more than a political one. Or rather, politics comes to assure a state of peace and freedom where reason can be exercised to its fullest potential. Observing at a world scale, the philosopher is trying to discern the emerging shape and direction of a new mode of existence, no matter how unfocused or shrouded by war and the conflict and clamor of politics.

I will leave to one side Arendt's substantial analysis of Kant's arguments concerning the legitimacy or not of violent revolutions and its deep connection to the demands of practical reason. To understand how the perspective of the world-spectator responds to the conflict of politics with morality, only two claims need to be addressed. The first claim derives from the transcendental principle of publicness, which is offered in "Perpetual Peace" as a maxim for judging political actions: "All actions affecting the rights of other human beings are wrong if their maxim is not compatible with their being made public" ("Perpetual Peace" 126); or as Arendt puts it, "Publicness is already the criterion of rightness in [Kant's] moral philosophy" (*Lectures* 49). Through the categorical imperative, an individual in his solitude can through his own reason affirm a self-consistent maxim for moral action. However, the real test of a maxim is to declare it openly and thus to subject it to public examination to find out if it is acceptable to others and if they are willing in turn to act on it in concert.

Kant's elevation of publicity to a transcendental principle also directs his view that the only legitimate justification for revolution arises in situations where freedom of opinion has been abolished; this is the ultimate tyranny and the only truly moral reason for overthrowing authority. In addition, the insistence on publicity as a transcendental principal transfers the private individual deliberations of practical reason to public politics, even revolutionary politics. Here one's reason is applied as a public legislator more than as a self-legislator—you must care not only for yourself but also for a community; your practical reason and your judgments must serve the polis. In these situations, morality will inevitably come into conflict with politics and therefore require judgments to assess the compromises that will inevitably arise. When such circumstances occur, Arendt notes, "Though it is true that, by resisting evil, you are likely to be involved in evil, your care for the world takes precedence in politics over your care for your self—whether this self is your body or your soul" (*Lectures* 50). This insight leads to the second claim, where in responding to criticism from Moses Mendelssohn in his essay "On the Common Saying: That May Be True in Theory, but It Does Not Apply in Practice," Kant defends his argument that human progress may be interrupted but it is never broken off and that evil is self-destructive by nature. While the action and aims of individuals may and will contradict and erode the arc of human progress toward a peaceful cosmopolitan existence, human progress in the whole is unstoppable in its evolution as long as an idea of reason guided by providence prevails in human actions.[45]

---

45. Kant's version of providence as an inhuman hand guiding history as a progressive force is open to perverse interpretations, as exemplified in the arguments of one of Eichmann's prosecutors who suggested that an unintended consequence of the attempted destruction of European Jewry was to bring the state of Israel into existence, as if the result was somehow foreordained in the entire history of the Jews. Arendt notes the proximity of such thinking to anti-Semitic

Mendelssohn recognized that one of the greatest difficulties in Kant's political writing, where Nature's providential hand guides human history, is to resolve or redeem the place of human freedom.[46] Here Arendt asserts again that the perspective of the onlooker is decisive for Kant because only through judging are human agents capable of recognizing nature's will and freely formulating it as a guide for practical reason. In other words, only through judging can one engage in a predictive history that interprets and evaluates how practical reason might guide the free actions of individuals in history, now or for the future. Judgment restores historical self-consciousness as a mode of practical reason applicable to others as well as oneself—this is philosophy's gift to politics. And in Kant's view, if the assumption of ineluctable progress is absent, then the drama of history looks either to risk despair (catastrophe is just around the corner) or nihilism (nothing will ever change).[47]

If conflict and discord are the forms of human action that drive history, then the ultimate test of philosophically reconciling politics with morality will be judgment's attitude to what Kant calls in §28 of the *Critique of the Power of Judgment* the sublime spectacle of war. Kant's essay "Perpetual Peace" provides further insight to why the world-observer and judge of history must withdraw from action in order to perceive the arc of history and to pass moral judgment on it. The spectator is perhaps drawn to the sublimity of war not because of its dramatic violence but rather because of his "taste" for the transcendent moral design inscribed there—the predictive knowledge that discord is the only path

---

opinions voiced in the Egyptian National Assembly at about the same time that Hitler was innocent of the slaughter of the Jews and instead a victim of the Zionists who "compelled him to perpetrate crimes that would eventually enable them to achieve their aim—the creation of the State of Israel" (Hannah Arendt, *Eichmann in Jerusalem: A Report on the Banality of Evil* [New York: Penguin Classics, 2006], 20).

46. This problem is raised by Kant himself with great precision: "What does nature do in relation to the end which man's own reason prescribes to him as a duty, i.e. how does nature help to promote his *moral purpose*? And how does nature guarantee that what man *ought* to do by the laws of his freedom (but does not do) will in fact be done through nature's compulsion, without prejudice to the free agency of man? This question arises, moreover, in all three areas of public right—in *political, international* and *cosmopolitan* right. For if I say that nature *wills* that this or that should happen, this does not mean that nature imposes on us a duty to do it, for duties can only be imposed by practical reason, acting without any external constraint. On the contrary, nature does it herself, whether we are willing or not: *fata volentem ducunt, nolentem trahunt*" (Fate leads the willing, drags the unwilling; "Perpetual Peace" 112; Kant's emphasis).

47. Compare, for example, Kant's assessment of the three possible forms of philosophical prophecy in "Contest of the Faculties," 178–80.

toward self-perpetuating peace, a path that providence has laid out for humanity as a whole, if Kant is to be believed. What is the moral duty of the judge of history here? As an individual among individuals, pursuing her own interests and resolving her own conflicts, the observer is as immersed in the contingent and haphazard flow of life's events as any other human agent. But through the imaginative enlargement of her representative thinking, the philosopher is drawn to events of world-historical impact or is able to picture the fact that events will have global historical consequences whose true meaning has yet to be fully discerned or decided. In this respect, the philosophical observer of history must be guided by the "moral-practical reason within us [that] pronounces the following irresistible veto: *There shall be no war.* . . . Thus it is no longer a question of whether perpetual peace is really possible or not, or whether we are not perhaps mistaken in our theoretical judgment if we assume that it is. On the contrary, we must simply act as if it could really come about . . . even if the fulfillment of this pacific intention were forever to remain a pious hope . . . for it is our duty to do so" (from the conclusion to *The Metaphysics of Morals*; cited in Arendt, *Lectures* 54). One easily discerns the command of duty in this passage from *The Metaphysics of Morals*, and in presenting this passage to her auditors, Arendt is arguing that judgments involve a moral claim where the world-spectator is pressed in her assessments to assume a duty for the future where her ideas and actions must serve a world to come. Physically at a distance in space and time from unfolding events, which she must maintain for her impartiality, the philosopher does not and cannot participate; yet she sees imaginatively the map according to which providence leads humanity collectively on its progressive path. Her moral duty is to preserve, maintain, and perpetuate this historical memory that makes of peace a direct duty for each individual who wishes to be worthy of human reason.

In this respect, unlike the individual who exercises practical reason through the modality of the categorical imperative, the world-spectator judges from the perspective of a community, whether real or imagined. As Kant insists on the fundamental importance of the public use of one's reason to avoid conflicts between politics and morality, what kind of community is appealed to here? Arendt's imagined world-spectator is a public figure who, unlike the isolation and contemplative solitude of Plato's or Aristotle's philosopher, makes her judgments in anticipation of a community who will share her sympathies and respond to them critically. Kant's insistence on the red line that demands that freedom of opinion shall not be abolished is also a demand for a freedom to publish, hence Arendt's emphasis on the importance of a reading and writing public as a kind of civil society who in their public judgments bear witness to the actions of rulers and governments. Arendt notes that the Prussian monarchy and "enlightened" bureaucracy under Frederick II did not constitute a public sphere; in the absence of real democracy, government was by definition unapproachable by the public and likewise had no desire or need to make its decisions and operations a matter of public debate. At the same time, Arendt notes after Kant that the qualities that made the French Revolution into a public spectacle of world-historical significance was the exaltation of the uninvolved public looking on in sympathy, and for Arendt the key to this observation is precisely their distance and nonparticipation. The fascinated spectators, whose participation was limited to their situation as a reading public, constituted the public sphere for the event and the public culture that memorialized it. And again, what draws this public ideally is less the sublime spectacle of the violent overthrow of a monarchy than it is their discernment of the historical appearance of a possible political reality guided by what Kant calls an idea of humanity, where perpetual progress toward freedom and peace are the compass points directing humanity's becoming human. As the second Critique makes clear, practical reason is moral reason, and it concerns the individual qua individual. But here the companion to practice is not theory but rather the *speculative* use of reason or, one might say, its futural use, not for the individual but for a polis or a people to come where the idea of humanity may become a political reality.

We are now in the tenth session and drawing toward the heart of Arendt's Kant lectures. At this point, Arendt states specifically that one must turn to Kant's critique of the powers of aesthetic judgment to understand the significance of his implicit potential political philosophy. (And this in spite of the fact that she has given over nine lectures to a fairly deep reading of Kant's political writings!) Here the problem of taste reappears to make distinctions between the respective roles of actors and spectators. Arendt is discussing §50 of the third Critique, where Kant introduces arguments about genius and the creation of art in contrast to the discerning judgment of art. There are echoes here of Arendt's discussion of *homo faber* in *The Human Condition* or her account in "The Crisis in Culture" of the simultaneous appreciation and contempt for fabricators in ancient Greece. The central point, however, is that even if genius may be required for the isolated creation of imaginatively compelling works, art fails if it does not express the power of initiating a public conversation. Creation must aim for communicability and the creation of its own public sphere no matter how small in scale. "The faculty that guides this communicability is taste," Arendt argues, "and taste or judgment is not the privilege of genius. The condition *sine qua non* for the existence of beautiful objects is communicability; the judgment of the spectator creates the space without which no such objects could appear at all. The public realm is constituted by the critics and the spectators, not by the actors or the makers. And this critic and spectator sits in every actor and fabricator; without this critical, judging faculty the doer or maker would be so isolated from the spectator that he would not even be perceived" (*Lectures* 63).

This passage is significant for at least two reasons. First, it demonstrates that the formation of a polis in collective acts of judgment is also the formation of a public sphere; in other words, this is another domain in which the artful conversations of judgment can be scaled up into a civil society constituted by a reading public. Equally important is Arendt's suggestion that the distinctions she has presented between the perspectives of the philosopher, the artist, and the *politikos* are not absolute but rather involve the possibility of a continuous rotation of perspectives depending on context—a spectator and critic reside within every actor and fabricator. This acknowledgment is key to understanding the thoughtful activities that inform public citizenship in constituting a new public sphere. One might say then that the French Revolution was made a world-historical event by the medium in which it entered into history, that is, how it was represented and memorialized by a writing and reading public. What made the French Revolution a phenomenon not to be forgotten, Arendt argues, "were not the deeds and misdeeds of the actors but the opinions, the enthusiastic approbation, of spectators, of persons who themselves were not involved. We also saw that these uninvolved and nonparticipating spectators—who, as it were, made the event at home in the history of mankind and thus for all future action *were* involved with one another (in contradistinction to the Pythagorean spectator at the Olympic games or the spectators

in the Platonic cave, who could not communicate with one another)"
(*Lectures* 65). From the attractions of art to the sublime spectacle of
wars and revolutions, taste draws spectators together and calls them
to judgment, thus creating a space of appearance forged in exchanges
of opinion and expressions of approbation or disapprobation toward
events. And at the same time, it is important to note that unlike the
philosopher or the artist in their solitude, spectators exist only in the
plural; the criteria of plurality and publicity are indissolubly linked.
When a judgment expresses its taste in an enthusiastic demand for
universal assent or in expressions of sympathy guided by speculative
reason, it is asking not only for a conversation but for a public conversation within a newly constituted public sphere.

I suggested above that what incited the enthusiasm of the Enlightenment observers of the French Revolution was less the historical spectacle itself than a sympathy for an idea of the human expressed through
the exercise of speculative reason in their judgments. In my reading,
what Arendt tries to define here is what one might call the historical
imagination of world-spectators as expressed by their taste, their enthusiastic approbation for the French Revolution. Think of the examples
above. The spectators in Plato's cave can hardly be called a polis because
they cannot communicate with another, which also means that they are
in no position to judge; their distance from the shadowy presentations
parading before them is not freely assumed but rather restricted by
enforced *doxa*. In his impartial distance from the game, the Pythagorean philosopher coolly judges and thus evaluates, but his particular
form of detachment also removes him from the sphere of public communication. In these examples, criteria of impartiality, publicness, and
communicability are out of sync and unbalanced.

This is why the *Critique of the Power of Judgment* is so important to
Arendt, for only in judgments of pure taste are these operations in sync
and mutually amplifying. Taste in the Kantian definition is the faculty
of judging a priori the power and potential of the communicability of
the feelings that are bound up with a representation, and the measure
of a judgment of pure taste is whether or not one is directly and empiri-
cally affected by events. In the third Critique, Kant is particularly concerned with encounters at a local level of reception; however, Arendt's
enlargement of judgment now places world-spectators at a remove
from the clamor of history where one's witnessing and understanding

is mediated by the reporting and testimony of others, and in this community, which is a political community, taste gives way to judgment. I argued in earlier sections that through the operations of imagination and reflection, external presentations and experiences become objects of thought; one might say they enter the domain not only of imagination but also of speculative reason as the medium for predictive history. As I have insisted, this activity also entails an imaginative remapping and revision of sense according to one's history of experience, both individually and as part of a collective. The act of imaginative seeing compresses and focalizes the manifold of sensation and experience—in seeing by the eyes of the mind one imagines the whole that gives meaning to particulars, and here one might also say that speculative reason intervenes through historical judgments to extract the singular idea whose meaning is clouded by the fog of actions.

After her discussion of imagination, Arendt rightly wonders if there are standards that one can apply to the operation of reflection. What are the criteria or conditions according to which judgment passes from an expression of taste to a philosophically informed evaluation? Are there maxims of judgment, analogous to those of pure and practical reason, that inform right judgment? Imagination is linked to taste because it chooses and discriminates according to the criterion of what pleases me or doesn't. Arendt suggests that reflection adds to imagination another choice where one may approve or disapprove of the very fact of pleasing. The operation of reflection inspires expressions of value as approbation or disapprobation and thus leads to conversations, whether of consensus or disagreement, whose fundamental character is to establish a public space of communicability and intersubjective exchange (if one does not first come to blows). But in judging events or experiences, how does one choose to give voice to approbation or disapprobation, that is, how does one know and test the worth of one's ideas and sympathies? Once again, the measure is given by Kant's transcendental principle of publicness. One never judges privately but rather as a member of a community, real or imagined, and the power of judgment to forge public communities in conversation arises on the ground of sensus communis, that extra mental capability, or *Menschenverstand*, that fits us into a community. Sensus communis is a specifically human sense because language depends upon it as an intersubjective medium of public exchange. Out of community sense comes the desire, even the

drive, to share judgments with others, which as Kant puts it, is a form
of reflection that takes account a priori of the mode of representation
of others in thought as if to compare one's judgment with the collective
reason of humanity. This is the first stage of thought's "enlargement"
in and through judgment, whereby projecting ourselves imaginatively
into the position or perspective of others we take account of their own
possible judgments, whether in agreement or disagreement with our
own. Here again we tend to assert a universal rule only to find it challenged as often as agreed with; yet out of conflict comes human conversation and sociability. Representative thinking is therefore the sine
qua non of right judgment, and community sense makes possible this
enlargement as the ground from which one imagines oneself as part of
a shared community. Communicability of experience is again the key
criterion, and the less idiosyncratic and the more impartial one's judgment, the better it can be represented to others. Here Arendt signals
an important passage from §41 of the third Critique. "If we admit the
impulse to society as natural to man," Kant writes,

> and his fitness for it, and his propension toward it, i.e., *sociability*, as
> a requisite for man as a being destined for society, and so as a prop-
> erty belonging to *being human and humaneness* [*Humanität*], we can-
> not escape from regarding taste as a faculty for judging everything in
> respect of which we can communicate our *feeling* to all other men,
> and so as a means of furthering that which everyone's natural inclina-
> tion desires. . . . [If] everyone expects and requires from everyone else
> this reference to general communication [of pleasure, of disinterested
> delight, then we have reached a point where it is as if there existed] an
> original compact, dictated by mankind itself. (as quoted in *Lectures* 73,
> 74; Kant's emphasis)

Arendt characterizes this compact as an idea of the human, which is
the necessary condition for the greatest possible enlargement of an
enlarged mentality. As Kant links the maxim of publicity and the condition of plurality to the ideal of a possible cosmopolitan existence, this
ideal is also a political idea that guides our reflections in their communicability but that also inspires our actions, thus suggesting a potential
bridge between actor and spectator:

> It is by virtue of this idea of mankind, present in every single man,
> that men are human, and they can be called civilized or humane to

the extent that this idea becomes the principle not only of their judgments but of their actions. It is at this point that actor and spectator become united; the maxim of the actor and the maxim, the "standard," according to which the spectator judges the spectacle of the world, become one. The, as it were, categorical imperative for action could read as follows: Always act on the maxim through which this original compact can be actualized into a general law. (*Lectures* 75)

From the ground of communicability and sensus communis, the futural ideal of a cosmopolitan existence, now visible to the world-spectator, becomes a political maxim for action as guided by judgment or insight.

Here Arendt makes a leap to discuss some of the key political principles embodied in "Perpetual Peace" as if they might be considered maxims for connecting reflective judgments to concrete actions. As such, her thought is instructive for imagining the kind of ethical standards that could moderate the judicious exchange of opinions and evaluation in the context of the inherent asocial sociability of humankind. For example, the sixth article states that that no combatant shall during conflict permit acts of hostility that would erode mutual confidence in a possible peace. This is something like Donald Davidson's principle of charity—one must not enter into conflict or dissensus without imagining that understanding and consensus will be possible if not completely achievable. In turn, Arendt says that the third article is the only one that follows most directly from the sociability and communicability of judgments embodied in Kant's idea of the human: "The law of world citizenship shall be limited to conditions of universal hospitality." For Arendt, who as a refugee knew only too well this situation, the right of temporary sojourn, the right to associate with others across borders in the larger human community, is considered an inalienable human right. In Kant's view, human beings are collectively responsible for the globe on which they live, and since even this territory is limited, ultimately human tribes cannot avoid one another but must finally learn to tolerate the presence of others, "[For] the common right to the face of the earth . . . belongs to human beings generally. . . . [All of which can be proved negatively by the fact] that a violation of rights in one place is felt throughout the world, [from which Kant concluded that] the idea of a law of world citizenship is no high-flown or exaggerated notion" ("Perpetual Peace," quoted with Arendt's interpolations in *Lectures* 75). Thus, Arendt concludes that as guided by one's community sense, one always judges as a member of a community, and in the last analysis we are also already all members of a world community, of a shared cosmopolitan existence, through the sheer fact of being human, especially in an increasingly interconnected world: "When one judges and when one acts in political matters, one is supposed to take one's bearings from the idea, not the actuality, of being a world citizen and, therefore, also a *Weltbetrachter*, a world spectator" (75–76). This is another way of saying that the speculative and anticipatory idea of being able to judge as if one represented the whole of humanity (since one is no less capable of becoming human than others) should be the standard guiding the imagination of a world-historical politics.[48]

At this point, Arendt arrives at a very open conclusion, which is nonetheless attentive to the ironies adhering to Kant's ideas about history and human progress. The perspective of the historical actors is partial—immersed in events, they cannot perceive the shape of the whole. Arendt says that this is true for all stories—they must conclude and reveal their finished shape before they can be fully understood. However, the same is not true for the beautiful, because for Kant, it is an end in itself: "All its possible meaning is contained within itself, without reference to others—without linkage, as it were, to other beautiful things" (*Lectures* 77). Objects of aesthetic experience are absolute singularities. And here is the ethical contradiction that arises in the contrast between aesthetic and historical judgments. As Arendt explains, for Kant "infinite Progress is the law of the human species; at the same time, man's dignity demands that he be seen (every single one of us) in his particularity and, as such, be seen—but without any comparison

---

48. In "Anthropology from a Pragmatic Point of View," Kant writes, "The character of the species, as it is known from the experience of all ages and by all peoples, is this: that, taken collectively (the human race as one whole), it is a multitude of persons, existing successively and side by side, who cannot *do without* being together peacefully and yet cannot *avoid* constantly being objectionable to one another. Consequently, they feel destined by nature to [develop], through mutual compulsion under laws that come from themselves, into a *cosmopolitan society* (*cosmopolitismus*) that is constantly threatened by disunion but generally progresses toward a coalition. In itself it is an unattainable idea but not a constitutive principle (the principle of anticipating lasting peace amid the most vigorous actions and reactions of human beings). Rather, it is only a regulative principle: to pursue this diligently as the destiny of the human race, not without grounded supposition of a natural tendency toward it." In Kant, *Anthropology, History, and Education*, ed. Günter Zöller and Robert B. Louden, trans. Mary Gregor, Paul Guyer, Robert B. Louden, Holly Wilson, Allen W. Wood, Günter Zöller, and Arnulf Zweig (Cambridge: Cambridge University Press, 2007), 427; Kant's emphasis.

and independent of time—as reflecting mankind in general. In other words, the very idea of progress—if it is more than a change in circumstances and an improvement of the world—contradicts Kant's notion of man's dignity. It is against human dignity to believe in progress" (75).

Teleology is an affront to human dignity because individuals want to be valued for their singularity and their capacity to choose freely where and how to exercise their will, rather than being understood as being the collective agents of transsubjective historical forces. Arendt's solution to this dilemma is to conclude that the idea of progress into infinity means that the end of the story itself is in infinity—there is no endpoint at which one can stand and look back with the retroactive glance of the historian.

From what place in space and time, then, does the world-spectator observe and judge? It may be that the meaning of a story only reveals itself at its end, yet if one accepts with Kant that human history is driven teleologically in the form of perpetual progress, no matter how failed or compromised in any of its chapters, then history cannot come to an end but only at best progress asymptotically toward its ideas and ideals of reason. One might think of this notion as the Enlightenment's particular utopia. But the temporal complexity of this attitude must also be considered—one always judges from within the flow of time, which is a complex space of becoming where at any given point the precise relation of the present to past and future is indiscernible. For Kant, the importance of an event is not judged retroactively but rather with a present evaluation of how it opens new horizons for the future and thus gives witness to the hope for future generations. (Arendt's principle of natality must soon come into play here.) The French Revolution was a world-historical event because attentive and sympathetic observers armed with speculative reason could discern that it contained the seeds of the future—it indicated possible divagations in the general arc of human history and perhaps planted the seeds of a new political culture.

From this idea Arendt concludes after Kant that history is the key to understanding all the possible dimensions of becoming human, that is, of achieving what Kant calls the conditions in which humanity's full capacities for the free exercise of reason may be deployed and developed. One reason why the essence of "man" cannot be determined is that the potential value of humankind's existence can only be revealed in the whole, which is always yet to come, and for this

reason progress is perpetual or self-perpetuating. The arc of progress
extends across and through generations of humanity toward an infinity
and thus tends toward an indeterminable end where the potential of
humankind's becoming human is "actualized, developed to the 'highest
pitch'—except that a highest one, in an absolute sense, does not exist"
(*Lectures* 59). This is one way of acknowledging Kant's view that human
conflict cannot be eliminated, for if so, a defining fact of the human, its
capacity for indeterminable development, would be lost. From another
perspective, these words give voice to Arendt's perfectionism as well as
her pragmatism: one is always working toward these ideals yet never
achieving them.

Despite the centrality of the concept for her argument, Arendt's
picture of the world-spectator or observer in the *Lectures* is curiously
incomplete. The main value of the *Lectures* for Arendt, I believe, is to
deepen her account of the modality of judgment as an ethical and
world-building practice where principles of plurality, publicity, communicability, sensus communis, imagination, and revisability are fundamental operations for building and maintaining a polis. However,
Arendt's open-ended remarks in her last lecture, and indeed her perceptible ambivalence toward the role of teleology in Kant's picture of
human history, point toward two unresolved problems. The first relates
to how Arendt's picture of the world-observer and historical judgments
are meant to reconcile politics with philosophy. A second conundrum
then arises wherein Arendt's important concept of natality directly confronts Kant's insistence on the role of providence in history. How do we
make judgments, and what do we make of judgment, when providence
is overturned by natality? Or in other words, how does judgment deal
with radical contingency in history? In both cases, Arendt's *Lectures*
are preparing the ground for arguments that are as yet unfinished and
inconclusive.

Alternatively, the preface to *Between Past and Future*, written ten
years before the Kant lectures, offers some intriguing insights into
how Arendt might have more fully characterized the world-spectator
as a historical perspective complexly located in space and time. In
this respect, it is interesting to note that "The Crisis in Culture" was
first published in *Daedalus* in 1960 and thus was ready for inclusion
as the last chapter of the first edition of *Between Past and Future* when
it appeared in 1961 at Viking Press. Arendt's assessment of a crisis in

modern culture is thus linked to the overarching theme of the book, which is concerned with what becomes of historical thinking when it is no longer guided by tradition. When moments of world-historical violence and catastrophe explode all certainties, when suddenly the great monuments are damaged, destroyed, suppressed, or forgotten, how does one reclaim a new sense of history? The urgent problem addressed here is how to give witness in the midst of catastrophe and to preserve what the witness has experienced in a testament for the future. This is where the historian is called to judge.

In her "Postscriptum" to *Thinking*, volume 1 of *The Life of the Mind*, Arendt links the faculty of judgment directly to the task of the historian. This is yet another imaginative extension of Kant's critique of the power of judgment, and I might add, a fourth perspective on Arendt's picture of "taste" and the range of problems to which it applies. Unsurprisingly, Arendt defines the concept of history by appealing to its classical origins, noting that "history" is derived from *historein*, "to inquire to tell how it was," or in the phrasing of Herodotus, *legein ta eonta*. But ultimately, Arendt claims that the meaning of history is Homeric in origins—the Homeric historian is the judge who evaluates the lasting sense of events and actions.

Why is it, though, that the historian must judge rather than simply recount, which is also to ask why the actions, words, and conflicts of human agents in history be subject to critical evaluation in analogy with taste? Arendt's answer is that in the wake of Hegel and Marx, problems of theory and practice, and reason and ethics, have pictured history as a teleological and progressive force acting through the collective actions of humanity. Whether one considers history as World Spirit realizing itself through human society or a force immanent to collective actions expressed in class conflict, questions of choice and freedom of action are left unaccounted for.[49] Here is one reason why Arendt's projected volume on judging was meant to follow her philo-

49. See for example Arendt's account of Marx and Lenin's surprise at the spontaneous uprisings of the Paris Commune and the Russian Revolution of 1905: "What struck them was not only the fact that they themselves were entirely unprepared for these events, but also that they knew they were confronted with a repetition unaccounted for by any conscious imitation or even mere remembrance of the past." Hannah Arendt, *On Revolution* (London: Penguin Books, 1991), 248. In other words, they had no historical or conceptual means for recognizing and understanding the force of natality in action.

sophical investigations of thinking and willing. For a philosopher facing
modernity's multiple historical and political crises, the choice is either
to follow Hegel in posing history as a metaphysical force expressing its
will through human conflict or to maintain with Kant the autonomy
of individual thought and will as faculties operating independently
from things as they are or have come into being. Hence the meaning,
perhaps, of the only known page of *Judging* written by Arendt's hand,
found in her typewriter at the time of her death in 1975. This lonely page
contains two epigrams. The second, from part 2 of Goethe's *Faust*, can
be understood as a direct rebuke to Hegel's metaphysics of history:
"Könnt' ich Magie von meinem Pfad entfernen, / Die Zaubersprüche
ganz und gar verlernen, / Stünd' ich, Natur, vor dir ein Mann allein,
/ Da wär's der Mühe wert, ein Mensch zu sein."[50] The first, however,
may hold the key to Arendt's thought of what it means to be a judge of
history, which is Cato's pronouncement, "'*Victrix causa deis placuit, sed
victa Catoni*' ('The victorious cause pleased the gods, but the defeated
one pleases Cato')."[51] The taste of the gods may be to rejoice at the
realization of their will in human conflict, but Cato, a philosopher alone
before them, asserts his autonomy and freedom to choose and to judge
otherwise if he so wills. In these terms, Arendt writes, "If judgment is
our faculty for dealing with the past, the historian is the inquiring man
who by relating it sits in judgment over it. If that is so, we may reclaim
our human dignity, win it back, as it were, from the pseudo-divinity
named History of the modern age, without denying history's importance but denying its right to be the ultimate judge" ("Postscriptum on
Thinking" in *Lectures* 5).

This problem is expressed concisely by the line from René Char
that opens the preface to *Between Past and Future*: "*Notre héritage n'est
précédé d'aucun testament*."[52] Already a significant poet when he joined

50. "If I could banish Sorcery from my track, / Unlearn the magic-spells that draw me
back, / And stand before you, Nature, as mere Man, / It would be worth the pain of being
Human." Trans. A. S. Kline (2003) 512. http://www.iowagrandmaster.org/Books%20in%20
pdf/Faust.pdf. Johann Wolfgang von Goethe: Der Tragödie zweiter Teil—Kapitel 59, Faust II
(5. Akt).

51. A facsimile of the page found in Arendt's typewriter is reproduced as the frontispiece
to *Lectures on Kant's Political Philosophy*. Arendt cites the line from Cato on multiple occasions.

52. "Preface: The Gap between Past and Future" in *Between Past and Future*, 3. The passage
appears as the 62nd aphorism in Char's *Feuillets d'Hypnos* (Paris: Éditions Gallimard, 1962).
Char's aphorism is also invoked in the introduction to *The Life of the Mind: Thinking* (12–13) as

the French Resistance in 1940 at the age of thirty-three, during the last year of fighting Char wrote an influential book of aphorisms, *Feuillets d'Hypnos*, from which this line is taken. The subtitle to Arendt's preface is "The Gap between Past and Future," and this chasm is precisely the dilemma that confronts Char as both actor and spectator of history.

In another line quoted by Arendt, Char gives personal testimony to the felt breach in history opened by war and resistance: "If I survive, I know that I shall have to break with the aroma of these essential years, silently reject (not repress) my treasure" (quoted in "Past and Future" 4). As if caught in the gap between past and future, in the first part of this line Char's writing occupies a present from which he cannot recognize a stabilizing past; in the second half, he anticipates the opening of a future with new and unforeseen ethical responsibilities. For all the deprivations of living covertly and in constant danger, one of Char's most important discoveries of resistance was the new possibilities of existential freedom, that is, of actively reinventing oneself in a context without precedent or, in other words, of making the choice to freely embrace, and be embraced by, the force of natality. Char describes this discovery as the naked satisfaction of newly creating a self by dropping the social and psychological masks behind which one insincerely negotiates a conventional life. In these lines, Arendt, herself writing as a world-observer, judges that Char and other resisters found themselves "visited for the first time in their lives by an apparition of freedom, not, to be sure, because they acted against tyranny and things worse than tyranny—this was true for every soldier in the Allied armies—but because they had become 'challengers,' had taken the initiative upon themselves and therefore, without knowing or even noticing it, had begun to create that public space between themselves where freedom could appear. 'At every meal that we eat together, freedom is invited to sit down. The chair remains vacant, but the place is set'" ("Past and Future" 4, citing Char, 131st aphorism). In looking back on the modern world history of revolution and resistance (America in 1776, Paris in 1789, Budapest in 1956, and now one could add many others up to and beyond the German *Wende* of 1989), Arendt characterizes the discovery of this existential freedom without precedent as "an age-old

---

a way of explaining the importance of a new vision of history after the modern demise of metaphysics, and in chapter 6 of *On Revolution*, "The Revolutionary Tradition and Its Lost Treasure."

treasure which, under the most varied circumstances, appears abruptly, unexpectedly, and disappears again, under different mysterious conditions, as though it were a fata morgana" (4). In a word, what becomes perceptible in the temporal nature of resistance and revolutions is the recurrent force of natality in conjunction with a will to act in concert, no matter how fragile or evanescent its forms of appearance.

It is important to emphasize that these forms of appearance are both public and collective. Char gives voice to the existential character of freedom and resistance yet knows that he is not the only one seated at the table, and that it is set for many. However, there is yet another important dimension to this experience, which powerfully relates to Arendt's discussions of culture and curation, history and memory. To have resistance and revolution as an inheritance means that one has been thrown into a gap between past and future where there is no "testament," no obvious document or monument that sets out for the actor the stable platform of a historical past from which a new future can be willed and achieved. As Arendt observes in *The Life of the Mind: Thinking*, "What has been lost is the continuity of the past as it seemed to be handed down from generation to generation, developing in the process its own consistency. . . . What you then are left with is still the past, but a fragmented past, which has lost its certainty of evaluation" (212). In short, the actor is suddenly caught floating in an abyss where the past as memory has crumbled and the future is opaque, unsettled, and unclaimed. In other words, to be without testament is to be without a tradition preserved in the continuity of curation, of discerning, selecting, naming, and thus indicating what the treasures are, where they are to be found, and what they are worth to a culture and its history. Without tradition, Arendt writes, "there seems to be no willed continuity in time and hence, humanly speaking, neither past nor future, only sempiternal change of the world and the biological cycle of living creatures in it" ("Past and Future" 5). There is, in fact, no culture and no human world; one must discover new worlds and new ways of becoming human.

I want to make clear that in my reading of Arendt, what is lost, and lost repeatedly and inevitability, is not just the historical memory of revolutions and their possibility but in a deeper sense, our full acknowledgment and embrace of the force of natality present in every lived moment. Arendt's evaluation of the power of natality to make unforeseen revolutions stands in stark contrast to her essay on the crisis in culture and its commitment to preserving and sustaining a culture through the potential immortality of its monuments: the treasure is lost not because of the violent adversity of historical circumstances but rather "because no tradition had foreseen its appearance or its reality, because no testament had willed it for the future" ("Past and Future" 5).

The loss that Char felt must be retroactively rejected but not repressed was perhaps the terror and passion of unexpectedly living in the gap between past and future, which opens a dilemma for both the present actor and the retroactive spectator. Destroying the bridge of tradition may open new possibilities of freedom, but it is also an abyss into which historical memory falls, for there is no memory without culture and tradition. How is it possible to make such an event meaningful for both the past and the future? Arendt writes that as one of the most important modes of thought, remembrance is almost helpless to sustain itself in time without an established historical frame of reference to provide it with continuity and causality. As an actor in the French Resistance, Char gives testimony to the loss of those who failed to remember the full force of their "treasure" because they were the first to grab hold of it and then found it strange that they could not even name it. To be fully immersed in action, it would seem, is to occupy a nameless time. Still, Arendt suggests that these philosophical dilemmas did not bother the actors in their time of resistance: "If they did not know their treasure, they knew well enough the meaning of what they did and that it was beyond victory and defeat: 'Action that has a meaning has value only for the dead, completion only in the minds that inherit and question it'" ("Past and Future" 6; Char, 187th aphorism). This last phrase throws the dilemma forward from the actor to the spectator, for the restoration of France after the occupation threatened to erase the memory of the existential freedom lived in resistance. "The point of the matter is," Arendt concludes, "that the 'completion,' which indeed every enacted event must have in the minds of those who then are to tell the story and to convey its meaning, eluded them; and without this thinking completion after the act, without the articulation accomplished by remembrance, there simply was no story left that could be told" (6). Consider Char, then, Arendt's first portrait of the modern historical observer whose nearly impossible task is to preserve in remembrance the freedom of will to action, whose poetic articulation serves as a new testament where future generations can inherit the memory of this freely willed action in history.

After the testament of Char's *Feuillets d'Hypnos*, Arendt turns to a second example of the crisis of thinking in the gap between past and future, a dilemma best characterized perhaps by de Tocqueville's observation that the mind wanders in obscurity when the past ceases to throw its light on the future. When the bridge of tradition collapses, thought drops into a maelstrom that violently separates it from reality. An only too natural reaction to this situation is passionate exasperation with strident calls for reason and rationality, whose voices are lost in the storm. The danger here is that the guiding light of thought is deflected or dispersed when historical reality is so shaken, and one either loses the capacity for thought or falls back on discredited beliefs and dogmas. From what new perspective can historical and critical thinking exert itself in this disorienting situation?

Arendt's second portrait of the thinking dilemma of the world-observer is more allegory than picture. Drawn from Kafka's short text "HE: Notes from the Year 1920," Arendt characterizes Kafka's parable not as throwing light into the tempest, but rather illuminating its edges and contours, or better, it functions as an X-ray that lays bare the inner structure of a mind struggling with the competing demands of past and future. Kafka's parable goes like this:

> He has two antagonists: the first presses him from behind, from the origin. The second blocks the road ahead. He gives battle to both. To be sure, the first supports him in his fight with the second, for he wants to push him forward, and in the same way the second supports him in his fight with the first, since he drives him back. But it is only theoretically so. For it is not only the two antagonists who are there, but he himself as well, and who really knows his intentions? His dream, though, is that some time in an unguarded moment—and this would require a night darker than any night has ever been yet—he will jump out of the fighting line and be promoted, on account of his experience in fighting, to the position of umpire over his antagonists in their fight with each other.[53]

53. Franz Kafka, "HE: Notes from the Year 1920"; Arendt's translation in "Past and Future," 7. Arendt returns to this parable in the concluding pages of *The Life of the Mind: Thinking* to describe with greater precision the "time sensation of the thinking ego" (202).

Kafka's parable is one response to Char's aphorism and the difficulties of negotiating a position where the lived continuity of time has been destroyed. In this respect, it is easy to imagine that there are not three actors in Kafka's story but rather only one, who struggles to occupy multiple perspectives in and on time. Rather like Paul Klee's *Angelus Novus* as interpreted by Walter Benjamin, while HE is thrown forward by the events of history accumulating at his back, progress is blocked by a still undetermined and unknowable future. The X-ray of Kafka's parable lays bare his protagonist's dream even though his intentions are opaque: to arrive at that unforeseeable moment, shrouded in night, when blind chance will allow him to leap above the fight and, because of his experience, achieve the position of the judge who can envision new bridges connecting past and future.

How can this story find a satisfactory conclusion, especially as Kafka's tales are in many instances famously open, incomplete, fragmentary, and unfinished? The struggle of Kafka's protagonist begins in the gap between past and future at precisely that moment when action comes to an end. And in order to avoid being lost to the mists of history, this fading memory awaits a perspective from which a narrative can be formulated that will give the completed action a future by linking it to the past. For he who will judge, the task now is to understand and give sense to what happened, "and this understanding," Arendt writes, "according to Hegel, is man's way of reconciling himself with reality; its actual end is to be at peace with the world. The trouble is that if the mind is unable to bring peace and to induce reconciliation, it finds itself immediately engaged in its own kind of warfare" ("Past and Future" 7).

Char's experience of the Resistance and its aftermath—especially the ironies of its forgetting and subsequent fabulation—are analogous to the dilemma of Kafka's anonymous protagonist. Arendt notes that Char is writing in the last months of the Resistance, "when liberation— which in our context meant liberation from action—loomed large, [and] concluded his reflections with an appeal to thought for the prospective survivors no less urgent and no less passionate than the appeal to action of those who preceded him" ("Past and Future" 8–9). Here is another compelling picture of the world-spectator, who must also cycle between action and thought, especially when significant actions have run their course. In this picture, the observer's mind stands revealed

as having been forced to turn full circle not once but twice, first when he escaped from thought into action, and then again when action, or rather having acted, forced him back into thought. Whereby it would be of some relevance to notice that the appeal to thought arose in the odd in-between period which sometimes inserts itself into historical time when not only the later historians but the actors and witnesses, the living themselves, become aware of an interval in time which is altogether determined by things that are no longer and by things that are not yet. In history, these intervals have shown more than once that they may contain the moment of truth. (9)

What is the nature of this moment of truth—which I would like to call the interval-event—where the line of chronology and tradition is broken and possibilities for thought and action are suspended between a disappeared past and a nonapparent future? Arendt presents Kafka's "thought-event" as the most advanced position from which to newly imagine a world-spectator. In her description, in this interval-event human thought is caught between countervailing temporal forces where, paradoxically, the past is not a tide that retreats but rather one that surges forward, and the future is neither an opening nor a path forward but rather the immoveable wall against which time breaks and splinters. This all-too-human perspective on time, at least from the standpoint of the thinking ego, falls between past and future in an interval that interrupts and diverts the successive and chronological flow of time. New thought and new perspectives on history and action emerge only in this gap, this *nunc stans*, or standing now, that makes all new beginnings possible. Man's insertion between past and future thus breaks up the inhuman and indifferent flow of unceasing change by giving it an aim—the unreachable human. Call this the insertion of human freedom to choose and to act, which can divert the flow of history in unpredictable ways.

The question thus arises: Into what space or time would Kafka's protagonist leap if he could transcend the fray and assume the position of judge? Arendt argues that what is missing from the picture of Kafka's thought-event is a spatial dimension where thought can assert itself without being forced out of human time—in other words, to renounce the absolutes of a metaphysical or providential perspective and remain an observer moored to the space and time of human actions. Arendt imagines that a human perspective on time breaks the continuum in which the forces of past and future clash and thus deflects them so that they no longer clash head-on but rather meet at an angle forming a "parallelogram of forces" ("Past and Future" 11).

This is Arendt's solution for negotiating the labyrinth of time, and we are now confronting some of the most difficult and densely argued passages of her writing. Arising out of the question of how to live and act in history, while also remembering it and assuring its transmission for future generations, her most urgent task now circles back to the first section of this book. In the context of imagining the world-observer or spectator of history, how does one picture that most elusive and most nonapparent activity—the activity of thought—for the world-spectator is ultimately a philosopher, indeed a philosopher who has emerged from the space of action of politics and must return to it.

Consider again the complex time-space that Arendt draws out from Kafka's parable. This time-space is a combat zone enveloped by the fog of conflict produced by the countervailing forces of future and past, where the observer struggles to find a space of action as well as a perspective from which to observe the battle. He dreams of being witness and judge, and not a combatant, and thus to cycle between action and thought. In Arendt's story, the combatant's one hope is to discover a line of flight along the diagonal that emerges from the point of intersection of the conflicting temporal forces where he occupies the gap as a thinking subject. This line differs from the inhuman pressures of past and future in an important aspect. One vector emerges from an infinite past, and the other points toward an infinite future; yet while both are unlimited with respect to their origins, each has a terminus, which is the point at which they continually clash. Arendt's diagonal cuts through this finite point as if a third dimension of time, or perhaps better, a new human perspective on time. The intersecting line has a determinate beginning, a point of origin, at the intersection of the antagonist forces; at the same time, its extension is infinite because it emerges from the concerted action of two forces that themselves spring from infinity. "This diagonal force, whose origin is known," writes Arendt,

> whose direction is determined by past and future, but whose eventual end lies in infinity, is the perfect metaphor for the activity of thought. If Kafka's "he" were able to exert his forces along this diagonal, in per-

fect equidistance from past and future, walking along this diagonal line, as it were, forward and backward, with the slow, ordered movements which are the proper motion for trains of thought, he would not have jumped out of the fighting-line and be above the melee as the parable demands, for this diagonal, though pointing toward the infinite, remains bound to and is rooted in the present; but he would have discovered—pressed as he was by his antagonists into the only direction from which he could properly see and survey what was most his own, what had come into being only with his own, self-inserting appearance—the enormous, ever-changing time-space which is created and limited by the forces of past and future; he would have found the place in time which is sufficiently removed from past and future to offer "the umpire" a position from which to judge the forces fighting with each other with an impartial eye. ("Past and Future" 11–12)[54]

I believe this to be Arendt's richest and most complex philosophical account of what it means to be a world-spectator. The achievement of this perspective, which is only a perspective in thought, is not without danger. Arendt observes that in Kafka's fictional universe, the more likely outcome is that while the protagonist may achieve some awareness of the gap of time into which he has been thrown, as the line of flight along the diagonal remains unknown to him, he is more likely than not to expire from the fatigue of his struggle. The philosopher might count himself lucky, then, that this conflict is limited to the terrain of thought and its dilemmas of historical understanding inherited from modernity's erosion of tradition's foundations and continuities. There is still something inhuman about this dilemma—with respect to

---

54. Arendt extends and deepens these arguments in section 20 of *The Life of the Mind: Thinking*, entitled, "The Gap between Past and Future: the *Nunc Stans*." The following passage is particularly informative: "For this diagonal, though pointing to some infinity, is limited, enclosed, as it were, by the forces of past and future, and thus protected against the void; it remains bound to and is rooted in the present—an entirely human present though it is fully actualized only in the thinking process and lasts no longer than this process lasts. It is the quiet of the Now in the time-pressed, time-tossed existence of man; it is somehow, to change the metaphor, the quiet in the center of a storm which, though totally unlike the storm, still belongs to it. In this gap between past and future, we find our place in time when we think, that is, when we are sufficiently removed from past and future to be relied on to find out their meaning, to assume the position of 'umpire,' of arbiter and judge over the manifold, never-ending affairs of human existence in the world, never arriving at a final solution to their riddles but ready with ever-new answers to the question of what it may be all about" (209–10).

historical or biographical time, it would seem to be senseless or incomprehensible since human beings mostly live in confidence of time's linearity and consistency. At the same time, Arendt is well aware that there is something uncanny about the very ordinary human capacity for thought when attention is focused on its own unceasing activity. For Arendt the activity of thinking always involves a withdrawal from the time of "life," as it were. Yet only when one withdraws into thought "does man in the full actuality of his concrete being live in this gap of time between past and future" ("Past and Future" 12). While such an experience might be all too rare, for Arendt, it remains something like an ontological given, or a fact of the human, coeval with the existence of humans on earth. "It may well be the region of the spirit," Arendt continues,

> or, rather, the path paved by thinking, this small track of non-time which the activity of thought beats within the time-space of mortal men and into which the trains of thought, of remembrance and anticipation, save whatever they touch from the ruin of historical and biographical time. This small non-time-space in the very heart of time, unlike the world and the culture into which we are born, can only be indicated, but cannot be inherited and handed down from the past; each new generation, indeed every new human being as he inserts himself between an infinite past and an infinite future, must discover and ploddingly pave it anew. (13)

Here is where the force of natality—which may well be another name for this diagonal line—intersects with the activity of thinking. Of course, most of us are as unprepared as Kafka's anonymous protagonist (who is no one, and thus everyone) to confront this mental and existential situation. Arendt writes that for many centuries the gap between past and futured was bridged by a concept of tradition inherited from Roman culture and thought, and in this respect, the vertigo induced when one becomes aware of this non-time-space at the heart of time was usually reserved for those who made thinking their primary business, that is, philosophers. However, in and after the twentieth century, modernity's erosions of tradition, metaphysical certainties, and consoling ideologies have made this experience of time and uncertainty "a tangible reality and perplexity for all; that is, it became a fact of political relevance" ("Past and Future"13).

What recourse do we, ordinary humans, have in this situation? Neither philosophy nor ideology nor religion can now authoritatively supply us with the certainties of tradition. When there is no longer any stable ground for belief, our only diagonal route, perhaps, is to continue to think, though this can only be, as Arendt liked to say, thinking without bannisters. Here there are no guideposts or guidelines, nothing to tell us with certainty what to think or to believe.[55]

The ultimate problem for Arendt, who is otherwise so deeply drawn to Kant's philosophy, is to imagine how to be a judge of history without the "bannister" of teleology or a belief in providence. The problem is analogous to the one posed in "Thinking and Moral Considerations"—the destructive character of thought means that there is no end to moral evaluation or self-criticism; that is, one must always judge reflectively without the aid of transcendental principles. This is why impartiality and nonparticipation are the observer's existential ground for discerning meaning in the course of historical events, even given the horror of the spectacular violence of wars and revolutions. One judges this meaning in the course of events according to the criterion of progress imagined as hope for the future and the promise the events hold for generations to come. However, these judgments do not and cannot give any principles or guidelines for action. One might say that they are entirely "theoretical"; the ethical stance of the world-spectator is a *bios theōrētikos*, from *theōrein*, to look at. However, in contrast to Plato or Aristotle, where to engage in philosophy is to withdraw from the company of others to contemplate what is eternal and unchanging, the theoretical perspective of judging, whose impartiality also requires withdrawal, turns from the unreachable sky back to the contingent and contradictory domain of concrete human actions in their interdepen-

---

55. In *The Life of the Mind: Thinking*, Arendt writes that Kafka's parable, for her, "describes the time sensation of the thinking ego. It analyzes poetically our 'inner state' in regard to time, of which we are aware when we have withdrawn from the appearances and find our mental activities recoiling characteristically upon themselves—*cogito me cogitare, volo me velle*, and so on. The inner time sensation arises when we are not entirely absorbed by the absent non-visibles we are thinking about but begin to direct our attention onto the activity itself. In this situation past and future are equally present precisely because they are equally absent from our sense; thus the no-longer of the past is transformed by virtue of the spatial metaphor into something lying *behind* us and the not-yet of the future into something that *approaches* us from ahead (the German *Zukunft*, like the French *avenir*, means, literally What comes toward). In Kafka, this scene is a battleground where the forces of past and future clash with each other" (202).

dency. In addition, what the classical philosopher kept to himself in his silent contemplation must now be made public. Impartiality and publicity are the two essential qualities of judgments. In this respect, for Arendt the world-spectator only "acts" as an agent of "the Tribunal of Reason before which the occurrences of the world appear" (*Lectures* 56). The impartiality and autonomy of judgment require that I stand before yet outside of the spectacle, thus relinquishing "the standpoint that determines my factual existence, with all its circumstantial, contingent conditions" (56). The judge is disinterested in the *doxa* of the actor who is not autonomous because his recognition and fame depend upon the acclaim of spectators. The philosopher has nothing to gain for himself but rather serves as a theoretical agent of history, assessing the expression of the moral character of mankind in collective events.

Socrates returns here as an exemplary artist of thought, the one who displays thinking and judgment as an expert performance, and there is no sure method or program for learning this art—it can only be exercised, rehearsed, and practiced. In my view, this is what Arendt calls education. The subtitle of *Between Past and Future* is *Eight Exercises in Political Thought.* "Exercise" is an activity, something that must be practiced, and thus like judgment thinking is not something "theoretical" but rather a skill or capacity whose power can only be maintained and enlarged through continuous rehearsal. In this respect, thinking differs from all those varieties of instrumental reason that claim certainty in their reproducible syllogisms, methods, algorithms, and other systems of symbolic calculation "whose logical rules of non-contradiction and inner consistency can be learned once and for all and then need only be applied" ("Past and Future" 13).

In writing this and other books and essays, Arendt does not and cannot teach us how to think or to judge but like Socrates, only offers us examples of how thought is exercised, practically, and thus, politically. Arendt confesses as much at the end of her preface. One might consider her exemplary thought in these exercises as experiments in working through such difficult problems as the concept of history after the modern break in tradition, questions of authority and freedom, culture and crisis, and truth and belief. In thinking and writing for herself, the only possible educative aim of these essays is, whether through writing, reading, or critical conversation, to discover a space where one may practice thinking and judgment. There are no formulas to learn or truths to gain as certainties in an uncertain world; much less are there transcendental bridges that link up or cover over the gaps and dislocated joins in the frayed threads of tradition. And so, Arendt writes, "Throughout these exercises the problem of truth is kept in abeyance; the concern is solely with how to move in this gap—the only region perhaps where truth eventually will appear" ("Past and Future" 14).

In these final lines, Arendt observes that thought emerges out of the actions and events of living experience, and if it is to open a space for criticism and action in this world, it must take its direction from the embrace of this experience with all of its contingency and indeterminacy. Kant's distant observer is attuned through sympathy to a pattern of human freedom and human rights emerging from violent conflict. Arendt's world-spectator is attuning herself to, and producing historical consciousness of, the force of natality (the enormous, ever-changing time-space that is created and limited by the forces of past and future) as a historical force through which human will and action become newly possible.

V. POLITICS AND PHILOSOPHY, OR RESTORING A COMMON WORLD

Absence of thought is not stupidity; it can be found in highly intelligent people, and a wicked heart is not its cause; it is probably the other way round, that wickedness may be caused by absence of thought.

HANNAH ARENDT, *The Life of the Mind: Thinking*

In the arc that extends from "The Crisis in Culture" to the *Lectures on Kant's Political Philosophy*, Arendt builds a picture of the world-spectator that occupies split perspectives in time: an orientation toward the past, which is curatorial, redemptive, and interpretive, and an orientation toward the future, anticipating what is to come as an affirmation of freedom and the capacity for progressive change. The writing of history and counterhistory is also important to Arendt as a form of action aimed at transforming our common spaces of understanding and debate, as exemplified not only in Arendt's reading of René Char or Franz Kafka but also in her own major works such as *The Origins of*

Totalitarianism, On Revolution, or *Eichmann in Jerusalem.* Judgments are always diagnostic of the state of a culture and the terms of possible discourse within it. With her concept of the *Weltbetrachter,* I read Arendt as trying to strike a balance between Kant's aesthetic and political writing by constructing a bridge from local spaces of engagement to a public space defined by a larger critical community, say, of engaged, informed, and interested writers and readers responsive to Kant's demand that one's reason be exercised publicly, whether on editorial pages, political meetings, demonstrations, or town halls, or even in the classroom. If the aim of judgment is to define the shape of a shared world but also the terms and frameworks of cultural kinship and common experience in that world, then the historical judgments of the world-observer are now tasked with discerning the ethical and political orientation of coming communities on a global scale with a view to recognizing their anticipatory powers. Aesthetic judgments are a model for the ongoing and interminable assessments of meaning and value in local communities. Historical judgments are framed not by immediate experience but rather by events unfolding at a distance in space and time. What judgment seeks to understand from a historical perspective is whether there is a possible or potential shape and direction of humanity as a whole in its conflictual, contradictory, and uneven progress toward an interconnected cosmopolitan existence.

In this context, the response to Kant's anthropological and ethical question—What does it mean to be human or to become more fully human, or to know that one can become so, and so engage more fully in a revisable ethical and political life?—is guided by the idea that the value of human existence can be revealed only in the whole, never in a single individual or generation, hence the importance of Arendt's concept of plurality. Where Arendt differs from Kant is that for her no teleology or transcendental force guides this progress, nor can one be assured, from moment to moment, of history's direction toward civilization or barbarism. Although not discussed as such in her *Lectures,* it may be that Arendt's world-observer is attuned less to the invisible and ineluctable inhuman unfolding of what Kant calls "providence" than to what Arendt calls the ever-present force of natality—the always recurrent possibility of human beginnings with their surprising and unforeseen possibilities and consequences. Natality is an ethical and existential criterion not only for defining the human, whose essence is always yet to be determined, but there is recognition that the fundamental importance of judgment is its capacity for interpreting and evaluating events in their singularity and contingency, often in the absence of tradition and without the aid of normative or transcendental criteria—both are qualities or dimensions of the freedom inherent in human actions. In the absence of providence, humans must continually negotiate, in plurality and community, the truth that defines their history and their actions, indeed their politics, and it is up to humankind, from moment to unpredictable moment, to define collectively the ethical shape of its common existence.

Within the humanities, the aim of an education in judgment is to preserve and enhance the possibilities of discernment, choice, deliberation, and decision for agents in their free subjectivity and thus to encourage their openness to intersubjective communication and ethical revisability. In a world where local conversations about matters of import and value are increasingly and fluidly integrated with global communications and social media marked by political tribalism and opinions of uncertain provenance, it is ever more important to practice judgment simultaneously in local and global contexts. Rather than acquiescing to the divisive and fragmenting forces of social media, perhaps one can imagine an alternative that considers the potentiality of our ever expansive and interconnected means of communication for encouraging a cosmopolitan perspective or at least their potential for amplifying understanding of our social interconnectedness and responsibility for one another.

Such ideas are no doubt utopian but no less important for that. Arendt was one of our greatest historical and political diagnosticians of modernity, and one must indeed wonder what she would have thought of our current situation. In her postwar writings, Arendt continually returned to the idea that the crisis of modernity was expressed in different and complex ways by the loss of a common world no less than the increasing difficulty of maintaining together, at whatever scale, our "community sense"—that no matter how different our respective viewpoints, political life, wherever it is found, emerges from the human desire to create a common world through our actions and discourse. The problem is that this process is as fragile as it is interminable. To the extent that it has a foundation, the process arises in what Kant called humanity's "asocial sociability," meaning that the human desire for building and enlarging communities is inseparable from misunderstanding and conflict that equally threatens the erosion or destruction of community. The negotiation of agreement and consensus is inseparable from discord and dissensus, and for this reason a new account of the role of the humanities for an education in judgment has never been more urgent.

This loss of a common world is the urgent problem addressed in Arendt's late essay "Truth and Politics," where she describes the maintenance and preservation of a common and factual reality as a political problem of the first order. The common reality that concerns Arendt is located, however evanescently, in what she calls the space of politics, which appears only where and when people speak and act together. One might think of politics as the aspiration to one's humanity in plurality. The loss of the common world is equivalent to the erosion of the possibility of politics in Arendt's specific sense of the word, which one might also think of as inhibiting the possibilities for becoming human. One of Arendt's most powerful responses to this dilemma is to ask philosophy to rededicate itself to one of its most ancient responsibilities, which is care of the polis through education in judgment.

Arendt's most astute diagnosis of this problem is developed in her 1954 text "Philosophy and Politics," which was delivered as the third and final part of a lecture series given at the University of Notre Dame on the problem of action and thought after the French Revolution. The central question addressed in this lecture is what are the possibilities for politics, of maintaining the health of a polis or human community guided by reason, when there are no absolute epistemological or moral standards, and political judgment means navigating one's way through the often contradictory and antagonist plurality of others' perspectives on the world? One of Arendt's responses is to present a picture of Socrates as a model thinker and citizen whose aim is to educate his interlocutors in virtue, which may be thought of as the exercise of good judgment, though not by *teaching* them but rather by exemplifying these qualities of judgment and thought in his public performance in the agora. In "Philosophy and Politics," Arendt is searching for a new political philosophy, that is, a politics that arises from and in a practice of philosophy that directs its attention to the myriad interconnected actions of humans engaged in their daily affairs.

But before turning to this important text, I want to leap forward

In time. The consequences arising from the loss of a common factual reality are addressed with renewed urgency in Arendt's later essay "Truth and Politics," first published in *The New Yorker* in 1967 and then included in a new edition of *Between Past and Future* as her seventh exercise in political thought. One key aim of an education in judgment is to provide the means for rebuilding and maintaining a common factual reality, which also includes knowing how to diagnose the collapse of a common world, to pass judgment on it, and to imagine alternatives. In comparing these two essays, the substitution of philosophy by "truth" is of great significance. In the earlier essay, Plato is shown as trying and failing to oppose the singular truth of philosophy to the plurality of the *dokei moi*—that is, the human truth of each citizen's perspective on his or her shared public existence. In her reading of the allegory of the cave in Plato's *Republic*, Arendt notes that Plato is skeptical about prospects for reconciling the solitary meditations of the philosopher with the cacophony of opinions echoing through the cavern, which to him are no more substantial than shadows. But what happens when the "truthteller" is just one citizen among others, even an exceptional seeker of truth like Socrates? On returning to the cave, the philosopher is forced to confront the brutal fact that the common world of human affairs is composed of nothing more nor less than the plurality of voices expressing and exchanging their *dokei moi*, and his is one voice and one view among others. The Platonic philosopher directs his thought to an inhuman world, but the shared space of appearance forged in the expression and exchange of opinion is the only human world; practically speaking, we have no other. Whether journalist, judge, legislator, educator, scientist, student, or simple citizen, the one who seeks truth in the realm of human affairs does not have the consolation of Platonic philosophy—there has been no journey to a transcendental realm of absolute knowledge nor the solitary comfort that one stands on earth apart from the polis in possession of unshakable truth or an unassailable method of reasoning. The din of human opinion defines the common world in which we live, with its conflicts, contradictions, anger, and resentments, along with its gestures of generosity and solidarity and agreements to act in concert for the betterment of all who share this world.

In defending Socrates after Plato, Arendt shrinks the distance separating philosophy from politics such that citizenship now means that every individual, each from his or her own shared perspective, is by turns observer, thinker, and historical actor, or as she puts it in "Truth and Politics," "In the world we live in, the last traces of this ancient antagonism between the philosopher's truth and the opinions in the market place have disappeared" (231). In "Truth and Politics," Arendt's truthteller is less a philosopher than a witness, one who gives testimony to his or her perspective on historical and political events. The deeper question here is the relation of testimony to judgment, where testimony might serve as the first draft of history, as it were, and judgment as the ground for preparing decision and action. This witness is in fact a *Weltbetrachter*, a world-spectator, but in contrast to Arendt's notes in her lectures on Kant, this spectator is fully immersed in the polis in which she or he lives—she is simultaneously an actor as well as a spectator because to give witness to facts and to know when and how to defend them when challenged is a political action par excellence.

"Truth and Politics" sets out with often alarming precision the difficulty of adjudicating the messy and unstable relation between truth and facts, while also mapping out ways in which power is exercised, or challenged, according to one's account of facts and what counts as truth. There are other essential observations to be made about the displacement of philosophy by truth in the later essay. In 1954, Arendt asks for a new political philosophy that arises out of thoughtful attention to the fact of human plurality. Readers will already recognize that in 1967, Kant's account of the power of pure judgments of taste and his other political and historical writings are guiding Arendt to just such a philosophy. But both the complexity and fascination of "Truth and Politics" arise out of Arendt's deep doubts and hesitations about the prospects for democratic politics in her times, which in turn leads her to work out in fearless detail the multiple and contradictory tactics that politics uses to deflect, derail, distort, or destroy factual truth in pursuit of its own interests. There is little hope now that politicians will respect the truth, that philosophers in turn can serve to arbitrate and adjudicate disputes over factual truth, or that factual or historical truth can be protected from its inherent flexibility, contingency, and context dependency. In short, what Arendt diagnoses as both a crisis in culture and a crisis in education in her other exercises in political thought is linked to a vertiginous feeling that even simple citizens can no longer hold onto and share a common factual reality, which seems to slip between their fingers like fish and or ubiquitous on the horizon like a fata morgana. Neither philosophers nor politicians, at least in their ideal guises, are going to be of much help in this situation. Citizens will have to judge for themselves and maintain for themselves a common culture of judgment. The key question of "Truth and Politics," then, is how to assess one's responsibility to the truth, and from what perspective. Philosophers cannot "educate" us, and politicians don't want to. From this perspective, the crisis in culture and the crisis in education are synonymous with the loss of a common world.

Plato could defend the philosopher's relation to the Real, the True, and the Good, because each single philosophical mind aims at the *eide*—unique and unchanging rational Forms. But without such a transcendental anchor, humans must continually negotiate, in plurality and community, the truth that defines their history and their actions, indeed, their politics. And on the battleground of truth, philosophy's antagonist is not *doxa* but rather dogma in the form of lack of imagination, unreflective belief, and a failure to judge. There is a radical change in perspective in the later essay "Truth and Politics" because the presumption of truth or factuality as some kind of common measure can no longer be taken for granted. Indeed, the central question of the essay is to examine whether there is an inherent and intractable antagonism between politics and truth that erodes the political culture of democratic societies no less forcefully than totalitarian ones.

One might also think of the problem as a conflict between power and politics. Arendt states clearly that what is at stake in her argument is a political problem of the first order: the maintenance and preservation of a common and factual reality both in the present as quotidian political exchanges and in the past through the monuments and archives to which these exchanges appeal to negotiate their common memory and their relation to history. To respond to this problem, one must ask if there is such a thing as "political 'truth'" in contrast to philosophical truth, and if so, how can it be defined and defended? In what ways and to what ends are facts mobilized in the realm of human politics, which is also a way of asking how to make judgments in given political situations about the relation of knowledge to power.

Let's begin with some of Arendt's fundamental assumptions about the nature of politics and the relation of truth to politics. In "Truth and Politics," the broad division between the singular truth of the philosopher and the plurality of opinion and the *dokei moi* is now parsed into finer distinctions that often shade into one another in provocative ways. Across the five sections of the essay there is a deliberate cast of characters, each of which has a particular relation to the truth, or rather, historical facts: the solitary philosopher; the impartial witness or truthteller; the politician, or deliberate liar; and the dogmatic adherent of unreflective belief. Unsurprisingly, these characters are further distinguished between spectators, like the philosopher and the witness-reporter, and actors who are principally prevaricating politicians. But implicitly, there is one other character who is the central focus of the essay—the public citizen and opinion holder—whose difficult task is to decide the value and meaning of what Arendt now calls "political truth" and to use it as the basis for forming opinions and, perhaps, planning political actions. In short, in a situation where a common factual world consists of little but lies, damn lies, and deep fakes, the citizen must learn how to discern and to make judgments about the truthfulness of historical and cultural facts.

And here another dilemma presents itself. Historical facts are no more trustworthy than the philosopher's axioms and, worse, as Arendt states in "Philosophy and Politics," there is no visible hallmark that marks off truth from opinion. In many instances, one would like truth to exhibit a coercive power that produces conviction in any skeptic. Arendt acknowledges that any assertion of truth, whether factual or rational, carries within itself an insistence that it be accepted without argument and thus includes an element of coercion. However, the grand arc of her argument is shaped by three observations, none of which will finally console Arendt's truthteller. First, because political combat means distorting facts to fit one's own perspective and aims, at least in the most cynical definition of politics, "it may be in the nature of the political realm to be at war with truth in all its forms, and hence to the question of why a commitment even to factual truth is felt to be an anti-political attitude" ("Truth and Politics" 235.) The second worry arises in the frank acceptance of the radical contingency of historical facts—that they always could have been otherwise and may always be pushed into contradictory interpretive contexts, or, worse, they may be erased or rewritten. Unlike natural scientific laws, which being time independent may always be rediscovered if forgotten, if human truth is lost to history, it may never be recovered. This is the paradox of factual truth in contrast to rational truth. Accepting that factual truths are both plural and pliable accounts equally for their democratic power (that they are debatable and revisable and in need of agreement and consent in conversations carried out in good faith) and for the facility with which they can be cynically and nihilistically challenged and rewritten. If factual truth is by its very nature open to revision, there is no guarantee of its progressive truthfulness or its power to challenge recalcitrant opinion as the expression of either pure self-interest or tribal allegiance. No accumulation and strength of evidence can anchor factual truth in certainty, and it is an unhappy fact that skeptics can always challenge factual truth as just another opinion.

Nevertheless, Arendt insists that the apparent arbitrariness and contingency of historical facts are the price of freedom. I will qualify and deepen this idea below. But let it be said for the moment that no matter how messy, infuriating, and troubling the capricious nature of facts may seem, if there is no self-evident standard, hallmark, or bright line separating opinion from truth, then what Arendt will call facts or even "political truths" are fundamentally noncoercive. You can't change a belief or produce conviction through force—everyone is free to view and communicate the world through his or her own *dokei moi*—which means that the conflict between truth and opinion, or to make judgments about how much historical truth adheres to a fact, must be fought on the terrain of persuasion, and there are no guarantees of success. No matter how well defended, factual truth has no claim to certainty. It will always be expressed and deployed in the realm of opinion—at best an interpretive and evaluative perspective on the world—and therefore its only political power relies on, as it were, talking things out. In other words, it has no coercive power, and this is its political strength, at least in fully democratic societies.

In this messy and uncertain context, the importance of testimony—of giving witness to historical events and perpetuating and preserving their memory—is ever more important. As I suggest above, facts and events are infinitely more fragile than axioms and natural laws, for they reside not in nature but rather on the outcome of the myriad contingent actions of human agents in political situations. The shape, content, and persistence of factual truth is in turn subject to deformation by power and the persistent framing of history and counterhistory. Factual truths are inherently fragile, mutable, and open to interpretation and reinterpretation. When politics seeks to filter, alter, or suppress factual truth according to its own means and ends, it erodes the value of human memory and history and deforms the space of a shared human culture.

While Arendt emphasizes the importance of witnessing and public testimony, her attitudes toward history and counterhistory are nuanced yet sometimes wrestle with the hazy line between facts and opinion. For example, while Arendt clearly acknowledges that the sense and implication of historical facts may be redirected by different interpretive contexts, whether valid or invalid, she still often insists on the brute historicity of the archive and documented facts as an implicit counterweight to the philosopher's dilemma in "Philosophy and Politics," where the appeal to absolute truth is eroded and clouded by the myriad expressions of *doxa* and each citizen's *dokei moi*. In Plato's view, there can be no terrestrial or human truth, that is, political truth. Still, in "Truth and Politics," against the absolute and unchallengeable claims of the rationalist philosopher and the cynicism of the politician who wishes to shape and alter facts as a means to an end, Arendt defends a kind of historical truth as materially shaped by the interdependent and multicausal actions of human witnesses and communities; these factual truths are established, defended, and given public expression by witnesses' commitment to proffering the most truthful picture they can. And in spite of the inherent fragility of facts, Arendt insists on maintaining the inviolability of certain historical truths such as "The Germans invaded Belgium in August 1914." The more governments seek to control and deform the flow of public information, the more urgent the need to maintain publicly a common and factual reality. "Freedom of opinion is a farce," Arendt insists, "unless factual information is guaranteed and the facts themselves are not in dispute. In other words, factual truth informs political thought just as rational truth informs philosophical speculation" ("Truth and Politics" 234).

Here again the question of freedom arises in complicated ways. Factual truth arises out of human actions and human communities. It is established by witnesses and depends on public testimony and is therefore political by nature. Though one must discern between facts supported by testimony and opinions sustained only by unreflective belief, for better or worse they belong to the same realm. And where the question of freedom is concerned, assertions of historical truth present their own danger. The assertion of a truth is always in some

degree coercive. Philosophical or scientific truths are absolutely so; historical truth is also coercive in the degree that it peremptorily asks to be acknowledged as beyond debate. However, Arendt rightly insists that debate is the essence of political life, and whenever a truth relies on coercion rather than persuasion, it discounts the need to take into account other people's opinions, which Arendt calls the hallmark of all strictly political thinking.

Still, one might wonder: Where does political truth sit on a spectrum defined on one side by the cynical deployment of "facts" by politics and on the other by the stubborn imperviousness of unreflective opinion?, which is another way of asking, Where does one draw the line between trying to persuade and demanding that a conviction be shared? (Note here that Arendt is trying to find more subtle ways to redefine and remap the relation among truth, fact, and opinion.) One arrives at political truths, no matter how precariously and provisionally, through engaging in and sharing authentically political thought, whose more common name is judgment. Most of section 3 of "Truth and Politics" is devoted to laying out the fundamental criteria for political thought, which are now familiar to you, patient reader, as the operations of judgment. Political thought is representative thought whose primary qualities are imagination, impartiality, and broad-mindedness. These three qualities are interrelated and mutually sustaining in important ways. Political thinking is representative in the degree that an opinion is formed by making it present to oneself and taking into account the perspective of others. As Arendt often insists, this thinking process is neither an expression of empathy nor the adaptation of one's will to majority opinion; rather, Arendt calls this kind of imaginative representative thought "being and thinking in my own identity where actually I am not" ("Truth and Politics" 237). Imagination plays another important role here as the means for expanding one's perspective intersubjectively and revising and deepening one's thoughts as challenged by the opinions and arguments of others. Or again, as Arendt puts it in an often-cited phrase, "The more people's standpoints I have present in my mind while I am pondering a given issue, and the better I can imagine how I would feel and think if I were in their place, the stronger will be my capacity for representative thinking and the more valid my final conclusions, my opinion" (237). Here Kant's enlarged mentality—what

I have called more simply broad-mindedness—is the capacity or skill of revising and expanding judgments in a way that never lets the fact of human plurality disappear from view. To engage in representative thinking is to see beyond the limits of one's own private interests, or at least to weigh them against the competing interests of the community. This is the most precise definition of the quality of impartiality—not that one is willing to give up on his or her own interests but rather that one allows those interests to be revised, deepened, and enlarged in community and accepts that one actually learns more from others than in solitary contemplation. Arendt insists that both the philosopher's solitude and the stubborn independence of a closed mind are illusions:

> The very process of opinion formation is determined by those in whose places somebody thinks and uses his own mind, and the only condition for this exertion of the imagination is disinterestedness, the liberation from one's own private interests. Hence, even if I shun all company or am completely isolated while forming an opinion, I am not simply together only with myself in the solitude of philosophical thought; I remain in this world of universal interdependence, where I can make myself the representative of everybody else. Of course, I can refuse to do this and form an opinion that takes only my own interests, or the interests of the group to which I belong, into account; nothing, indeed, is more common, even among highly sophisticated people, than the blind obstinacy that becomes manifest in lack of imagination and failure to judge. But the very quality of an opinion, as of a judgment, depends upon the degree of its impartiality. (237)

Perhaps what Arendt calls conscience is the voice of this impartiality where the capacity for imaginative and representative thought arises from that inner plurality and internal division that Arendt calls the "two-in-one" of thinking.

In mapping out the spectrum between opinion and truth, Arendt tries to sort out some of the difficulties in judging factual truths to evaluate their claims to veracity and their relation to political thinking. No opinion, no matter how deeply held, is self-evident, of course, and this is its potential strength. Unlike matters of rational truth, which seek to be revised toward unshakable certainty, representative thinking leaps from one particularity to another; it causes the imagination to go traveling, Arendt says, through widely divergent contexts and alternative views until it finally settles on a generality whose persuasiveness derives from its impartiality. Arendt depicts this process as forcing a particular issue or question to open itself and to show itself from all sides and from every available perspective "until it is flooded and made transparent by the full light of human comprehension" ("Truth and Politics" 238).

Alternatively, Arendt argues, a statement of truth is characterized by a certain opaqueness, or even a quality of unsettledness. What does Arendt mean by opacity or opaqueness, which she asserts is a quality of both rational and factual truth? With respect to factual truth, the problem has to do with the relation of facts to history and their openness to interpretation. On one hand, historical truths demand to be accepted as settled fact; on the other, Arendt admits that "facts have no conclusive reason whatever for being what they are; they could always have been otherwise, and this annoying contingency is literally unlimited" ("Truth and Politics" 238). Arendt says again that this apparent arbitrariness and contingency is the price of freedom, and one might add, the price of political freedom as the freedom to judge, and to choose one's companions, values, and communities, which in turn relies on a certain open-mindedness as the freedom to persuade and to be persuaded, to shift one's perspective and, therefore, to create the freedom to initiate new actions. Here terrestrial historical truth confronts the same dilemma as celestial philosophical truth—both their power and fragility are exposed in the plurality of perspectives, the *dokei moi*, that constitute a polis at any given moment. Again, one arrives at the unsettling conclusion that in the degree that factual truth is contingent, context dependent, and open to interpretation, it is no more self-evident than opinion. Despite her appeal to the powers of witnessing and testimony, Arendt frankly acknowledges that as a basis for historical truth, eyewitness testimonies are notoriously unreliable, and supporting records and documents can always be suspected as forgeries. In cases of conflict and disagreement, there is no alternative but to call upon more testimony and more documents, none of which can appeal to a higher standard of proof than others, and even the appeal to majority opinion may simply reveal and reinforce the power of entrenched dogmas.[56]

---

56. Arendt presents another picture of this dilemma in "Lying in Politics: Reflections on the Pentagon Papers": "The deliberate falsehood deals with *contingent* facts; that is, with matters that

Falling in an unsettled way between the coercive demands of natural law, philosophical truth, and moral or historical absolutes, political truth must acknowledge that its variable and contingent validity can only be decided through discursive and representative thinking in acts of judgment, that is, through persuasion and dissuasion in a context that assures the free exchange of opinion and the potential for revised thinking. The counterexample to this acknowledgment is full awareness that pervasive and deliberate lying is also a form of political action, and often the predominant one. Political mendacity blurs and shifts the frontier between factual truth and lying. In this situation, the opposite of factual or historical truth is neither error nor opinion but rather the intentional perpetuation of falsehoods, whose worst cases involve the deliberate suppression, rewriting, or falsification of history. Since all facts require interpretive context, such falsifications may lead to a reformulation of history, of rearranging (if not outright fabricating) the facts and telling another story. In any case, the key idea here is that attempts to change the historical record are forms of action, and indeed political action. Worse, there is no effective means of contradicting the deliberate liar or recalcitrant believer because he or she will insist that his or her "opinion" is just as valid as any other. And owing to the contingent nature of facts, the chances are more than good that the political liar will be more persuasive than the truthteller.

In this situation, the truthteller confronts a terrible dilemma, whose only solution in Arendt's view is to insist on the independence and autonomy of the witness or truthteller as spectator. Persuasion is the only means at the truthteller's disposal if she wishes to enter the fray of political action to serve some partial interest, perspective, or political group. Here Arendt recapitulates another dilemma recounted in "Philosophy and Politics": even if the philosopher manages to win over the polis with his eloquence, his arguments are diluted when absorbed or

---

carry no inherent truth within themselves, no necessity to be as they are. Factual truths are never compellingly true. The historian knows how vulnerable is the whole texture of facts in which we spend our daily life; it is always in danger of being perforated by single lies or torn to shreds by the organized lying of groups, nations, or classes, or denied and distorted, often carefully covered up by reams of falsehoods or simply allowed to fall into oblivion. Facts need testimony to be remembered and trustworthy witnesses to be established in order to find a secure dwelling place in the domain of human affairs. From this, it follows that no factual statement can ever be beyond doubt—as secure and shielded against attack as, for instance, the statement that two and two make four." In *Crises of the Republic* (San Diego: Harcourt, Brace, 1972), 6.

framed by the multiple and partial perspectives of his fellows; misunderstandings proliferate, and his victory is at best Pyrrhic. By the same
token, when the teller of factual truth commits himself to some partial
interest or power formation and thus enters the domain of politics, he
invariably "compromises on the only quality that could have made his
truth appear plausible, namely, his personal truthfulness, guaranteed by
impartiality, integrity, independence" ("Truth and Politics" 245–46).

It would seem that a deep irony connects the truthteller to the deliberate political liar. Arendt says that the deliberate liar is an actor by
nature with his own motives, aims, and values, no matter how shal-
low, misguided, or despicable. In addition, the deliberate political liar
claims an almost absolute power to publicize his values, for who shall
contradict him with arguments and convince him to revise his ironclad
beliefs whether sincere or not? At the same time, if he violently rear-
ranges the facts, interprets or suppresses them selectively, and sets out
to rewrite history, he is still answering a fundamentally human calling:
he wants to change the world, and he is exercising his freedom to do
so no matter what the consequences. Through his speech and actions,
the deliberate political liar shows that "our ability to lie—but not necessarily our ability to tell the truth—belongs among the few obvious,
demonstrable data that confirm human freedom. That we can change
the circumstances under which we live at all is because we are relatively
free from them, and it is this freedom that is abused and perverted
through mendacity" ("Truth and Politics" 246). Ironically, when the
professional politician yields to the temptation to misstate and mis-
represent facts, or even to pull "facts" from thin air, he is nonetheless
exercising in plain sight freedoms of choice and action that belong to
every human even if he is abusing them.

And yet, mustering her usual practicality and subtlety, Arendt does
not find this situation to hopelessly undermine prospects for positive
political change. The absolute contingency of human facts is, after all,
an affirmation of human freedom, just as the force of natality holds in
reserve an ever-present possibility for unforeseen events and circumstances to surprisingly assert themselves and to unexpectedly rearrange
the historical context and prospects for meaning and action. Moreover,
Arendt knows full well that in the realm of practical politics, factual
matters disclosed to the public by more or less trusted political institutions and organizations can encourage and strengthen the claims

for justice by disadvantaged and disenfranchised groups; these institutions are not to be discounted. Alternatively, as history has shown many times, and present times are not excluded, when a government or community undertakes organized programs of deliberate and universal lying, the political circumstances and responsibilities of truthtellers shift in fundamental ways. Like the confirmed liar, they too want to change the world, but with different sets of aims and values: "Where everybody lies about everything of importance," Arendt insists, "the truthteller, whether he knows it or not, has begun to act; he, too, has engaged himself in political business, for, in the unlikely event that he survives, he has made a start toward changing the world" ("Truth and Politics" 247). In these trying situations, the truthteller must struggle to preserve the authority of her independence so as to preserve and publicly disseminate her account of the facts in ways that try to weave a persuasive story that can hold the frayed strands of a common factual reality together.

Neither lying nor truth telling can claim an absolute power to persuade or convince, which means that the deliberate liar's hold on political power is just as fragile as any honest assertions of factual truth. For example, Arendt observes that the most successful liars often fall prey to their own fabrications. Moreover, within the new world network of global communications, no existing power has the capability to make its political image and version of history seamless and foolproof. Complexity, contradiction, natality, and uneven and asynchronous flows of information lead to multiple and contradictory versions of "reality," all of which are subject to critique as well as the tendency to collapse under the weight of their untruthfulness.[57] One of Arendt's key points is that despite every effort, power can neither completely control the historical narrative nor entirely alter the documented experience of the past, and even though political power relies on the unsettled nature of facts and the variability of opinion, it is no more able than its critics and adversaries to preserve its story against all challenges. Wherever

---

57. In her essay "Lying in Politics: Reflections on the Pentagon Papers," Arendt adds that "Under normal circumstances the liar is defeated by reality, for which there is no substitute; no matter how large the tissue of falsehood that an experienced liar has to offer, it will never be large enough, even if he enlists the help of computers, to cover the immensity of factuality. The liar, who may get away with any number of single falsehoods, will find it impossible to get away with lying on principle." In *Crises of the Republic*, 7.

one stands on the political spectrum, the relation between truth and opinion remains just as slippery.[58]

Nonetheless, for Arendt the past has a certain density, as if it were a sort of collective memory that settles and congeals in libraries, museums, and archives in ways that make the historical record independent of present human actions and politics. In her view, history will always trump power, and facts are as resilient as they are fragile. Even though they are the residue of human actions, once facts pass into history they persevere with remarkable tenacity, even if hidden or ignored for a time, and may often come to light again whether through accident or assiduous research. For Arendt facts are less transitory than power formations, and in their powers of endurance they are superior to power. Politics is always expressed in human actions, which appear and pass away along the arc of their performance. And for this reason, Arendt insists that power is "a highly unreliable instrument for achieving permanence of any kind," which means that "not only truth and facts are insecure in its hands but untruth and non-facts as well" ("Truth and Politics" 254). Here, the contingency of historical truths is an advantage. Historical facts are forged out of the performance of human actions and as such they are always an expression of human freedom. By the same token, the writing of history and the memorialization of the past occur in the same dimension where freedom is exercised in the interpretation and recounting of the meaning and value of historical facts. Arendt therefore resolutely focuses her argument on powers of freedom, whether

---

58. In *Eichmann in Jerusalem*, Arendt provides the following example: "It is true that totalitarian domination tried to establish these holes of oblivion into which all deeds, good and evil, would disappear, but just as the Nazis' feverish attempts, from June, 1942, on, to erase all traces of the massacres—through cremation, through burning in open pits, through the use of explosives and flame-throwers and bone-crushing machinery—were doomed to failure, so all efforts to let their opponents 'disappear in silent anonymity' were in vain. The holes of oblivion do not exist. Nothing human is that perfect, and there are simply too many people in the world to make oblivion possible. One man will always be left alive to tell the story. Hence, nothing can ever be 'practically useless,' at least, not in the long run. It would be of great practical usefulness for Germany today, not merely for her prestige abroad but for her sadly confused inner condition, if there were more such stories to be told. For the lesson of such stories is simple and within everybody's grasp. Politically speaking, it is that under conditions of terror most people will comply but some people will not, just as the lesson of the countries to which the Final Solution was proposed is that 'it could happen' in most places but it did not happen everywhere. Humanly speaking, no more is required, and no more can reasonably be asked, for this planet to remain a place fit for human habitation" (232–33).

in the form of natality or in contingent decisions to act in concert. To guide political attitudes toward facts, one must always steer between two equally undesirable alternatives—on one hand, the assumption of historical necessity, which is no less a feature of totalitarian regimes than is Kantian providence or Hegel's World Spirit; on the other, the nihilist danger of denying facts or trying to manipulate them out of the world.

We have come a long way together on the conceptual pathways that Arendt has laid out for her readers, all of which converge on a horizon called judgment. That judgment was the last and most persistent problem with which Arendt was occupied testifies to her resolute desire to reconcile philosophy and politics or, in other words, thinking alone or perhaps in company, and acting in concert with others. The concept of the world-spectator and the activities of historical judgment both respond to a problem that is present to almost all of Arendt's postwar writing, where the ancient conflict between philosophy and politics opens a gulf between the positions of spectator and actor in relation to thought and action. And indeed, one key theme threading throughout her scattered texts on judgment is the need to find that point of intersection where observing and acting meet and find their point of reconciliation.

Arendt's most astute diagnosis of this problem is developed in her 1954 text "Philosophy and Politics." With her usual care and imagination, in this lecture Arendt critically reimagines the conflict between philosophy and politics as two forms of life that must be reconciled if a new role is to be found for philosophy in the exercise of an active citizenship informed by the capacity for making and sharing critical judgments. Moreover, comparing the two texts on truth, philosophy, and politics broadens and deepens Arendt's perspective on the relation between truth and opinion, as if to examine the problem from two distinct and contrary ethical positions, which are nonetheless connected in important ways. If "Truth and Politics" focuses attention on the power of the liar as political actor and the problem of ascertaining political truth, "Philosophy and Politics" presents a picture of the philosopher as educator and an exemplar for how to navigate the tricky pathways between truth and opinion as a companionable working through of the interminable dilemmas of judgment.

The history of philosophy inherited from much Greek is the ideal of the *bios theōrētikos* as a form of life lived apart from the city as an alternative to the polis, whose most famous examples were Plato's Academy and Aristotle's Lyceum. As laid out in book 10 of Aristotle's *Nicomachean Ethics*, the highest ethical virtue is the silent and isolate contemplation of the *nous*, the freest and most independent activity with the deepest pleasure precisely because of its independence from the demands of life and the city. Here *theōrein* is no longer even the Pythagorean observation of the "Great Games" and the diversity of social life but rather Platonic contemplation of the eternal and unchanging Forms. As Arendt notes, the source of Plato's despair of polis life was the trial and death of Socrates, especially Plato's skepticism toward the rhetorical arts of persuasion, or *peithein*, which the Greeks considered as the specifically political form of speech. From the side of philosophy, a darker interpretation of the circular and inconclusive nature of the Socratic elenchus is exactly its powerlessness to induce conviction and certainty, or even to encourage any kind of action in concert apart from the public performance of thinking in conversation with others. In contrast to the *bios theōrētikos* and the purest forms of contemplation, even though the exercise of Socratic *dialegesthai* requires both publicity and plurality, it still remains, one might say, a theoretical art. Not only was Socrates unable to persuade his judges that his speech and actions were in the best interest of the city, ultimately, he also could not convince his friends. Plato's conclusion was that the city had no use for philosophers, and philosophy's friends had no use for political argumentation. One might then conclude with Plato that city life was inhospitable to philosophy to the point of erasing the memory of great thinkers through exile and execution, in short, "de-memorializing" them.

Plato's disenchantment with rhetoric and persuasion drove him to seek absolute standards by which human actions could be judged and human thought achieve a measure of reliability that was beyond earthly dispute. Arendt calls this the primary impulse of Plato's political philosophy, whose most powerful testament is the *Republic*. But in many respects, according to Arendt's own criteria it is hard to imagine Plato's vision of philosophy as being "political" in any concrete sense. In fact, the impossibility of a Platonic political philosophy is one lesson that could be drawn from the allegory of the cave in book 7 of the *Republic*—when the philosopher returns underground with his celestial vision of the unchanging realm of Ideas, his testimony is drowned out and diluted by the din of *doxa* or opinion, and his picture of an ideally ordered life diffused and dissolved. What Arendt seeks to understand, then, is not Plato's political philosophy, but rather the exemplarity of the Socratic elenchus as a way of conducting a political and philosophical life in the city. Here the relation between *doxa* and truth, and truth and politics, will be judged very differently. Within the domain of judgment, whose exemplary instances are the Socratic elenchus with its exercise of dialectic or *dialegesthai*, one might seek conviction, perhaps, but not certainty.

The central point of contention here is defining the possible good of philosophy; in the present day, the humanities find themselves in a similar defensive posture. Aristotle, for example, defends the philosophical life and the exercise of *theōrein* as the highest good in his *Nicomachean Ethics*, yet he also observes that while exemplary philosophers such as Anaxagoras and Thales were wise men, they lacked understanding of what is good or beneficial for humanity as such.[59] Present here already is a problem that Arendt wrestles with in later essays and the *Lectures on Kant's Political Philosophy*, which is the Greek prejudice that accuses the *sophos*, or wise man, of not understanding what is good for himself, much less for the city, in stark contrast to the *phronimos*, whose insight into worldly affairs qualifies him for active citizenship and life in the polis. Plato's response, of course, was not to reconcile the activities of *theōrein* and *phronēsis*, or contemplation and insight, but rather to shift the ethical standard to a higher plane where only those adept at beholding eternal ideas are capable of ruling according to an absolute standard of the good, whose value is greater than any earthly measure. "Only if the realm of ideas is illuminated by the idea of the good," Arendt observes, "could Plato use the ideas for political purposes and, in the *Laws*, erect his ideocracy, in which eternal ideas were translated into human laws" ("Philosophy and Politics" 77). Of course, both the beauty and danger of Socrates was his constant denial that he was a *sophos* and that irony was the only proper response to the Delphic oracle's pronouncement in his favor: only the one whose sole certainty is that men cannot be wise could be the wisest of all men, and

---

59. See, for example, *Nicomachean Ethics*, 1140 a 25–30, 1141 b 4–8.

therefore, Arendt concludes, "as a philosopher he truly had nothing to teach his fellow citizens" ("Philosophy and Politics" 78).

In this framework, Plato developed a distinction, accepted as well by Aristotle, that promoted *dialegesthai*, or dialectic, as a specifically philosophical form of speech in contrast to *peithein*, or persuasion. Persuasion is a political art in that it is always addressed to a multitude, whereas dialectic is only possible as a dialogue between two interlocutors. In Arendt's reading, Plato views the tragedy of Socrates's death as insisting on defending himself before his judges in the form of dialectic: "Socrates insisted in talking the matter through with his judges as he used to talk about all kinds of things with single Athenian citizens or with his pupils; and he believed that he could arrive at some truth thereby and persuade the others of it. Yet persuasion does not come from truth, it comes from opinions, and only persuasion reckons and knows how to deal with the multitude" ("Philosophy and Politics" 79). At the same time, political persuasion in this sense is also a means to impose one's own opinion on the plural opinions of others, and in this respect, persuasion is not an alternative to rule by violence but rather another tactic of enforcing order on the chaos of opinion. Indeed, the edifice of interlocking myths and allegories that constitute the dramatic and conceptual form of Plato's *Republic* may be understood as the erection of a tyranny of truth against the multitude whose very plurality must submit to the order of an absolute standard of the good, which is understood only by a philosophical elite. Plato's *Republic* can be read as philosophy's rebuke to Athenian democracy, especially with respect to its aim to separate, classify, and order individuals in hierarchies according to their capacity to be ruled by truth, whose essence is to be eternal and immutable. Plato wanted to contain and channel the *doxa* of the many to cordon off the truth, not because it is dangerous to the many but rather because for him the many dilute and dissolve the compelling nature of truth.

Understanding this context is important because the principle aim of Arendt's lecture is a redemptive exercise in which Socrates, as citizen and educator as well as philosopher, is rescued not only from Plato's division of philosophy from politics but also his imposition of philosophy *on* politics. With her usual care and subtlety, Arendt offers her auditors a more nuanced reading of the Socratic power of *dialegesthai*, of talking something through with somebody, where persuasion is no longer a term foreign to philosophy and the expression of opinion, the presentation of how the world appears from one's individual perspective, is no longer a descent into illusion but rather the ground on which a reasoned ethical or political conversation might blossom. Here emerges one of the key terms of Arendt's postwar philosophy, where *doxa* is the spoken presentation of *dokei moi*, the "it seems to me" of one's individual take on the appearances that constitute a common world or the world as it opens itself to singular perspectives situated together in a particular space and time. This is by no means a lapse into perspectivism or relativism but rather an acknowledgment that plurality's deepest meaning is that we can only arrive at a common understanding of the world, no matter how contested and fragile, by sharing our perspectives on and in it. In Arendt's reading, the *dokei moi* of ancient Athens

> was not, therefore, subjective fantasy and arbitrariness, but also not something absolute and valid for all. The assumption was that the world opens up differently to every man, according to his position in it; and that the "sameness" of the world, its commonness (*koinon*, as the Greeks would say, common to all) or "objectivity" (as we would say from the subjective viewpoint of modern philosophy) resides in the fact that the same world opens up to everyone and that despite all differences between men and their positions in the world—and consequently their *doxai* (opinions)—"both you and I are human." ("Philosophy and Politics" 80)

Most interesting here is Arendt's insistence on what might be considered the interlocking ontologies of worldly appearance and what Stanley Cavell calls in *The Claim of Reason* the internal relation of each human being with all others. In contrast to Cavell, however, the persistent dilemmas of skepticism—of doubts concerning the knownness of others or the world—is completely elided in Arendt's perspective. The presentation and sharing of one's *dokei moi* is the dynamic forging of a common space of appearance, a public space in which judgment becomes possible as a form of world-building and the means for deciding how the world is to look, how it is to be valued and interpreted, and who belongs together in it. As such, it shares common territory with Kant's projection of a community sense as the human ground of judgment. The Socratic *dialegesthai*, then, does not begin in doubt

concerning the existence of common world in the others who share
it with me but rather in acknowledging that the internal relation of each
human with all others is the common ground on which intersubjective
relations are constructed and maintained.[60]

In Arendt's account, *doxa* is not a limitation of perspective but rather
the passageway through plurality and publicity into a shared space of
appearance. The *dokei moi* is one's point of entry into the political realm
as a public sphere wherein everyone can appear and present who they
are in the company of others. The expression of the *dokei moi* was what
publicity meant in the Greek polis, and there was no politics without
it, and for philosophy to exile itself from the polis indicated its refusal
to entertain seriously *doxa* as an important feature of life in plurality,
whether this meant opinion, splendor, or fame.

This is where Arendt disengages a picture of Socrates that overturns
or reverses Plato's view of him in important ways. Both Plato and Aristotle define dialectic as a form of reasoned argument that aims to compel
conviction in one's adversary and thus bring him or her closer to an
inescapable truth. (This is one model of education, though perhaps not
the best one.) But in this respect, one might also imagine dialectic so
conceived as an expression of force and as a restriction of the freedom
of the other, both of which were antithetical to the ideals of the Greek
polis. Alternatively, Arendt has already suggested that for Socrates,
dialegesthai means something more modest, namely, to engage in conversation about matters of value and importance as in talking things
over with a friend. In the first section of this book, I argued alongside

---

60. Very early in *The Life of the Mind: Thinking*, Arendt proposes an extraordinary argument
concerning the coincidence of Being and Appearance in connection with spectatorship and
plurality. Arendt characterizes the coincidence of Being and Appearing as the phenomenal
nature of the world in which all existent things, whether natural or artificial, have in common
the quality of appearance: "They are meant to be perceived by sentient creatures endowed
with appropriate sense organs" (19). This idea leads to two further insights. First, if Being and
Appearing are of one ontological substance, then all Being presupposes a spectator, and this
leads in turn to the fact of plurality. No existence or identity is singular. Things, humans, and
animals are interdependent, rely on each other for their existence, but as or more importantly,
"everything that is is meant to be perceived by somebody," including humans by their fellows.
"Not Man but men inhabit this planet. Plurality is the law of the earth" (19). All living enti-
ties are of the world, and only belong in it together through their codependence, "and this is
precisely because they are subject and objects—perceiving and being perceived—at the same
time" (20). This plurality is not only human and social; it is also an existential condition that
connects and envelops human social interdependency with all that exists.

Arendt that there is no "content" to Socrates's philosophy and so indeed he had nothing to teach others and no certainties to convey. But what Socrates did accomplish was to make of *dialegesthai* the art of maieutic or midwifery—what Socrates was after in his incessant and excitable probing of others was to help his interlocutors give birth to their own thoughts and to bring those thoughts into the light of a public conversation. Only in this way can one know what one thinks and assess whether those thoughts seem reasonable and communicable to others.

Again, if Socrates is not chasing truth or certainty, what is he after? In one of the most important passages in "Philosophy and Politics," Arendt explains that the style of Socratic conversation is shaped by the acknowledgment that every person has his or her own *doxa*, his or her own opening on to the world and perspective on it, but these thoughts and opinions are invisible to others, and perhaps as yet unclear, unshaped, or not yet fully acknowledged to oneself. This is why Socrates always begins with questions: "He cannot know beforehand what kind of *dokei moi*, of it-appears-to-me, the other possesses. He must make sure of the other's position in the common world. Yet, just as nobody can know beforehand the other's *doxa*, so nobody can know by himself and without further effort the inherent truth of his own opinion. Socrates wanted to bring out this truth which everyone potentially possesses" ("Philosophy and Politics" 81). In other words, the path to knowing one's own mind begins with the quest to know the other's mind. Socrates thought of himself as a midwife because he wanted to make the city more truthful by delivering each citizen of their *doxa*, their specific truth, by bringing it forth to a common space of appearance. In this respect, the aim of *dialegesthai*, of talking something through, was not to destroy *doxa* according to an absolute standard of truth but rather to examine publicly the shifting boundaries of truth, its claims and criteria, as held within the localized perspective of the *dokei moi* shared between friends or in common community. (How different this picture is from the culture of political lying depicted in "Truth and Politics," where there are no friends but only allies, adversaries, and victims.) For Socrates, the health of the city and the conversations through which it is governed is best assured not by imposing truth on the multitude or by governing through a culture of lies, deception, and ideology but rather only in helping each citizen to discover his or her own mind and to deliver his or her own thoughts and opinions to a shared public space of critical conversation. "The role of the philosopher, then," in Arendt's account, "is not to rule the city but to be its 'gadfly,' not to tell philosophical truths but to make citizens more truthful. The difference with Plato is decisive: Socrates did not want to educate the citizens so much as he wanted to improve their *doxai*, which constituted the political life in which he too took part. To Socrates, maieutic was a political activity, a give and take, fundamentally on a basis of strict equality, the fruits of which could not be measured by the result of arriving at this or that general truth" (81). In short, the art of maieutic was not teaching or convincing so much as showing by example that the potential of achieving right judgment in a critical exchange is based less on conviction or certainty than it is on taking account of one's own limits and doubts. The aim is to achieve a measure of self-knowledge that is communicable to others and revisable in the light of one's own expressed *doxa*.

In this respect, it is important that one's interlocutor be less an adversary than a friend. As a means for comparing and testing shared perspectives on a common world, the dialectic functions best under conditions of equality, which does not mean, of course, remaining blind to difference and differences. Arendt presents Socratic conversation as a model of politics and political discourse that poses an alternative to what she describes as the Athenian agonal spirit that "consisted of an intense and uninterrupted contest of all against all, of *aei aristeuein*, ceaselessly showing oneself to be the best of all" ("Philosophy and Politics" 82). This picture of politics as combat or warfare whose goal is to gather and maintain power by vanquishing one's opponents is not unknown to contemporary democracies; indeed, it is the picture of politics that Arendt presents in "Truth and Politics." The great failing of Athenian political life was to consider the polis as drawn by the walls of the city and the boundaries of its laws rather than something experienced and maintained in the quality of relationships arising between citizens in their daily interactions. In Arendt's Socratic perspective, in the *dialegesthai* citizens are not rivals because there are no winners or losers, much less conclusions to be drawn of one against the other. What is at stake, rather, is the dynamic and open construction of a common world, indeed a world in common discovered and shared among friends. At the same time, the aim of dialogue is neither to establish hierarchies nor to erase differences but rather to forge community in recognition and acknowledgment that in spite of all frictions and disagreements, each participant's *dokei moi* is of equal value and contains its own measure of shareable truth. In the realm of friendship, everyone is equal because everyone is different. Certainly, in every community stark asymmetries inevitably arise from the unequal distribution of wealth, power, and social standing. However, following Aristotle, Arendt defends friendship as a path toward political equalization because of its independence from more material and self-regarding forms of rivalry. The goal of equalization in friendship, Arendt writes, does not mean that friends become similar in every respect but rather that they become partners with equal standing in a common world— that they together constitute a community.

What does friendship mean here? Through friendship the dialectic aims for an ethical situation where in spite of every potential for miscommunication and misfires of meaning, conversants agree to participate under conditions of symmetry and impartiality. In a modern context, one would say that friendship means building conversations according to Donald Davidson's principle of charity. As Arendt puts it, the political element in friendship is that each participant works to understand the truth inhering in the other's opinion: "More than his friend as a person, one friend understands how and in what specific articulateness the common world appears to the other, who as a person is forever unequal or different. This kind of understanding—seeing the world (as we rather tritely say today) from the other fellow's point of view—is the political kind of insight *par excellence*" ("Philosophy and Politics" 83–84).

Another striking feature of political communities based on friendship is that they are self-legislating through such forms of rational accommodation. No external force or judge is needed to manage or adjudicate differences—no *politikos* or statesman is needed if everyone can fully assume the ethical responsibilities of citizenship. To achieve citizenship informed by insight comes back to the power of representative thinking, where one strives to comprehend the greatest number and variety of those realities presented by others through their *doxa*. "If such an understanding—and action inspired by it—were to take place without the help of the statesman," Arendt concludes, "then the prerequisite would be for each citizen to be articulate enough to show his opinion in its truthfulness and therefore to understand his fellow

citizens. Socrates seems to have believed that the political function of
the philosopher was to help establish this kind of common world, built
on the understanding of friendship, in which no rulership is needed"
("Philosophy and Politics" 84).

Philosophy and politics are connected here in that the reach of
one's representative thinking requires work on one's self as well as the
recognition that assessing the truth of one's own *dokei moi* involves
accepting how this perspective is bounded within a larger plurality.
In this way, Arendt presents the Delphic command to know thyself
as meaning that one only achieves a relation to truth through coming
to know what appears to me from the perspective of my own location
and concrete existence. Socrates's claim to know nothing embraces the
realization that an absolute truth, which would be the same for all, is
both impossible for mortals and an impediment to earthly politics.
For ordinary humans, the most important act is to try to see the truth,
no matter how partial, that adheres to every *dokei moi* because every
doxa opens onto the shared perspective of a world lived in common,
and in turn to learn to communicate one's *doxa* such that the truth of
one's opinion reveals itself to oneself and to others. The fundamental lesson of the Sophists, Socrates's greatest adversaries, was the *dyo
logoi*, in which every matter can be discussed in two different ways
and from competing and contradictory perspectives; in this world, so
similar to the picture of political life drawn in "Truth and Politics,"
there is no truth, only opinion, and no friends, only adversaries. For
Arendt, Socrates's more radical philosophical and political view was
that there are or should be as many reasons as there are individuals
to articulate them in common conversation, and these reasons collectively form the human world. Again, the emphasis here is on how a
common space of appearance shapes and is shaped by the plurality of
shared (though partial) perspectives bound together in rough consensus rather than competition.

Socrates's probing of his partners in conversation has another aim,
which is not just for them to acknowledge and to make present the
shape and content of their opinions but also to test the consistency
of their beliefs and reasons. The truth of one's *dokei moi* as uncovered
in Socratic conversation is not measured by certainty but rather by
consistency, meaning that the aim of reasoning out one's opinions is to
avoid self-contradiction and to come into agreement with one's self. As

I suggested in my account of "Thinking and Moral Considerations," this test is as much ethical as epistemological. Arendt presents here an early version of her picture of *eme emautô*, of being two-in-one in thought, where thinking is characterized as a form of friendship because it requires harboring a friend, even a probing and critical friend, within one's self. Only someone with experience of this internal critical conversation of self with self is capable of being a friend and in a spirit of rational accommodation to open his or her beliefs and opinions to criticism and revision. To the extent that thinking means living with myself in conversation through the two-in-one of thought, even individuals alone with their internal reflections are representative of the fact of human plurality.

Here the principle of noncontradiction takes on a fearsome existential quality because in the absence of this internal friend who continually tests the consistency of my thought and moral standing, I would be entirely alone, which is tantamount to being banished from the human community. Arendt takes a somewhat different view, however. The philosopher's wish to leave politics and to retire to a *bios theōrētikos* is an inhuman illusion, for one lives in the condition of plurality even when alone, and therefore, the plural condition of humankind can never be abolished. Plurality is another fact of the human, and philosophical solitude can only be viewed ironically: "The philosopher who, trying to escape the human condition of plurality, takes his flight into absolute solitude, is more radically delivered to this plurality inherent in every human being than anybody else, because it is the companionship with others which, calling me out of the dialogue of thought, makes me one again—one single, unique human being speaking with but one voice and recognizable as such by all others" ("Philosophy and Politics" 86).

The most fundamental fact that associates plurality with politics is that living together with others means living together with one's self. It is as if that internal relation of self to self that Arendt calls conscience makes of every human a polis in microcosm. Perhaps this is another way of asserting that every being who aspires to be human carries that possibility within him- or herself as a shared community sense. Living together with others, then, starts with learning how best to live with one's self without internal conflict or self-contradiction, unless of course one chooses not to think at all. This is the dark side of a *doxa* untested by critical reflection and conversation, which always remains

the same whether from ignorance or from unearned conviction. Since
even in solitude you are never alone, you can and must give witness and
expression to your own reality, your own *dokei moi*. Socrates therefore
advises, "Be as you would like to appear to others," which might also
mean, become the person whose company and community you would
really like to share. This is why Arendt insists,

> Men not only exist in the plural as do all earthly beings, but have an
> indication of this plurality within themselves. Yet the self with whom
> I am together in solitude can never itself assume the same definite and
> unique shape or distinction which all other people have for me; rather,
> this self remains always changeable and somewhat equivocal. It is in
> the form of this changeability and equivocality that this self represents
> to me, while I am by myself, all men, the humanity of all men. What I
> expect other people to do—and this expectation is prior to all experi-
> ences and survives them all—is to a large extent determined by the
> ever-changing potentialities of the self with whom I live together. . . .
> In this sense, and to the extent that we still live with ourselves, we all
> change the human world constantly, for better and for worse, even if
> we do not act at all. ("Philosophy and Politics" 88)

One of the key lessons of these lines is that even in solitude, through
his or her internal plurality each individual represents the polis and is
present to a polis. At the same time, if conscience as self-consciousness
arises out of this silent examination of self by self, thinking becomes
an ethical practice that is ineluctably linked to politics; thinking and
moral consideration are parts of one and the same process. Ethics and
politics are inseparable in the extent to which conscience arises with
self-consciousness, and this is why Socrates believed that ethical bad
conscience and self-contradiction were fundamentally the same phenomenon. This observation also means that there is no ontological
gap between thinking and acting. If plurality is the law of the earth or,
at least, of human community, the image that others have of me is not
congruent with the dynamic shape of a self engaged in thought and a
life lived in history and in time. The fact that one's thinking self is so
dynamic and plastic is a fact of the human and shared by all humans
endowed with reason and the capacity for self-revision guided by conscience. Without the plurality that I experience internally as the dialogue of self with self, I would be incapable of intersubjective relations

and action within a larger community of others. Socrates's belief that virtue could be taught as a means of improving individuals and citizens is an acknowledgment that humans are thinking and acting beings in one, and thus virtue is the constant awareness that thinking invariably and unavoidably accompanies one's actions. Keeping one's thoughts consistent and in good order is therefore the fundamental ground of citizenship as an ethical practice wherein all the qualities of right judgment are displayed: discernment, insight, impartiality, representative thinking, critical self-consciousness or self-awareness, openness to revisability, and generosity or fellow feeling.

If one accepts Arendt's argument that acting is inescapably accompanied by thinking and that thinking itself is acting as a kind of artful performance actualized in speech and conversation, then the philosopher's intentional withdrawal from politics seems misguided, both philosophically and politically. Perhaps philosophy's reticence before politics is also the recognition of a terrible power? How many of Socrates's dialogues, inconclusive as they are, end in friendship? As often as not, Socrates's interlocutors part his company not with more truthful opinions but with no opinions at all. (The abyss opening between truth and opinion is the problem that Arendt later confronts in "Truth and Politics.") Arendt acknowledges that in so much as philosophical truth has the power to destroy *doxa*, it is also capable of threatening the specific political reality of citizens—hence the danger inherent in the elenchus, which undermines and overturns all opinions but offers no secure truths to replace them. Socrates wanted to make philosophy relevant for the polis, not by playing a political role, but in presenting the idea that virtue could be taught, making of the philosopher an educator whose practice of performative thinking exemplifies right judgment. After the death of Socrates, and Plato's disappointment with politics, comes Aristotle's withdrawal of philosophy from the city (when philosophers were not in fact exiled or forced to flee, experiences familiar to both Plato and Aristotle). From this point forward, philosophers no longer felt responsible for the city and its citizens, and in turn, the only thing that philosophers wanted from the city was the right to be left alone and to be given the freedom to think. Arendt calls this the parting of the man of thought from the man of action. However, even though the commitment to a *bios theōrētikos* involves devotion to the solitary contemplation of what is unearthly and more than human, the philosopher nonetheless remains a human being and therefore embodies within himself and his mode of existence an unresolved conflict between politics and philosophy, and between community and self.

Philosophy's division of thought from action is presented in Aristotle's distinction of *phronēsis* from *theōrein*, and in both Plato and Aristotle's location of philosophical experience in *thaumazein*, the speechless beholding of Being, or the unchanging order of everything that is. Arendt notes that this stupefied beholding of existence is a philosophical *pathos*, something the philosopher wordlessly endures, and as such it occupies a different dimension than *doxazein*, that is, forming an opinion about something specific, concrete, and shareable with others through speech. The wonder that befalls the philosopher cannot be communicated because it is too general for words. At best it leads only to those questions of great existential import whose common denominator is that they cannot be answered conclusively: What is being? What meaning has life? What is death? What does it mean to be human? and so on. For Arendt, the pathos of *thaumazein* produces wonder rather than despair because its result can only be the Socratic discovery that "now I know what it means not to know; *now* I know that I do not know" ("Philosophy and Politics" 98). Arendt continues by observing,

> It is from the actual experience of not-knowing, in which one of the basic aspects of the human condition on earth reveals itself, that the ultimate questions arise—not from the rationalized, demonstrable fact that there are things man does not know, which believers in progress hope to see fully amended one day, or which positivists may discard as irrelevant. In asking the ultimate, unanswerable questions, man establishes himself as a question-asking being. This is the reason that science, which asks answerable questions, owes its origin to philosophy, an origin that remains its ever-present source throughout the generations. Were man ever to lose the faculty of asking ultimate questions, he would by the same token lose his faculty of asking answerable questions. He would cease to be a question-asking being, which would be the end, not only of philosophy, but of science as well. (98–99)

Perhaps the one most conclusive existential fact of the human is the inescapable desire to pose such inconclusive questions, which is in fact the engine driving the human capacity for thinking.

Arendt has now arrived at the heart of the conflict that drives the argument of her lecture. If *thaumazein* is the defining experience of philosophy, then its conditions of solitude and silence transport the philosopher outside of the realm where the capacity for speech and humanity's asocial sociability define political experience and life in plurality. One experiences the shock of philosophical wonder alone and from within one's own interiority; Arendt writes that the experience "strikes man in his singularity that is, neither in his equality with all others nor in his absolute distinctness from them" ("Philosophy and Politics" 100). In his unrelenting metaphysical focus on the eternity of existence, the philosopher turns away from the polis, life in plurality, and the concerns of daily existence in the city, and in his strange singularity is thus viewed by citizens with suspicion. The philosopher does not fit into the common world, which Socrates accepted and even valued, whose shared space of appearance is woven dynamically out of the intersubjective experience of acknowledging, expressing, and exchanging *doxai*. Here each individual's presentation of their *dokei moi* is an expression of his or her shared plurality rather than singularity.

In the first section of this book, I emphasized Arendt's observation that the experience of thinking invariably produces disorientation, doubt, and an internal questioning of epistemological and moral certainties. Critical thinking risks shaking the ground beneath one's feet and imposing distance and misunderstanding between the thinker and his fellows. Moreover, because there is no more mortal threat to authoritarian societies than freely thinking, as Arendt says, thinking is a dangerous business, as Socrates knew only too well at the end. However, without diminishing the power of philosophical wonder, what Arendt wants from philosophy is return from its solitude and rededication to Socrates's vision of its critical and educational role in the life of the city. There is no philosophy without politics and no politics without philosophy.

Arendt's deep and thoughtful reconsideration of the relation between philosophy and politics, and thinking and acting, is an act of redemption that wants to reclaim Socrates's insight that in order to maintain a healthy climate for the sharing of *doxa*, and thus the political life of the city, citizens need to rehearse continually the art of *dialegesthai*, of reasoned conversation among friends. Call this daily exercise in the art of judgment, which is in fact the principle aim of humanistic education. Plato's dialogues report that Socrates could stand motionless for hours in rapt meditation. But the picture of Socrales performing the elenchus and engaging citizens in dialogue displays another emphasis. Socrates always returns to the city and its citizens— his life, his mode of existence, is primarily city life, and he is constantly concerned for the philosophical and political health and well-being of its citizens. For Arendt, in its essential points thinking is not solitary contemplation, no matter how alone the thinker, but rather an internal dialogue or the two-in-one of thinking where the philosopher is never alone but always accompanied by a friend. This kind of solitude, Arendt concludes, "is an integral part of being and living together with others, and in this solitude the philosopher, too, cannot help but form opinions—he, too, arrives at his own *doxa*. His distinction from his fellow citizens is not that he possesses any special truth from which the multitude is excluded, but that he remains always ready to endure the *pathos* of wonder and thereby avoids the dogmatism of mere opinion holders" ("Philosophy and Politics" 101). Plato's insistence on turning away from the city and the *doxai* of its citizens, and his resolute focus on the singular contemplation of all that is eternal and inhuman is indeed the remaking of a mode of existence and a retreat from political life, but in so doing philosophy risks destroying the plurality of the human condition that resides in each individual.

After more than two thousand years, the situation in which we find ourselves today, in Arendt's view, is that we live in a world where not even common sense makes sense any longer, whether for philosophy or politics, which is of course the great dilemma of "Truth and Politics." Plato's or Aristotle's ideal of philosophical existence outside of and beyond the city was never realized; indeed, in Arendt's view it was unrealizable. As a result, the utility of philosophy has had to be defended across the centuries since, in fact, critical thinking can yield no practicable results, at least from the ends-directed perspective of political action. Still, even if Plato ultimately directed philosophy away from political concerns, philosophy's primary charge has persevered, which is to maintain the health of human thinking and moral reasoning. Despite the variety of its paths and directions, philosophy after Plato continued and continues to define and clarify criteria according to which judgments of human affairs, culture, and history can be understood and evaluated, debated, and revised. In other words, philosophy has always sought to provide an education in judgment for the human community. In turning to the example of Socrates, Arendt makes the case that our only chance for restoring a common world, of rebuilding a shared world and a common culture of sense, is to rebuild the connection between politics and philosophy, but in order to do so, the aims of philosophy will have to be redirected in more earthly directions. "Philosophy, political philosophy," she concludes, "like all its other branches, will never be able to deny its origin in *thaumazein*, in the wonder at that which is as it is. If philosophers, despite their necessary estrangement from the everyday life of human affairs, were ever to arrive at a true political philosophy they would have to make the plurality of man, out of which arises the whole realm of human affairs—in its grandeur and misery—the object of their *thaumazein*" ("Philosophy and Politics" 103).

Any reconciliation of philosophy and politics will have to find a bridge between thought and action as well as acknowledge that every road to truth passes through a plurality of competing perspectives. If philosophy cannot offer us grounds for certainty, how can it instead produce the possibility of conviction, no matter how fragile? This question defines the terrain where politics meets the dilemmas raised by the connection of thinking to moral considerations.

"Philosophy and Politics" is a text that consistently links moral reasoning with the dilemmas of political thinking as exemplified in the figure of Socrates. As a thinking person in the singular, the philosopher may convince himself to articulate and live by a moral principle, such as Socrates's maxim, "It is better to suffer wrong than to do wrong." A self-given maxim is compelling because the thinker's actions are checked by his conscience, that is, the two-in-one of thinking or the silent companion in thought whose health and integrity must be assured. This is surely one of the key ethical aims of philosophy.

However, the philosopher's moral axioms address man in the singular and not humans in their messy plural and intersubjective lives as political citizens who must together, and often in conflict, care for their shared world. It is highly unlikely that a philosopher's maxim will carry moral weight for others or translate well into common customs or commandments. Philosophical truth is unpolitical by nature because it concerns humans only in their singularity. Within the marketplace and the plural opinions of others, the philosopher is unlikely to be convincing and from this experience despair of the value of truth. Where truth fails to compel belief in its self-evidence or transcendental significance, we are thrown once again into the realm of opinion and a plurality of competing perspectives.

And yet, even given the frequency of Socrates's failures to bring others around to his arguments about truth, justice, morality, and so forth, his ethical principles and arguments had far-reaching impact even if they did not, perhaps could not, be translated into political principles. Socrates convinced no one of the truth of his philosophical convictions, which remain opinions and not truth; how then to understand and do justice to his powers of persuasion? From where did Socrates gain his authority to influence others, no matter how temporarily, and to serve as a representative of human dilemmas of thinking? From where does persuasion derive a power to encourage others to revise their thinking and modes of behaviors without in any way impinging on their freedom to think and choose? In other words, why was and is Socrates accepted as something like a time-honored ethical exemplar?

At this point, Arendt arrives at an interesting conclusion, which is to defend the power of teaching by example, to teach or persuade by serving as an inspiration for others. As I have strongly suggested elsewhere in this book, Arendt (and many others) consider Socrates as a representative human and a model for thinking, judging, and acting, and this despite his failures to reach conclusions or to persuade friend and foe alike of his arguments. Arendt insists that the continuing power of Socrates to elicit thought, argument, and counterargument ultimately derives not from his speech but from display of his ethical choices and actions. Socrates became a powerful philosophical exemplar not when he appeared before the Athenian tribunal, where his dialectic, no matter how eloquent, fell upon deaf ears, but when he chose death by his own hand rather than exile from the polis. From this action, Arendt comes to the conclusion that teaching by example is the only means of persuasion that philosophical truth is capable of without perversion or distortion: "Philosophical truth can become 'practical' and inspire action without violating the rules of the political realm only when it manages to become manifest in the guise of an example. This is the only chance for an ethical principle to be verified as well as validated" ("Truth and Politics" 343).

Arendt supports this argument by reviewing Kant's distinction between examples and schemata in the third Critique. Recall the key role that Kant's notion of exemplary validity plays at the end of Arendt's

Lectures on Kant's Political Philosophy.[61] One assumes that every particular object in the world has a corresponding conceptual schema by which it is recognized. This could be a Platonic idea, a Kantian schema, or even a cognitive mental construct. However, one more possibility remains, which is that one may encounter an object, a real object that one feels compelled to judge aesthetically as the best possible example of something, whose very existence is the criterion for assessing the excellence of comparative objects. Like all others, such judgments are open to debate. Nevertheless, the exemplar remains an existential particular that in its very particularity gives rise to a comparative general criterion that cannot otherwise be defined. The intense attraction one feels to an idea or sensation in aesthetic experience is an intuition of exemplarity. Schemata are a cognitive power produced by the human mind by means of a formal imagination, but in "Truth and Politics" Arendt suggests that examples are primarily cultural and that aesthetic and historical experiences open up different fields of imagination and occasions for exercising and assessing the power of judgment.[62] Or to return to earlier sections of this book, one might consider cultural archives as repositories of creative and intellectual exemplarity preserved for future use and assessment. Arendt notes that the comparative general criterion that arises when judgment assesses exemplarity often takes the form of similes or metaphors, for example, Socrates as a midwife who delivers forth for public examination the as yet unformed thoughts of others. These expressions interject poetic forms into philosophy—as aesthetic expressions they spin out, often through artful conversation, further chains of meaning that encircle and flow from the exemplary instance like waves in a pond in ways that broaden and deepen the original intuitions of sense.

I have said that Socrates's exemplarity is defined by his actions as well as his speech. Socrates is the exemplary philosopher as teacher because of his open display of thinking as a public performance. When the philosopher sets out to persuade openly in the market-

---

61. Arendt's most replete discussion of the distinction between examples and schemata occurs in her lecture notes on "Imagination," which appear as an addendum to *Lectures on Kant's Political Philosophy*, 79–85.

62. In his essay "Anthropology from a Pragmatic Point of View," Kant similarly points to the importance of world history, biographies, novels, and plays as aids to human understanding, even if they are imprecise sources for anthropology. See *Anthropology, History, and Education*, 233.

place, he has transitioned from thinking to action and thus serves as a
model for moving fluidly between the external world of appearances
and internal reflection on the meaning of appearances. He has made
thinking an act pictured by his whole moral being as an exemplary
mode of existence. In Arendt's view, only moral philosophy has this
power to transform theoretical argument into exemplary truth. The
moral for the philosopher here is to embrace the knowledge that
"inspiration of and manifestation in human action may not be able
to compete with the compelling evidence of truth, but they can compete . . . with the persuasiveness inherent in opinion" ("Truth and
Politics" 239).

Of course, in present times, philosophy, like the humanities, has very
few possibilities for politically threatening the polis, and so the force
of philosophical exemplarity is weakened. (I would hope that Arendt
herself, as philosopher, witness, and teacher, is a counterexample to this
dilemma.) At the same time, Arendt feels that the witness, the reporter,
the academic, that is, the tellers of factual truth, are even worse off, for
factual statements contain no principles that can guide human action
and even their contents defy verification by exemplary action. "A teller
of factual truth, in the unlikely event that he wished to stake his life on a
particular fact, would achieve a kind of miscarriage," Arendt concludes.
"What would become manifest in his act would be his courage or, perhaps, his stubbornness but neither the truth of what he had to say nor
even his own truthfulness. For why shouldn't a liar stick to his lies with
great courage, especially in politics, where he might be motivated by
patriotism or some other kind of legitimate group partiality?" ("Truth
and Politics" 244).

In this situation, one of the great dilemmas of modernity is how one
can maintain one's bearings in our present and actual political worlds
when conditions for making judgments about truth and falsehood are
so deeply eroded. How then to defend the "truth," or at least actionable
versions of the truth, where contingency will always trump certainty?
There are no guarantees from either side.

Yet questions remain. Who are the truthtellers and what are their
responsibilities, political or otherwise? The model of Socrates as por-
trayed in "Philosophy and Politics," "Truth and Politics," *The Life of the
Mind*, and indeed in many other writings by Arendt is one example. In
"Truth and Politics," after Arendt traces the sinuous and blurry line that

threads from philosophical truth to deliberate political lying, a project whose frankness risks despair or, worse, nihilism, she arrives at some hopeful observations. In its conflict with political power, factual truth faces severe disadvantages that undermine its powers to persuade and to persist as historical fact. Yet Arendt insists that factual truth has powers of its own that should not be discounted. Her first conviction, as I describe above, is that no matter how deep, widespread, and consistent political lies become, they cannot invent a viable and lasting substitute for political reality. "Persuasion and violence can destroy truth," she writes, "but they cannot replace it" ("Truth and Politics" 255). The other irony is that the truthteller's integrity diminishes in proportion to her acceptance of her partiality and partisan commitments to political actions. In other words, as Arendt has insisted many times before, the witness is not an actor but rather a spectator or observer, and witnesses forfeit their independence and impartiality, thus their power to persuade as dispassionate voices, if they try to "interfere directly in human affairs and to speak the language of persuasion or of violence" (255). With so many people—our neighbors and colleagues and especially young people, our students—passionately committed to political action, this attitude appears to be conservative at best, quietist at worse. At this point, then, I want to insist again that the roles and responsibilities, the ways of life or modes of existence, of the spectator, the actor, the *politikos*, and even the artist and aesthete are not settled and invariable. In the best of worlds, and in relation to the exercise of judgment, we cycle frequently between these roles and, hopefully, through the aid of insight, choose to exercise them wisely and in the right historical and cultural contexts.

In times of political and historical crisis, we tend to become more aware of what Arendt calls the nonpolitical and even antipolitical nature of truth. Note the irony of this observation: the deliberate political liar undermines, even destroys, the relation between truth and politics, while in order to maintain their impartiality, integrity, and independence, and to defend what Arendt calls political truth, the historical observer must stand at a distance from politics. In this respect, Arendt wants to enlist support for and confidence in one more paradox in the conflict between truth and politics, one which is more hopeful and positive. In most democracies, and even nations and cultures where full democratic participation is limited, there exist public institutions, both governmental and nongovernmental, where "contrary to all political rules, truth and truthfulness have always constituted the highest criterion of speech and endeavor" ("Truth and Politics" 255–56). Arendt's primary examples are an independent judiciary and, interestingly, universities. (One would think that a free and independent press should ideally also take its place here.) These institutions have always been imperfect, of course, and today one must acknowledge that they are undergoing extreme stress. Distantly related to Plato's Academy, Arendt portrays these institutions, at least ideally, as standing outside of yet next to the rough-and-tumble conflicts of politics. Practical minds will recognize that politics is unceasingly challenging and eroding the borders that are supposed to insulate these institutions from politics. Yet Arendt wants us to recognize equally that

> very unwelcome truths have emerged from the universities, and very unwelcome judgments have been handed down from the bench time and again; and these institutions, like other refuges of truth, have remained exposed to all the dangers arising from social and political power. Yet the chances for truth to prevail in public are, of course, greatly improved by the mere existence of such places and by the organization of independent, supposedly disinterested scholars associated with them. And it can hardly be denied that, at least in constitutionally ruled countries, the political realm has recognized, even in the event of conflict, that it has a stake in the existence of men and institutions over which it has no power. (256)

The unwelcome truths that Arendt points to in these lines are not the truth of the philosopher but rather a factual truth meant to shape and serve the judgments that educated citizens are called on to make in the domain of practical politics. One of the disturbing paradoxes of Arendt's essay "Truth and Politics" is the way she appears to persistently associate politics with lying. What, then, is "'political' truth"? Political truth stands at the far end from the rational truth of the philosopher, and at the same time political truth is not the opposite of lying nor exactly its contrary. Political truth is a domain whose borders are defined on one side by lying and on the other by independent reporting and analysis—in the middle resides, in all their variety and variability, the many forms of *doxa*, such as belief, opinion, and ideology. In its ideal form, political truth would be defined by the reporting, analysis, and criticism from independent and impartial witnesses, spectators, who investigate politics at its edges, next to it yet not in it, so to speak; in this respect, their judgment restrains them from acting. Nevertheless, as I have already suggested, this stark conclusion, which seems to draw sharp distinctions between political observers and actors, is complicated by three ideas that reappear with some consistency in Arendt's thoughts about judgment. First, to the extent that judgment is a political faculty, Arendt suggests that one aim of the impartial testimony and reporting of historical observers is to inspire political action by shaping our understanding and evaluation of historical events. Moreover, there are historical circumstances where political lying becomes so dominant and universal that it threatens to substitute ideology for reality, thus restricting or even eliminating the possibility of choosing freely how one wants to live and with whom and under what conditions of thought and solidarity; in other words, here power restricts possibilities for self-government at every scale. In these extreme situations, the very persistence of independent thought becomes a tactic of resistance and, therefore, action. Finally, Arendt suggests that depending on circumstances, every individual is capable of rotating between the roles of spectator and actor, which is evidence that just as Socrates moves freely between the external world of appearances and internal reflection on the meaning of appearances, the exercise of judgment is a bridge that leads from observations and evaluations of the shape and sense of the world to decisions regarding where we choose to exercise our freedom to change it. If judgment is a political faculty, it is our best means for navigating the difficult terrain populated by varying and variable accounts where the distinction between factual truth and fabricated truth may be difficult to discern. And in turn, it points us toward actions by which we may exercise our freedom to choose and to imagine and remodel a different world.

In the last paragraph of "Truth and Politics," Arendt addresses the lack of balance in her perspective, which seems to oppose a life guided by critical reason with an unbridled quest for power and dominance that asserts itself only with the most cynical regard for truth. Arendt writes that this extreme view of political actors coincides only with the lowest level of human affairs, which is distinct from both reasonable disagreements of opinion and "the actual content of political life—of the joy and the gratification that arise out of being in company with

our peers, out of acting together and appearing in public, out of insert
ing ourselves into the world by word and deed, thus acquiring and
sustaining our personal identity and beginning something entirely
new" ("Truth and Politics" 259). In Arendtian terms, politics is also
the realm of human action, and more importantly, of acting in concert
and solidarity with our peers in shaping and revising a shared world.
However, despite the centrality of politics to human life in community,
there are important matters of worldly reason and truth that politics
cannot alter or replace. Beyond the pleasures of acting in concert, the
very aim of all politics is to exercise one's freedom to change the world.
But this freedom is not exercised in a vacuum. It is bounded by existential particulars where the gravity of the past meets the force of the
future. In any present moment where actions take place, the future
emerges through natality, the ever-present possibility of the new and
the unexpected, and at the same time, every choice is weighted by the
past in the form of human history.

The great lesson of Arendt's essay is to present judgment as a political
faculty that is exercised at a distance, both actually and ethically, from
the space of politics itself. Judgment is also distinct from the writing
of history, which shapes the perspectives from which recorded and
memorialized human actions must be reviewed and evaluated. What
preserves truth in relation to judgment and history is what Arendt calls
a curious passion for intellectual integrity at any price, whose ideals are
shaped by an independent pursuit of the truth marked by impartiality
and freedom from self-interest in thought and judgment. Surely these
ethical ideals shape the aims of teaching and research in the humanities, regardless of the diversity of their pursuits. And if Socrates offers
for the humanities a distinct and exemplary existential model—that of
philosopher, educator, and citizen—the only thing that can be learned
from him is that in his teaching the philosopher neither transmits
knowledge nor tries to convince or persuade anyone to a position or
point of view. What Socrates seeks to teach by example is his capacity
for self-questioning and self-revision as well as his endless curiosity and
care for his fellow citizens, which is allied with the humanities' obligation to encourage not only criticism and curiosity but also discernment, insight, reflexivity, and revisable representative thinking. There
are no sure methods for teaching these qualities, yet the possibilities
for exemplifying them are endless and limited only by our imagination.

VI. AN AS YET UNDETERMINED ANIMAL

Teaching is more difficult than learning because what teaching calls for is this: to let learn. The real teacher, in fact, lets nothing else be learned than—learning.

MARTIN HEIDEGGER, *What Is Called Thinking?*

In the past fifteen years, one of my greatest pleasures has been to teach full or part time in departments of studio art. A central component of creative arts education is the studio "crit" session. These critical response sessions can take many forms. However, the Department of Visual Arts at the University of Chicago has developed a format that I find to be especially instructive.

MFA critiques at Chicago are an all-day affair, and all faculty and all students are invited to participate; taking breakfast and lunch together present occasions for collegiality and informal discussion, with multiple crit sessions taking place in the morning and afternoon. An individual session lasts forty-five minutes, and in the first twenty minutes or so, the young artist whose work is being evaluated is usually not allowed to speak. Beyond the great pleasure I take in being a member of this community, in the past few years and unbeknownst to my colleagues and students, this activity has taken on for me an intense ethnographic interest as one model for the practice of judgment and artful conversation, especially at a local level.

Think, then, of our community as a kind of polis, a gathering of like minds brought together with a common (educational) purpose, which disperses again as soon as that purpose is accomplished. This disappearance is not final, however, because the community continues to exist in virtual form, a recurrent possibility ready to be reconvened as the need arises. This community is based on qualities of mutual respect and openness to the expressed thoughts and perspectives of others; everyone is free to express his or her opinion or not under conditions of equality.

These qualities are no doubt important, but what interests me most in the studio critique is the following. We are a perambulatory community and wander from place to place in a directed way to engage with creative works intended to be works of art. Let's say, for example, that a student has created a construction in three dimensions, something

whose reception requires viewers to regard the work from all sides with
a kind of ever-shifting gaze. It may be that on first glance, I take the
work to be uninteresting or unfinished. But happily, to the extent that
the work exists, that it creates and occupies a space of appearance, my
perspective is not the only one in which it takes on sense and value.
Rather, the work's appearing occurs in the dynamic interleaving of multiple perspectives, diverse *dokei moi*, regarding it from various angles
and distances as well as historical and conceptual frameworks, though
these perspectives only become apparent when my collaborators in
criticism publicly disclose their opinions and offer them for agreement,
disagreement, and revision.

The formation of this community and its public sharing of opinion
and aesthetic experience, no matter how temporary and occasional, is
already a precious event worth remarking upon. However, I have so far
left out what is most essential and remarkable about the experience. I
see a physical work in space, but at the same time it occupies my imagination, and as I look attentively and listen thoughtfully to the opinions
of others, sudden shifts begin to occur in my own internal perspective.
The object itself does not physically change of course. It presents completely to view all that it has to offer in terms of form, material, shape,
color, texture, composition, and so forth, but this does not mean that
I or others "see" everything—there are inevitable gaps in our vision
and understanding. Or rather, this is the place to fully recognize how
the physical act of seeing is inseparable from imaginative processes of
understanding, indeed what Kant calls imagination and the operation
of reflection. This imaginative reflection is equally informed by my past
history of aesthetic experience and my knowledge of the history of art,
as well as my present experience of reflecting upon the opinions of others. In offering my views and listening to the contrasting or contrary
views of others, I gain new insight and powers of discernment—the
object becomes different. As Wittgenstein would say, it begins to shift
its appearance under different aspects. In other words, while no possible information has been added to or subtracted from the work itself,
when artful conversation with others encourages me to frame it in different contexts or to see it from different perspectives, its possibilities
of sense and value shift—for me it becomes a new work; I see it differently, and accordingly, I revise my opinion. The student whose work
is subject to critique must also practice the expression and defense of

reasons and learn how to explain her or his creative convictions. The student is also learning how to listen and to learn and to better understand how his work might inspire unintended meanings and ethical stances or consequences. Or how in the course of time the work may take on meanings and values that are entirely unanticipated by either the artist or his present community. The work is built with the hand, but its possibilities of meaning and value are shaped by judgment.

In the course of conversation, I and others learn from each other new vocabularies, styles of argument, and frameworks for observing and interpreting. The contributions of each participant subtly shift the descriptive language of the community and, therefore, our ways of seeing and understanding. Together we build a new picture of the object that appears in the overlapping edges of each individual's acts of discursive framing. This is not necessarily a fully consensual picture—an achievement that is rarely possible—but it is a more complete picture that accounts for possible new routes of sensemaking and evaluation. And even though these descriptions rarely agree in all points, together they bring otherwise unseen aspects of the object into a common space of appearance that all can recognize. As I reflect on the opinions of my colleagues and students, some aspects of the work recede and others come into the foreground; what was previously nonapparent becomes visible. I may find that the work suddenly acquires new depths of interest and possibilities of pleasure or decide I have new reasons for disliking it. Yet in almost every case I arrive at new depths of understanding, and I call this learning. I assess my own conviction and its reasons yet accept that I may not have the final say. Each and every one of us is offering judgments of this work that include reasons for our opinions and sense of conviction, but no judgment is final, and in fact our assessments are continually being revised, individually and collectively, for as long as conversation about the work lasts.

Stop for a moment to consider some of the key qualities of these acts of judgment. Judgment requires plurality—it has no claim to value or permanence unless shared with others. This plurality appears in a space where each participant grants her or his fellows the freedom to think and to express themselves under conditions of equality—judgment requires that each interlocutor extend the principle of charity to all members of the community. The sharing of judgments requests the giving and receiving of reasons and an open examination of one's con-

fictional. In giving voice to my opinions and making them present to others, I must face them publicly and nakedly, as it were. I test my convictions and assumptions of prior agreement or disagreement as well as my implied or unarticulated criteria for evaluating and making sense of experience. The possibility of revision and self-revision, to alter one's perspective and to change one's mind, is essential here; otherwise the power to broaden one's mind and to occupy imaginatively the perspective of others is lost. In sharing my judgments, I have changed, and perhaps the whole community has changed as well. We affirm (and disaffirm) together the degree to which we are a community of like minds and shared interests, and in so doing, commit ourselves to act collectively for the benefit of others who wholly or partly share our sensibilities and interests and to fight for the right of sharing and revising opinion in a free and open space of speech and action.

The collective studio critique differs from ideal cases of judgment, but those differences focalize what I want to call the educative aims of judgment. The first difference occurs at the initiating moment of judgment, which I have described as close to the philosophical experience of *thaumazein*, or speechless wonder. We have all had the experience of being stopped in our tracks by the intensity of a painting; of a passage of fiction, poetry, music, cinema, or philosophy; or even news of a political event, leading to intensified perception, rapt attention, and then to a state of apperception, which I call looking, listening, or reading while thinking, all the while sorting out what aspects of a work attract my interest, which is discernment.

This kind of aesthetic experience often arises in chance encounters, which Kant pictures as a singular encounter with a unique object. In contrast, the studio critique involves a preconstituted community of teachers and students who have come together in a spirit of care and education. Although it might happen, it is rarely the case that the judgments offered in these situations either want or need universal agreement. Nevertheless, these judgments are made with sincerity and conviction and follow the need to give voice to the reasons for that conviction and to test it in a public context.

However, in its educative aim the community solidarity that arises in the sharing of judgments of taste is secondary to another interest, which is to share counsel with the student artist. Some of this advice is certainly practical. Would using another kind of material, altering the composition, reimagining the conditions of display, or constructing on a different scale enhance the perceptual impact of the work? Moreover, the sharing of judgments might also involve important lessons in history, especially in this example, art history. This knowledge is important for its own sake. In realizing reasons, as it were, of discovering, communicating, and revising them, one also recovers and reviews their history. This is an idea appealed to in Arendt but for the most part missing in Kant. Judgments of taste do not emerge from individuals ex nihilo. No matter how singular and subjective the judgment, all reasons appeal to criteria, both personal and collective, that emerge from a more or less common stock of critical experience such as histories of viewing and experiencing, acquired frameworks and contexts for interpretation and evaluation, and learned conceptual inventories. One is testing not only one's judgment and values but also the relevance and power of this stock of experience. At the same time, these history lessons also suggest how the sense of the work can shift by clarifying its evident or unacknowledged family resemblances and its genealogical connections to prior works and art historical styles or movements. This is what education in judgment looks like.

Our department offers a course on "critique," but how can this skill be taught? In fact, it cannot—it can only be rehearsed and practiced, and solitary study will not deepen it—companionship is required for its exercise. As judgment cannot be taught, only practiced, in all essential aspects there is no distinction between teacher and student in the exchange of opinion. In classes where I have derived the most satisfaction, I have learned together with my students, who almost invariably offer new ideas and contexts for interpretation and evaluation that I had not yet seen, despite long years of research and learning. Something that we are learning together and sharing beyond the content of any given course is not only ideas but also examples of judgment and how judgment can be practiced concretely. Is one example better than another? No more or less so than one opinion is necessarily better than another, for there are no transcendental criteria that can be appealed to. Perhaps I have rehearsed my powers of judgment for longer than my students; this gives me experience and perhaps I can pass that experience along by example, but my experience does not make my judgments or opinions necessarily better than those of my students. In every given instance or example, we are all equally exposed to the testing of opinion and the surprise of an unforeseen idea or argument.

I have said that judgment cannot be taught except through its continual practice. And it may well be the case that when one ceases to practice judgment routinely, its powers decline like those of a dancer or musician who loses the desire to pursue his or her art. What can a philosophy of the humanities offer in these situations? If a primary aim of the humanities is to proffer an education in judgment, then the first task of its philosophy, if one should become apparent, would be to investigate critically exemplary instances of judgment in order to delineate with perspicuity its activities and operations, which is one task I hope to have begun in this book. If our powers of judgment can be strengthened, deepened, broadened, and intensified, then a philosophy of the humanities can diagnose those areas in which our powers of judgment have declined, weakened, or atrophied and offer directions for their exercise and restoration. (There is a reason why every advanced degree in the humanities confers the title of "doctor of philosophy.")

This experience is messy and governed by few explicit rules. No one is fully aware of engaging in operations of discernment, apperception, insight, imaginative reflection, and acts of revision and self-revision as they engage in the free play of judgment's improvisational conversations. Good judgment can be practiced intuitively and thoughtfully without the self-consciousness, reflexivity, and introspection necessary for philosophical investigation. Nevertheless, if a philosophy of the humanities can bring these operations into the full light of comprehension and give them conceptual clarity, then perhaps judgment can be practiced with greater care and self-attention by teachers and students alike. Introspection as an act of phenomenological description is a key strategy here, where the thinker reflexively makes an account of her or his experiences and activities when making judgments—this is a critical self-examination of thought and judgment in the course of their happening. The educative aim of a philosophy of the humanities is to understand what we do when deploying the operations of judgment and how this understanding might improve our capacity to discern and describe, to understand and evaluate, and to defend our convictions in ways that enhance our solidarity with others. Will a philosophy of the humanities guide us in perfecting our judgments? It would perhaps be better to follow the advice of Samuel Beckett and to imagine these acts as "Ever tried. Ever failed. No matter. Try Again. Fail again. Fail better."[63]

63. *Worstward Ho* (New York: Grove, 1983), 7.

As is often the case in Beckett's writing, there is hope in even his bleakest lines. Whatever progress can be made in human perfectionism will inevitably occur in activities of experimentation, or trying out opinions, ideas, and arguments in public situations where failure or embarrassment are standing possibilities. I have said that a directive aim of the humanities is to define and describe criteria for evaluating judgments, whether criticizing or affirming them, especially because there are no external standards that assure the quality of our judgments or guarantee their permanence, much less their teachability. Is there danger of infinite regress in this account? Appeals to reflective judgments are both widespread and common because we are called routinely to make judgments whenever and wherever we need to make sense of and evaluate an action, event, or experience. At the same time, because judgments are always context dependent and can rely on no external standards, infinite regress is a standing risk, just as the open-ended and unfinished character of thought can find no conclusive point of rest. This risk is ever present because in judgment's activity of critical evaluation, the standards evoked are as much subject to debate as the opinions expressed, and there is no end to this criticism.

In the absence of either providence or any transcendental legislation of meaning and value, perhaps the best we can do in these circumstances, as I have already suggested, is to negotiate continually, in plurality and community, the truth that defines our history and actions from moment to unpredictable moment. Arendt never ceases to argue that the activities of thinking and judgment are bound tightly together in every assessment of meaning or value. In Arendt's view and mine, the fact that thinking yields no practicable or utilitarian results and operates best when continually revising itself is closely tied to the open-endedness of judgments in relation to singular circumstances. Thinking of the paragraph above, it may be that the risk of infinite regress in critical thought and judgment is our best chance of not falling into dogma, prejudice, and the capacity for evil. The problem, and the advantage, is that there are no guarantees of success—both thinking and judgment occur "without bannisters," as Arendt liked to say, and perhaps one does not even have the next landing in view on these ever-spiraling stairs.

At the beginning of this book I noted that Kant's fourth question of urgent concern for philosophy, "What are humans?" follows closely on the heels of his other three questions—What can I know? What

should I do? What can I hope for?—and is intimately related to them.
Kant's most focused response to this question, which guided the lectures on anthropology that he offered annually for the last twenty-two years of his teaching career, are set out in his late essay "Anthropology from a Pragmatic Point of View." This far-ranging text offers exhaustive accounts of the physiology and psychology of humans, but ultimately the question provokes responses that are more ethical than empirical or ontological. Kant was among the first philosophers to imagine becoming human as a direction in species history. In the preface to the essay, Kant defines anthropology as concerned less with the physiological nature of *Homo sapiens* than with "the investigation of what [the human] as a free-acting being makes of himself, or can and should make of himself" ("Anthropology" 231). This knowledge is speculative in nature and its pragmatism limits philosophy to establishing certain facts of the human—that humans are beings endowed with the capacity of reason and moral self-legislation, that they exhibit a sense of common community defined paradoxically by their asocial sociability, and that in their capacity to exercise judgment they express a need for the free and public exercise of thought and opinion. In this context, certain questions of existential import inevitably arise: What can I know of myself and others? What should I do to enhance my possibilities for achieving the human? What is my hope for a new life shared with others in a cosmopolitan existence? Without certain knowledge of a next world, what hopes do I have for myself and others in this one? Humans are creatures who, whether instinctually or willfully, design their lives by engaging with these questions, and it is Arendt's contention that if judgment is closely associated with politics, then all of these questions seek avenues of response based on the condition of plurality, that is, of considering human perfectionism as a collective project, regardless of its checkered history, which includes as many abject failures as successes.

In its educative aims, pragmatic anthropology promotes "knowledge of the human being as a *citizen of the world*" ("Anthropology" 231; Kant's emphasis) or at least as a creature with the capacity to become such a citizen.[64] However, it is also clear from Kant's political and his-

64. "All cultural progress, by means of which the human being advances his education, has the goal of applying this acquired knowledge and skill for the world's use. But the most impor-

torical writing that achieving the human is an unfinished project, and therefore, the human is something of a moving target as a subject of philosophical investigation and ethical direction. One can imagine that becoming human is something that may never be fully or finally achieved, yet it persists as a perfectionist aim for all who can imagine it or be educated toward it. The most one can claim for it is the definition of an idea or ideal of the human as the ever-receding horizon toward which this speculative philosophy directs itself. Kant conceives this project as a direction in cultural history that is often detoured, stymied, or even reversed. It is a difficult path where some progress has been made but whose endpoint is still so far distant as to be barely visible. As Nietzsche wrote, man is the as yet undetermined animal.[65] Yet, if philosophy can imagine humanity's becoming, this means at least that we are on the path no matter how badly marked, neglected, or uncultivated.

As I read Arendt and Kant, I first imagine two routes of response to Kant's last question. I wrote earlier that for every individual born to history, the potential and possibility for becoming human is universal but also a path that might be only rarely taken or never finally nor completely achieved. If this observation has any value, then one might first try to better understand certain facts of the human, that is, powers and capacities that all humans share even if they are only dimly recognized and unevenly practiced. The second line of investigation would be to identify and examine the nature and consequences of failures of reasoning and ethical responsiveness as roadblocks on this path. In this approach, an idea of the human becomes apparent only in its failures, which may often have catastrophic consequences. I will suggest a third

---

tant object in the world to which he can apply them is the human being: because the human being is his own final end.—Therefore to know the human being according to his species as an earthly being endowed with reason especially deserves to be called *knowledge of the world*, even though he constitutes only one part of the creatures on earth" (preface to "Anthropology" 231; Kant's emphasis).

65. I am thinking here of Heidegger's comment in *What Is Called Thinking?* that "within the purview of his thinking, Nietzsche calls man as he has been till now 'the last man.' This is not to say that all human existence will end with the man so named. Rather, the last man is the man who is no longer able to look beyond himself, to rise above himself for once up to the level of his task, and undertake that task in a way that is essentially right. Man so far is incapable of it, because he has not yet come into his own full nature. Nietzsche declares that man's essential nature is not yet determined—it has neither been found nor been secured. This is why Nietzsche says: 'Man is the as yet undetermined animal'" (57–58).

approach in a moment, but in each one of these instances human powers of judgment must come to our aid.

Hannah Arendt has offered some of the clearest examples of human failing while describing their consequences with clear vision and courage. A first failing is ironically a charge against philosophy itself. By this I mean Arendt's daring accusation that Aristotle's *bios theōrētikos* is an inhuman form of life because of its solitude. However, this accusation is also a negative proof that the human condition is defined by a political life characterized by plurality and sociality and that the humanity of humans manifests itself in terms of communicability and sociability in the sharing of judgments and opinions. There is human need to imagine and design a life in common despite inevitable conflicts, misunderstandings, and misfires of reason. Human culture is nourished on the terrain of sensus communis and the asocial sociability that inspires conflict but also sometimes leads to agreement and shifts in opinions and beliefs. Judgment is a political faculty in Arendt's sense in the extent to which it generates critical communities in these terms. There is no right or wrong in aesthetic conversation, only disagreement or agreement about the reasonableness of our interpretations and evaluations. As such, aesthetic conversations are models for managing conflict and negotiating terms of agreement and consensus in our daily lives. What is asked for here is not assent to a conclusion but rather a mutual seeking out of overlapping patterns of understanding and partial agreement.

A second failure is exemplified by the case against Adolf Eichmann's sins of conformity to ideology as characterized by his lack of imagination, his failures of thinking, and the atrophy of his moral reasoning and his capacity to judge. Lest one believe this is a unique case, in "Truth and Politics" Arendt also examines the nihilism of the political liar who ruthlessly exploits the contingency of facts and the instability of truth. And in "The Crisis in Culture" Arendt worries about not only a certain philistinism but also a barbarism that I read as meaning the risk of becoming uncultured, uncivilized, being uncivil, or not open to conversation and the revision of belief and moral attitudes—in other words, of being impervious to both self-examination and external persuasion. Responding to the crisis in culture is not about making better works of art or learning how to preserve them but, rather, changing the terms of our relationship to art and the conversations we have about it. Yet, there is a deeper issue at stake. Arendt writes, "A life without thinking is quite possible; it then fails to develop its own essence—it is not merely meaningless, it is not fully alive. Men who do not think are like sleepwalkers" (*Life of the Mind: Thinking* 191). These somnambulists have not fully embraced, or have simply ignored, their capacity for becoming human. Nevertheless, in these near hopeless situations, where critical thinking, whether private or public, falls into deep slumbers and atrophies from lack of exercise, Arendt insists that the few who continue to think and to reason become political actors such that the very act of thinking becomes a kind of active resistance that displays a human need for reason and the public expression of opinion that cannot be suppressed.[66] As importantly, Arendt also notes that even the political liar displays a fundamental human attribute: he is exercising his freedom to change the world, even if the consequences for the rest of humanity are disastrous. As I remarked in the last section, the contingency of facts, that circumstances could have been otherwise, is an affirmation of human freedom. The deep ethical question then becomes, What kind of world do I hope for and how do I exercise my freedom to imagine and achieve that world?

I have said that in the humanities both teacher and student learn together and share beyond the content of any given course examples of judgment and how judgment can be practiced concretely. The important question embedded here is, What does exercising judgment educate us to? Every occasion to exercise humanistic reasoning, whether

66. In *The Life of the Mind: Thinking*, Arendt expands her picture of thinking in emergencies in the existential terms of Karl Jaspers's "boundary situations": "In Jaspers, the term gets it suggestive plausibility less from specific experiences than from the simple fact that life itself, limited by birth and death, is a boundary affair insofar as my worldly existence always forces me to take into account a past when I was not yet and a future when I shall be no more. Here the point is that whenever I transcend the limits of my own life-span and begin to reflect on this past, judging it, and this future, forming projects by willing, thinking ceases to be a politically marginal activity. And such reflections will inevitably arise in political emergencies. When everybody is swept away unthinkingly by what everybody else does and believes in, those who think are drawn out of hiding because their refusal to join is conspicuous and thereby becomes a kind of action. In such emergencies, it turns out that the purging element in thinking (Socrates' midwifery, that brings out the implications of unexamined opinions and thereby destroys them—values, doctrines, theories, and even convictions) is political by implication. For this destruction has a liberating effect on another human faculty, the faculty of judgment, which one may call, with some justification, the most political of man's mental abilities. It is the faculty that judges *particulars* without subsuming them under those general rules which can be taught and learned until they grow into habits that can be replaced by other habits and rules" (192–93).

Inside or outside of the classroom, is an opportunity to practice good judgment in a public context, and to practice judgment with others is to bestow the gift of freedom. In ideal situations, the public practice of judgment is an opportunity to learn how to accept and exercise one's freedom to think and to speak and to feel that freedom in solidarity with others. In this case, the classroom can function as something like a temporary autonomous zone that hosts a critical community based on generosity, community, and common care. Education means not to inculcate knowledge or belief but to learn how to judge freely with a capacity for charity and a willingness to alter one's beliefs and opinions. One should not ignore that there can be an intense pleasure felt in sharing judgments with others. This pleasure arises in feelings of sociability and solidarity, in the freedom to think and to think differently, to be in communication with others, and to persuade and be persuaded by them as a measure of belonging to the community. In such communities of judgment, one does not have to seek complete and total agreement but rather only feel attuned to the modes of reasoning and patterns of coming to agreement or in disagreeing, that one is speaking and listening on the same terms.

Beyond achieving clear understanding of the operations of judgment, are there any compass points that can orient the educative aims of the humanities? Arendt claims that Socrates expressed few positive statements, and apart from the practice of the elenchus as a kind of conceptual midwifery, offered no guidelines for judgment. Alternatively, throughout his voluminous writings, Kant offers implicit or explicit maxims for guiding human thought and behavior in its quest for achieving the human. (This is the third response to Kant's question.) It is important to emphasize that maxims are not rules, but rather closer to what Wittgenstein sometimes called reminders. Maxims are neither prescriptive nor proscriptive. For Kant, and for Arendt, they are not matters of cognition and are thus not compulsory; rather, they are standards against which to measure the quality of one's thoughts and judgments. As Arendt explains, "Just as, in moral matters, one's maxim of conduct testifies to the quality of one's will, so the maxims of judgment testify to one's 'turn of thought' (*Denkungsart*) in the worldly matters that are ruled by the community sense" (*Lectures* 71).

I asked earlier whether there are maxims of judgment for the humanities. Arendt certainly thinks there are. The best known are foregrounded in her *Lectures on Kant's Political Philosophy* as what Arendt calls the maxims of sensus communis: "Think for oneself (the maxim of enlightenment); Put oneself in thought in the place of everyone else (the maxim of the enlarged mentality); and, the maxim of consistency, Be in agreement with oneself ('mit sich selbst Einstimmung denken')" (*Lectures* 71). In particular, Kant considered the recommendation always to think consistently and in agreement with oneself (*Jederzeit mit sich selbst einstimmig denken*) to be among the "unchangeable commandments for the class of thinkers" ("Anthropology" 270). Returning again to Socrates in *The Life of the Mind: Thinking*, Arendt emphasizes the ethical dimension of this maxim in writing, "The only criterion of Socratic thinking is agreement, to be consistent with oneself, *homologein autos heautô*; its opposite, to be in contradiction with oneself, *enantia legein autos hautô*, actually means to become one's adversary" (186). Note that in its deepest meaning this is an ethical principle. All knowledge and meaning are always incomplete, partial, and potentially self-contradicting, and if this were not so, thought would lose its restless dynamic energy. Self-consistency thus means observing a self-given imperative: aspire to be true to your thinking self as thinking self.

Arendt is correct to call these maxims of sensus communis in that they imply a directionality where the solitary activity of thought reaches out to request public exercise in the practice of an enlarged mentality that includes the thoughts and opinions of others and applies to them the same tests of consistency. This outward and public-facing movement is also characteristic of some of the implied maxims presented in "Perpetual Peace." Among the most important is the transcendental principle of publicity: "All actions affecting the rights of other human beings are wrong if their maxim is not compatible with their being made public," which I interpret as meaning that all candidates for named rights must be made subject to the widest tests of public criticism if they are finally to be considered as universal human rights. This proposition is another link between judgment and Kant's moral philosophy in that the categorical imperative asks to be imagined as applying universally. Recall Kant's recommendation to act only according to that maxim whereby you can, at the same time, will that it should become a *universal* law. Implied here is the idea that moral imperatives should be imagined as what counts as being good for the whole of humanity and not just for one's self. The idea seems to me close to the universal assent demanded in judgments of taste and just as open to public testing, disagreement, and debate.

I also understood how some of the key political principles embodied in "Perpetual Peace" might be considered maxims for connecting reflective judgments to concrete actions. For example, the basis of the sixth article is the maxim that one must not enter into conflict or dissensus without imagining that understanding and consensus will be possible if not completely achievable. I argued in turn that the third article follows most directly from the sociability and communicability of judgments embodied in Kant's idea of a human community sense: "The law of world citizenship shall be limited to conditions of universal hospitality." Kant considers that the right of temporary sojourn, the right to associate with others across borders in the larger human community, should be considered an inalienable human right. I understand this maxim as a political application of Arendt's and Kant's insistence on representative thinking, and perhaps enlarging this circle of understanding is one of the acts that assures the internal relation of each human being to all others. Guided by one's community sense means judging as a member of a community, and in the last analysis we are already all members of a world community, of a shared cosmopolitan existence, through the sheer fact of being human.

As maxims of sensus communis, each one of these recommendations does not ask that I judge myself as who I am but rather as who I can become in the company of others. Each imagines a quality of the human and expresses the speculative and anticipatory idea of being able to judge as if one represented the whole of humanity, since, as I said, one is no less capable of becoming human than others. Kant imagines these maxims as guidelines that will assure humankind's eventual progress toward a universal cosmopolitan existence. The ideal aspired to here is not so much the establishment of an external legislative power such as a world government but rather to imagine the creation of conditions of existence for a human culture that sustains for everyone internal or self-given powers of becoming human: the capacity to choose and to act freely according to the limits of reason, to impose upon oneself universally applicable moral laws, and to acquire the capacity to exercise right judgment in the company of others.

Nowadays, this kind of seemingly intangible knowledge is widely treated with suspicion, especially by worried parents and the administrators of our increasingly financially distressed institutions of higher learning. Today, as in Arendt's time, universities are increasingly dominated by professional schools, the natural sciences, and technology and engineering, all of which are fundamental research endeavors, of course, yet all of which traffic in certainty, quantitative methods, metrical verification, and "transferrable knowledge." This is the nature of their economic and social utility. Yet this professionalization of knowledge, whose institutional organizations and value structures are so close to the ends-directed and utilitarian demands of corporatism and capitalism, have little or nothing to do with the practice of judgment. Does education in judgment have no role in the modern university, then? In moments of despair there is certainly doubt, giving rise to multiple reports about the crisis in the humanities and the erosion of their support in many academic institutions. However (and this is Arendt's central point and mine), there is no democracy without impartial and independent criticism, testimony, and the exercise of good judgment. In this respect, Arendt states that while no one will deny the myriad positive accomplishments of the sciences and professional schools, their importance is not political. Rather, history and the humanities are politically of far greater relevance because their aim is to discern, define, preserve, and interpret factual truth as expressed and transmitted in the documents of culture.

The activity of judgment as a practice of world building that is both ethical and political is key to Arendt's vision of humanism and humanistic education as both cultural and political activities. For example, the essay "Truth and Politics" stakes out the position of the citizen witness and historical observer who must negotiate a place that mediates between the celestial truth of the philosopher, the noisy *doxai* of earthly citizens, and the lies and half-truths of politics. The whole argument might be read as Arendt's account of how an education in judgment should serve to enhance one's ability to exercise *phronēsis*, or political insight, which in her reinterpretation of Aristotle is a kind of practical intelligence in social and political life connected to, yet distinct from, the solitary theoretical intelligence of philosophy. An education in judgment aims not only at the cultivation of "taste" but also the exercise of prudence or practical wisdom in negotiating the terms for evaluating and revising the factual history of a shared world. I observed earlier that the ancient Greeks referred to this educative practice as *paideia*, which in current times seems newly relevant. For example, in a 2017 editorial in the *New York Times*, David

Brooks commented, as if in direct sympathetic response to "Truth and Politics," that

> Paideia is the process by which we educate one another for citizenship. Paideia is based on the idea that a healthy democracy requires a certain sort of honorable citizen—that if we're not willing to tell one another the truth, devote our lives to common purposes or defer to a shared moral order, then we'll succumb to the shallowness of a purely commercial civilization, we'll be torn asunder by the centrifugal forces of extreme individualism, we'll rip one another to shreds in the naked struggle for power.... As the brilliant Spanish philosopher Javier Gomá Lanzón reminds us, most moral education happens by power of example. We publish the book of our lives every day through our actions, and through our conduct we teach one another what is worthy of admiration and what is worthy of disdain.[67]

Arendt's essay "The Crisis in Education" approaches an education in judgment from a different but related direction. Arendt's main idea here is that the essence of education is natality, which is not only an introduction of new humans to "life"—this complex and contradictory human-made world, both cultural and political, that the child must learn to navigate—but also that this world is only renewable, that lines of history can only be broken and deviated, by the appearance of new and unforeseen actions and ideas. Simply put, education aims at providing the conceptual and cultural resources for cultivating the freedom in which the possibility and potentiality of the new finds a space of appearance. Like her friend Walter Benjamin, for Arendt the spectator of history is sensitive to the fact that historical experience is marked less by its continuities than by the ineluctable recurrence of "emergency situations" where both common sense and a common reality have become fragile to the point of disintegration.[68] Basically, Arendt writes,

---

67. "The Essential John McCain," October 19, 2017, 25. Contemporary politics makes strange bedfellows. While I have often disagreed with many of Brooks's political recommendations and still do, he and the rest of the *New York Times* editorial board have becomes valuable voices of reason in challenging times, and from time to time, good examples of Arendt's hopes for the press as impartial arbiters of political and historical facts. Fortunately, they have not been alone.

68. See Benjamin's "On the Concept of History," §VIII, in *Walter Benjamin: Selected Writings* vol. 4, *1938–1940* (Cambridge, MA: Harvard University Press, 2006).

We are always educating for a world that is or is becoming out of joint, for this is the basic human situation, in which the world is created by mortal hands to serve mortals for a limited time as home. Because the world is made by mortals it wears out; and because it continuously changes its inhabitants it runs the risk of becoming as mortal as they. To preserve the world against the mortality of its creators and inhabitants it must be constantly set right anew. The problem is simply to educate in such a way that a setting-right remains actually possible, even though it can, of course, never be assured. Our hope always hangs on the new which every generation brings; but precisely because we can base our hope only on this, we destroy everything if we so try to control the new that we, the old, can dictate how it will look.[69]

Cultures and their meanings and values are no less marked by finitude than their human inhabitants—this is why the concept of natality is so important for Arendt. If the appearance of each new human breaks into the world as an "infinite improbability," then "education is the point at which we decide whether we love the world enough to assume responsibility for it and by the same token save it from that ruin which, except for renewal, except for the coming of the new and young, would be inevitable" ("The Crisis in Education" 193).

An education in judgment is one of the most important tasks of the humanities because here one prepares oneself and others, both within and across generations, to respond imaginatively and critically to the emergency situations in which we find ourselves while forging new ethical terms for lives held in common. In the past three thousand years, it may well be possible that philosophy has taught us nothing conclusively, but perhaps, through philosophy and the artful giving and receiving of judgments, we have learned how to learn.

69. "The Crisis in Education," in *Between Past and Future*, 189.

Acknowledgments

In the research and writing of this book, I have had the good fortune to spend the last three years as a senior research fellow with the Kolleg-Forschergruppe, Cinepoetics–Poetologien audiovisueller Bilder at the Freie Universität, Berlin. I would like to give special thanks to the directors, Hermann Kappelhoff and Michael Wedel, for their invitation and hospitality, and to all the other fellows and colleagues for their conversation and collegiality. During this time, it was also my great privilege to engage with the editorial board working on the international critical edition of Hannah Arendt's complete works, who are also attached to the Cinepoetics institute. This group provided an incomparable opportunity to deepen my research on Arendt as an important voice for a possible philosophy of the humanities, which included presenting my early thought and arguments in a lecture to the group on Arendt's account of thinking as a performative practice and subsequently participating in the Hannah Arendt Herausgebertreffen/Symposion, which took place at the Freie Universität in June 2017. At the invitation of Bernd Herzogenrath, I presented another paper from my research, "Hannah Arendt's Care for Culture," as part of the Frankfurt Lectures in Literary and Cultural Studies at the Goethe Universität in Frankfurt am Main, also in June 2017, and again in Paris in May 2018 for the Laboratoire de Recherches sur les Cultures Anglophones, Université Paris Diderot and Centre National de la Recherche Scientifique. I would like to thank Martine Beugnet and the late François Brunet for their invitations and the seminar participants for their lively discussion of my work. In June 2018, I co-organized with Hermann Kappelhoff and Barbara Hahn an international workshop on Hannah Arendt and the problem of judgment at the University of Chicago Center in Paris, guided by the theme "The Public Sphere and Common Sense." These conversations were inspiring and deeply informed the central arguments for this book. At an early stage of my writing, Richard McKirahan provided invaluable advice on interpreting many Greek terms, mystifying to me, that are central to Arendt's arguments. And, as will be clear toward the end of this book, I am deeply indebted to conversations with my colleagues and students at MFA critiques in the University of Chicago Department of Visual Arts, as well as the undergraduate students in my Core Seminar on Philosophical Perspectives in the Humanities.

An early version of the opening section of this book appeared in German as "Hannah Arendts Denkungsart" in the 2019 edition of the *Internationales Jahrbuch für Medienphilosophie*, edited by Dieter Mersch and Katerina Krtilova. I thank them both for their encouragement, support, and constructive feedback. Other friends whose support for this project was instrumental include Nora Alter, Johannes von Moltke, James McFarland, Arnaud Coulombel, and my Chicago colleague Robert Pippin.

Finally, I would like to thank Alan Thomas, Randy Petilos, and Kyle Wagner at University of Chicago Press for ushering this project toward publication, as well as the two anonymous readers (one of whom, Thomas Bartscherer, has unmasked himself as my most assiduous and helpful critic) whose reports provided precious advice midway through the composition of this book.

Index

Adorno, Theodor, 29
aesthetics: art and, contemporary
threat to the potential autonomy
of, 45; beauty, quality of, 38 (*see also*
beauty); judgments of, connection
of beauty to appearance and, 39–44;
judgments of, criteria provoking,
36–37; judgments of taste (*see* judgments of taste); Kant's condition for
judgments of, 45
Anaxagoras, 40n27, 129
anti-Semitism, 85–86n45
Aristotle: dialectic, definition of, 132;
persuasion and dialectic, contrast of,
57, 130; philosophy's separation from
the city, 128–29, 139–40, 160
art: aesthetics and, contemporary
threat to the potential autonomy
of, 45; artist and craftsperson,
confusing of, 62; as culture, time
and, 36–38; durability of artworks,
70; exemplary as constitutive of
culture, 46; judgments about, time
and, 31–32, 71; making and judging,
distinction between, 62; philistinism
and, 29–31; politics and, relation
between, 47–50, 62–65; proper mode
of intercourse with, 46–47; public
conversation and, 89; studio critique
sessions, 151–55

asocial sociability of humankind, 77–
78, 93, 112, 141, 158, 160

barbarism/barbarity/barbarous:
Greeks distinguished from, 64;
history's directions toward, Arendt's
fears of, 111, 160; lapse into, risk of,
55; love of beauty or wisdom and,
48, 60, 64; meaning of, 60; taste and,
68n36; vice of effeminacy attributed
to, 48n, 64
beauty: conflict between Arendt's and
Kant's account of, 44, 68; connection to appearance as the basis of
aesthetic judgments, 39–44; imagination and, 42, 44, 53; judgment
and, 38–39; judgments of taste and,
12n, 41–44, 49, 53–56, 66–68; love of,
politics and, 47–48, 60, 65; monuments and, 66; Plato on, 39–41;
problems arising from Arendt's position on, 67–68; wisdom, contrasted
with, 60
Beckett, Samuel, 156–57
Beiner, Ronald, xii
Benhabib, Seyla, xii, xv
Benjamin, Walter, 103, 166
Bernstein, Richard, xii
Between Past and Future (Arendt):
Char's aphorisms in the preface

tions with others and, 138; political friendship in the polis, role of, 135–36; possibility of politics in the absence of epistemological or moral standards, question of, 113; Socrates's conversations beginning with questions, reason for, 133; Socrates's denial of wisdom meant he had nothing to teach fellow citizens, 130; Socrates's effort to persuade at his trial, 130; Socrates's "sterility," characterization of, 14n; Socratic conversation as an alternative to the Athenian contest of all against all, 134; solitude as an integral part of being and living together with others, 142; a true political philosophy requires making the plurality of man the object of thought, 143; truth and opinion, lack of visible hallmark distinguishing, 117; "Truth and Politics" and, comparison of, 114, 127

Philosophy's Artful Conversation (Rodowick), 2, 6, 76n39

Plato: allegory of the cave, 90, 114, 128–29; Arendt's gloss on *eidos*, 40–41; dialectic, definition of, 132; dialectic and persuasion, distinction between, 129; *erōs* as the most powerful manifestation of the beautiful, 39–40; the Forms as transcendental anchor for, 116, 128–29; inverse ratio between perceiving and reasoning in the epistemology of, 12n; ironic view of writing held by, 11; philosophy and city life, separation of, 128, 139–40, 142; political philosophy of, impossibility of, 128; *Republic* as rebuke to Athenian democracy, 130; Socrates (*see* Socrates); Socratic dialogues require two or more for active thinking, 21–22; Socratic "teaching" as getting rid of the bad opinions of others without giving them good/truth, 14; thinking, definition of, 22;

thinking and *erōs*, relation between, 19–20

plurality: Arendt's concept of, xiv, 111; building/maintaining a polis and, 96; of the *dokei moi*, 114, 117–19, 122, 141, 152; fact of, coincidence of Being and Appearance in connection with, 132n; as a fact of becoming human, 26; inner, 121; judgment and, 153; participation/negotiation in, 75, 112, 116; politics and/or humanity, as a fact of, 26, 113, 115, 121, 137; publicity and, linkage of, 90, 92; shared space of appearance and, 132; singular existence and, 22

polis/polity, the: as the actions, words, and memories of its participants, 48–49; auto-constitution of, 59; formation of a public sphere and formation of, 89; imagination and, 96, 152 (*see also* imagination); judgments and, 54, 59; persuasion in, 57; as scalable, 77; self-regulating, 64; space of appearance of, 49–50, 70

politics: Arendt's definition of, xvii; art and, relation between, 47–50, 62–65; dimensions of reason leading to, 22–23; ethics and, 76, 138; friendship in the dialectic of, 135–37, 139; judgments of taste and, 29, 43, 49, 58, 61, 64–66, 115 (*see also* judgments of taste); loss of a common world and, 112–13; morality and, conflict between, 84–88; philosophy and, relationship of, 74–77, 82, 114–15, 127–50; plurality and, 26, 113, 115, 121, 137; power and, conflict between, 116; power in, limitations of, 126; the problem of judgment and the connection of the humanities to, 28–29; representative thinking and (*see* representative thinking); truth and, 115–18, 120–26 (*see also* truth). *See also* citizen(s)/citizenship

of, 75; universal capacity/right to exercise, 62

Thales, 129

"Thinking and Moral Considerations" (Arendt): dangers of thinking, nihilism and, 18–19; education in judgment exemplified in, 3; moral evil, diminished capacity for judgment can lead to, 3; moral judgments based on concepts/principles, rejection of, 57, 108; the problem of judgment as a bridge connecting this work to other works, 28; thinking and judgment, connection of, 4, 25, 44; thinking characterized as a form of friendship, 137

thinking/thought: acting and, 138–41; without bannisters, 108, 157; beyond sensory perception and common-sense, drawn to matters of, 5–6, 9; "boundary situations" and, 161n; conflict between "common sense" and, 8–9; conscience and, 4, 23–24; consciousness and, 21–22; dangers of, 141; enlargement of, through judgment, 92; *erōs* and, relation between, 19–20; evil, ability/inability to think and the problem of, 9–10, 20; friendship as a form of, 137; in the gap between past and future, 105–8; in the gap between past and future, Char and the first example of, 98–102; in the gap between past and future, Kafka and the second example of, 102–5; human need for recurring exercise of, 7–9, 19–20, 26; imagination and, 9–10, 81, 120–21 (*see also* imagination); as "impracticable," 10; judgment and, relation of, 3–4, 7, 17–19, 24–25, 27–28, 44–45n, 157; knowing and, distinction between, 8, 10; a life without, 160–61; the maxim of consistency and, 21; as meditation/aimless thought, 13–14; natality and, 107 (*see also* natality);

normative values and moral judgment, potential impact on, 17–18; as an ordinary human capacity, 10, 15, 20, 24, 68; paralysis of, nihilism and, 18–19; as political and antiauthoritarian, 24; representative (*see* representative thinking); as a skill or capacity that needs to be exercised, 109–10; sociality and, tension between, 9; as solitary but not cut off from others, 81; wickedness and the absence of, 110; by the world-observer, 105–7 (*see also* world-observer/spectator). *See also* critique(s); reason

thinking/thought, public activity of: criterion of publicity for, 16–17, 20–21; everyday speech and the, 12–13; exemplarity and, 144–46; Kant on, 15–16; the Socratic elenchus, aim of, 17–18; the Socratic elenchus, truth and, 57; the Socratic elenchus as the exemplar of, 10–15, 27, 129

Thucydides, 47, 64

time: breach in the continuity of, interval events as, 99–105; crisis in culture and, 34–37; entertainment as filling up "leftover," 32–33; judgments about art/culture based on, 31–32, 71; vacant, erosion of the inventory of available, 32–33

truth: absolute as an impediment to politics, 136; coercion associated with assertions of, 120; collective definition of, in the absence of providence, 112; contingency of historical, 115, 122, 126; facts and, 115–18; factual, difficulties in judging, 121–22; factual in contrast to rational, paradox of, 117–18; impartiality and, 121–22, 124, 147, 150 (*see also* impartiality); inviolability of certain historical, 119; lying and, 123–26, 147–49, 160–61; meaning distinguished from, 6; nonpolitical/antipolitical nature of, 147; opinion